CAVING

SIERRA CLUB GUIDES TO OUTDOOR ACTIVITIES

CAVING

The Sierra Club Guide to Spelunking

Lane Larson and Peggy Larson

SIERRA CLUB BOOKS   SAN FRANCISCO

COPYRIGHT © 1982 BY LANE LARSON AND PEGGY LARSON

LIBRARY OF CONGRESS CATALOGING IN PUBLICATION DATA

Larson, Lane, 1953
CAVING: *The Sierra Club Guide to Spelunking.*

Bibliography: p. 305
Includes index.
1. Caving—North America—Guide-books.
I. Larson, Peggy, 1931—joint author.
II. Sierra Club. III. Title.

GV200.66.N67L37   796.5'25'097   80-23110
ISBN 0-87156-246-4 (pbk.)

Cover photograph by Lane Larson
Book design by Jon Goodchild
Illustrations by Lane Larson and Cherie Wilson

Printed in the United States of America
10   9   8   7   6   5   4   3   2   1

for
Ryan, newest caver . . .
may all his leads go
L.L., P.L.

and for
Walter Bossler,
a good friend
remembered always
L.L.

ACKNOWLEDGMENTS

We wish to express gratitude to the following individuals who provided assistance in the preparation of this book. Their suggestions were greatly appreciated. If any errors or inadequacies have inadvertently occurred in the finished product, however, these are ours and not theirs.

Tom Rea, President, National Speleological Society; Pat Stevens and Janet McCormick; and Fred Anders, geologist, each read and critiqued the entire manuscript. Sheck Exley, Cave Diving Section, National Speleological Society, and Terry Leitheuser, National Association for Cave Diving, both read and advised regarding the chapter on cave diving. Bob Buecher, a caving friend, offered helpful advice on the chapters dealing with vertical caving.

We are also appreciative of the help extended to us by official personnel of the NSS, who searched for— and found—specific information when requested. Special thanks, also, to James Cohee, our editor. And, finally, thanks and acknowledgment to good caving companions who have helped, over the years, to make caving trips pleasant, successful, and often memorable.

Lane Larson, Peggy Larson
Tucson, Arizona. August 1981

CONTENTS

1

DARK WILDERNESS

THROUGH INNUMERABLE generations, extending back to a distant time when man was neither *sapiens* nor even *Homo*, both he and other animals have sought caves. There many of the early inhabitants sheltered, birthed, died, and decomposed. However, it was only shallow caves or near cavern entrances that man routinely made a home. Subterranean passages are often cold, damp, precipitous, and difficult to negotiate; darkness of a far greater intensity than that of the familiar night is a constant cavern condition; and the unknown, or fear of the known, may loom large in the dark, silent voids. Little wonder that early men, equipped only with burning torches and primitive weapons probably seldom ventured into the innermost recesses. We conclude today that on the occasions when they did dare the depths, their motivation often may have been the very strong one of fulfilling religious or mystical purposes, as evidenced by the cave paintings, sculpture, artifacts, or burials occasionally left in these locations. Thus for long ages, man lived largely on the outer perimeters of caves, affecting the inner portions of the caverns only to a very limited degree.

Some two to three centuries ago, man became increasingly interested in caves, not for the protection they could afford him, but rather as fascinating entities in themselves. Armed with candles, tinder boxes, lanterns, and miners' headlamps; using cumbersome, heavy ropes and rope-and-wood ladders; and developing methods by trial and error, these first explorers accomplished magnificent feats of cave exploration and amassed impressive amounts of scientific information regarding caves and their contents.

In the last thirty years the art of cave exploration has been revolutionized by radical improvements in caving equipment and the adoption of new techniques, many of these adapted from mountaineering. These improvements have spawned a virtual explosion of cave exploration and scientific investigation. Suddenly man has dropped deeper and crawled farther underground in natural caverns, and done so in greater safety, than he has ever before been privileged to accomplish—and there are greater depths, longer passages, and scientific questions begging answers. All beckon today's cave enthusiast.

There have long been individuals, their thinking in advance of their times, who have called for and practiced what today we term a land ethic, conservation, or environmental protection. Theirs were too often the proverbial voices crying out in the wilderness as the wilderness disappeared around them, but in the last quarter century a national and international conscience regarding the environment has emerged. Thus the accelerated development of ecological conscience has coincided with the rapid acceleration of cave exploration. One is almost tempted, cautiously and hopefully, to conjecture that man's dark wilderness heritage has largely been saved for him until he has at last developed the good sense to appreciate it fully and to protect it.

Today, as a group, serious cavers are among the most conservation- and ecology-oriented members of society. Protection of caves is a matter of concern and pride to them. So must it be for all who enter caves, neophytes as well as dedicated cavers. It takes but a single vandal, or even a well-intentioned but unknowledgeable or careless explorer, to harm or destroy what vast amounts of time have built and hundreds of other cavers have zealously protected. It must be realized that caves are basically nonrenewable resources, frequently bearing important scientific evidence, and enclosing extremely delicate ecosystems that often contain animal species living nowhere on the surface of the earth and some so limited in distribution as to be found in but a single cave.

Admittedly, it is too late to save a good many caves —their formations smashed or carried away, their unique animal life senselessly or inadvertently destroyed, their rivers fouled by sewage, their archaeological and paleontological treasures pirated and lost, their walls scarred by graffiti or quarried away. But there is yet time and ever the responsibility to repair the repairable, to prevent further destruction of damaged caves, and to preserve the known undefiled caves, as well as those yet to be discovered. Be advised: this is the message with which we begin this book, it is the one with which we will end it, and it is a major theme upon which variations will be presented throughout the text.

What motivates modern cavers to enter the subterranean depths? They are curious; they seek beauty; they search for scientific answers and intellectual satisfaction; they strive to become familiar with a most distinctive and interesting ecosystem. Some enter to test themselves in a strenuous, demanding sport, or against an exacting environment. Excitement, adventure, and the challenge of the unexpected are other motivations. Because it is different; because it provides a retreat from the everyday world and its routines; because there is good comradeship in exploration; because it helps put oneself in perspective; and because it is enjoyable—all these are valid reasons. Caves represent a relatively new wilderness and unexplored frontier, both powerful challenges. Therefore, the chance to be an explorer with the hope of experiencing the thrill and accomplishment of discovery or the setting of new records—the possibility of being where no person has ever been before—is a very strong incentive for cave exploration in today's world, where so much exploration and so many discoveries have preceded us in the sunlit wilderness.

Beginning cavers may be motivated by one or a few factors. If they continue to pursue the sport they often find their motivational base broadening. The person who came originally to partake in a strenuous sport soon finds himself curious about the things he sees in the cave. There is much of interest and many recreational, aesthetic, and intellectual diversions provided by the cave environment. A good many cavers who first enter a cave "just to look around" soon find themselves with a full-fledged, lifelong hobby. There are even some fortunate enthusiasts—speleologists, or cave scientists—who have been able to combine to varying degrees their vocation and avocation, so that, unlike the majority of us, even their profession need not distract from their hobby.

What, exactly, is a cave? There are as many definitions of the word as there are definers. Webster's provides more than twenty, most of which have little to do with the geological phenomena we are considering here. It does supply the information that the word is derived from the Greek word meaning "hollow," and one of the definitions reads as follows: "a hollowed out chamber in the earth or in the side of a cliff or a hill . . . a natural underground chamber (as one produced in limestone by running water) with an opening to the surface."

Speleologists usually define the word in more specific terms. They agree that a cave is a naturally occurring subterranean cavity or series of cavities (thus man-made mines are not included). They often state that the cavity must be such that it can be penetrated for an appreciable distance. Some cavers would say this must be of an extent that the distance traversable extends beyond the entrance twilight zone into complete darkness; however, some natural earth cavities, such as sea caves, that are commonly accepted under the term cave do not extend into total darkness. It is generally accepted that to be termed a cave, the cavity must be large enough for a person to enter, thereby inferring also, that there is an entrance to the cavity

4

from the surface.

These latter points are a little tricky and can become ludicrous if one cares to debate the matter. A small, thin caver may be able to enter a cavity that a more corpulent one cannot (although cavers, for good reason, tend not be be obese); thus a cave for one person may not be, technically, a cave for another. And occasionally a cave may not have an open connection to the surface until the eager cavers dig one. Has the cave been a cave all along or did it suddenly become one when man and shovel triumphed? Carol Hill, in the excellent book *Cave Minerals*, defines a cave as "a naturally occurring subterranean opening, cavity, or series of cavities; the implication is that it is man-sized and connected to the surface but neither are necessary in the definition."

One of the basic points in all definitions is that a cave is a cavity, series of cavities, hollowed-out chamber, orifice, void, hole, opening, or whatever similar term the writer may use. In other words, a cave is a space, not an object, and in specifying the extent of a cave, we are identifying the boundaries of a space. It's somewhat akin to the old query: does the hole make the doughnut or the doughnut make the hole—does space make the cave or do walls make the cave? With doughnuts the hole is expected, but not essential; with caves the hole is the vital element, but cannot exist without the essential matrix that encloses it.

For purposes of general discussion, we will consider a cave to be a natural subterranean cavity, ordinarily but not necessarily with an opening to the surface, the cavity large enough to allow a person to enter and to penetrate for an appreciable distance within, generally but not always to an area characterized by complete darkness.

Caves are amazingly varied in their form and appearance, and this is part of their attraction. Caves can be grouped according to the type of matrix in which they occur and their mode of formation. The best known and most numerous caves of the world are solution caves, those hollowed out of limestone or a few other types of rock by the dissolving power of weakly acidified water. A second type is the lava tube cave formed as a river of molten lava flows downslope from its source. The outer surface of this stream cools more rapidly than the interior; an outer crust solidifies and the inner molten material continues to flow downhill, leaving behind a hollow lava tube. Glacier caves are those in or beneath glaciers, formed in the glacial ice by summer streams flowing from the glaciers and by evaporation of the glacial ice. Sea caves are carved in rocks along coastlines by the powerful erosive action of ocean waves. Talus caves, usually small, may be formed in the voids of large piles of talus—blocks of rock that have broken off mountain cliffs and accumulated at their bases. There are additional types of caves and near-caves that fall into a miscellaneous category, including rock shelters or "sandstone caves," snow caves, fissure caves, and others. In the following chapters we will be discussing the various types, their genesis, and their characteristic conditions in more detail.

As the types of caves are varied, so too are the conditions within them, and these will also be discussed as we consider individual cave types. However, there are some general conditions often met in caves, particularly those formed in limestone, that we may consider typical.

Total darkness is one. Even on the darkest night our eyes are capable of limited sight, discerning a hand held in front of the face or dark shapes looming ahead. It is different deep in a cave where there is absolutely no light. A hand held an inch in front of the eyes is not visible, and photographic film exposed for long periods registers nothing without the addition of a light source. Complete absence of light is the dominating factor within a cave and exerts a profound limiting effect upon what kinds of living things can survive there.

Most caves tend to be on the cool side. Their interior temperatures closely approximate the average annual temperature registered above ground in their particular locations, and seldom vary more than one or two degrees.

Many caves are wet, with pools or moving streams

and dripping water. Relative humidity is high, the air at or near the saturation point.

Silence is characteristic of caves, at times complete, at times broken only by the monotonous dripping of water, the hollow gurgle and splash of a moving stream, the roar of a waterfall, the voices of bats, the passage of an animal in the darkness.

Cave air is largely free of pollen and smog. It tends to waft through the cave with a light, often imperceptible movement, but under certain conditions, when funneled through a narrow passage, may produce a strong breeze. For the human visitor the air carries various cave odors—wet earth, dry dust, water, the ammoniacal fumes of bat urine, the fetid odor of guano, decay, and a special, typical cave odor thought to be due to the action of bacteria within the cave soil. Whatever elements are present, in combination the odor is distinctive, and cavers sometimes refer to the whole as "cave perfume."

When man intrudes with lights, he notes other cave features often present: stalactites, stalagmites, and other decorations and formations; immense chambers; deep pits; high domes; spacious hallways; passages blocked by rock breakdown, filled with water, or of a size barely navigable by a human-sized crawler; mud; massive, rough, rock walls; and animal inhabitants, such as spiders, beetles, cave crickets, and fish.

A typical cave is a roofed, enclosed, dark space where the sun never shines, and although water and ice may be present, it never rains or snows. Its silence may be deafening, its beauties dissimilar to those of the sunlit world. No green plants grow within, and the animal life present includes numerous types of which many people have erroneously been taught an unreasoning fear or dislike. The cave is a harsh, demanding, uncompromising environment. It is greatly unlike the physical world in which we live, which is a primary reason it so strongly attracts some people and equally strongly repels others. Inasmuch as you are reading this, we assume you are among the former.

The Greek word for cave is *spelaion*. The English

language has adapted from this a most convenient combining term, *speleo-*, and words beginning with or including *speleo-* abound in cave literature and cave conversations. One of the most familiar of these is the term *speleology*, which is variously defined as the scientific study of caves and related phenomena; or of caves and their contents; or of the total cave environment, including both physical and biological features. In short, speleology is the scientific study of caves. It is a multidisciplinary science, for the cave is a total, distinctive environment, and specialized knowledge from many areas of science must be combined in order to understand it. Thus caves may be investigated by geologists, mineralogists, hydrologists, biologists, ecologists, chemists, physicists, climatologists, surveyors, paleontologists, archaeologists, anthropologists, and others. A *speleologist* is a person who studies caves within any of the various scientific disciplines. In some cases terms may be combined to transmit a finer distinction; for example, a biospeleologist is a scientist who studies the living things—plants and animals—in the cave environment.

In the past, the terms speleologist and speleology have tended to denote the scientific aspect of cave exploration. Their less scientific counterparts are the terms cavers and caving, or spelunkers and spelunking. Increasingly, these terms are blending in popular usage. A scientist may be both a caver and a speleologist. Quite often a caver may not carry a science degree, yet may be sufficiently interested in the cave environment to pursue knowledge in depth in related fields, thereby entering the field of speleology to a certain extent. Increasingly, as a group, experienced cavers seek to become knowledgeable regarding the cave environment, and increasingly the term speleology is also being applied to cave exploration that is conducted by people who aren't scientists but who are vitally interested in the cave as a whole, and who in conducting their explorations are bound by scientific understanding of the fragile nature of the cave environment.

Cavers and speleologists tend to be down-to-earth

types, in both their activities and their attitudes. When explorers are crawling belly-down through mud, wading waist deep in cold water, or slogging through fresh bat guano, the distinctions between them are not as likely to be scientific degrees as they are to be the differences in personality, capability, and dedication between each individual on that particular speleological undertaking. This freedom from class distinction is also reflected by the national cave organization in the United States and its membership. The National Speleological Society (NSS) strongly promotes the scientific exploration of the cave world: additionally, it promotes safe, intelligent caving and cave conservation. Its members certainly include speleologists, but its membership is more largely composed of people who simply like caves and caving and have allied themselves with the national organization for information, education, cave conservation, and an opportunity to meet and get to know other cavers.

On the basis of the foregoing, in this book we shall often use the term speleology in a broad sense, and we will approach the subject of caves from a combined scientific and recreational viewpoint. The individual interested in the sport of cave exploration needs to know something of the science in order to understand better the environment through which he moves, both for his own enjoyment and for the protection of the cave world.

One other thing. The English language shows its age. Pronouns are difficult. It is tiresome always to write "he and she," "him and her," and so on. Also, when referring to human beings in the sense of people in general, it is sometimes difficult to find nonsexist terms that do not become repetitious or cumbersome. Therefore, in this book we often will use the traditional "him," "man," "mankind," and similar terms when we're really including both genders. Certainly caving is a sport enjoyed by both males and females, and there are outstanding female cavers and speleologists as well as male ones. Despite the pronouns, this book is for both sexes. After all, it is written by one of each.

2
LIMESTONE CAVE DEVELOPMENT

THERE ARE THREE BASIC rock types: sedimentary rocks, formed from mechanical, chemical, or organic sediment; igneous rocks, formed by solidification of a molten magma: and metaphoric rocks formed from rocks of the other two types that have been changed by pressure, heat, or chemical action. Limestone fits into the first of these three categories, being a sedimentary rock composed principally of calcite ($CaCO_3$), one form of calcium carbonate. Over eons of geological time, in shallow seas that covered vast areas of the earth, various types of marine plants and animals secreted calcium carbonate as a part of their metabolic processes; for some, portions of their body, such as skeletons and shells, were formed of this material. Upon death, their calcareous remains, in the form of complete shells, or as bits and pieces of limy bodies, or as grains as fine as sand, drifted to the sea floor and accumulated there in beds of great thickness. Limestone formed from sediments transported to a point of deposition is known as *allochthonous* limestone.

Through compacting pressure, deposition in the pore spaces of the sediments of calcium carbonate carried there in solution, and other changes, these sediments underwent lithification—that is, the formation of rock from particulate matter. Such layers of sediments varied greatly in their makeup due to numerous factors affecting them; for example, the plants and animals involved; the rate of buildup; the occasional deposition upon them of other materials; location, such as in a lagoon or in the ocean depths; water currents; beds being uplifted and inundated again; the inclusion in their cementing matrix of other materials; the degree of pressure exerted upon them; and others. So, too, the resulting limestones vary in texture and structure. This process of limestone formation continues within the seas today. Some limestone beds, however, were removed from the sea's influence long ago by changes in sea levels or by powerful tectonic action —that is, by movements within the earth—which in time lifted many of the beds above sea level, often tilting or otherwise reorienting them in the process.

In some cases limestone has been formed from animal remains that have remained in place and not been transported. One example is limestone formed from coral reefs, where coral grew upon coral, building up masses of organic material that remained in position and eventually became limestone through the lithification process. Limestone formed *in situ* is known as *autochthonous* limestone; it often lacks the stratification we will discuss later as an important feature of allochthonous limestone.

Organic calcareous remains are not the only source of limestone deposits. As Sweeting states in *Karst Landforms*, "Limestones are partly detrital, partly chemical, partly organic and partly metasomatic" (formed as a result of chemical metamorphism). For a rock to be classed as limestone it must be composed of a minimum of 50 percent carbonate; however, most rocks commonly called limestones consist of at least 90 percent calcite. Among the wide variety of noncalcareous items that may be included in the lime sediments are silica (organic sand, silt, and clay, and organic skeletal remains), volcanic dust, and noncalcareous organic remains. Also, chemical reactions may eventually take place in the limestone to produce minerals within it such as clay minerals, pyrite and other iron sulfides and iron oxides, flint or chert nodules (varieties of quartz), and others. In certain locations magnesium is present in sea water. The introduction of magnesium into the calcite molecule results in rock called dolomite, and layers or rhombs of dolomite thus may occasionally be found in limestone.

Certain characteristic features of limestone have a vital bearing upon the formation of caves within it, and knowing something about these helps the caver to understand the cave he is exploring. Most limestone is composed of distinct beds separated by *bedding planes*, the surfaces or fractures present between two layers of sedimentary rocks. Bedding planes form when an interruption or change in the steady deposition of calcium carbonate occurs. This interruption can have a variety of causes, but a common one is the inflow of clastic sediment (composed of fragments of preexisting rocks) from nearby rivers. The flows cover the deposits to varying depths. Other causes include the uplifting of a bed above the water, resultant drying and erosion, and resubmergence and further deposition; a change in the size of grains being deposited; or a chemical change, as in the formation of dolomite.

Limestone is marked by numerous fractures caused by the force of tectonic movements. Of these fractures, *joints* are cracks in the rock mass and occur in parallel groups or sets, usually more or less vertically oriented in relation to the bedding planes. Other joint sets of a less vertical orientation may also be present. Joints often pass through only a single bed, but may at times pass vertically through two or three, or occasionally through several beds. Joints that pass through a great thickness of beds are often called master joints.

Faults are fractures in the earth's crust accompanied by a displacement of one side of the fracture in relationship to the other. Faults may cut across several limestone beds, and their earth-wrenching movements may bring a bed of one type in contact with that of another.

Other small fractures and cracks, neither faults nor joints, are also present in limestone; these are often called *diaclases*.

In a generalized manner, we have described the slow development of limestone beds lying generally horizontal to the earth's surface, layered by the presence of occasional bedding planes, marked by minor fractures, fissured by primarily vertical joint sets, and at times deeply fractured by faults. In certain locations today we find such horizontal limestone beds, although all are considerably more complex than our brief review would suggest. Such generally horizontal limestone often promises long cave systems, and indeed the longest known cave in the world, the Flint Mammoth Cave System in Kentucky, with over 224 miles (about 339 kilometers) of passages surveyed, is in largely horizontal limestone. Many limestone beds, however, have been subjected to major earth stresses that have tilted or folded them, and the beds are inclined, arched, have portions inverted, or are greatly modified in any number of other ways. The joints and other fractures already present at the time of these great movements rotated with them. However, the new stresses and later ones also affected the beds, causing additional fractures and many other profound and diverse changes, all of which add to the great variety and complexity of caves that may be formed in this limestone. It is in the greatly uplifted, tilted, massive limestone beds that the world's deepest caves have been found; currently the record holder is Gouffre Jean Bernard located in France. It's approximately 1,410 meters in depth.

Limestone lifted above the sea's surface is exposed to forces that begin its eventual dissolution. Calcium carbonate is slightly soluble in pure water and much more soluble in acidified water. Limestone is composed of calcium carbonate in the form of calcite, hence it is soluble. In order for any appreciable solution of the limestone to take place, however, water must be acidified and must have sufficient access to the rock.

Water becomes acidified by addition of the carbon dioxide in the form of a water-soluble gas. The carbon dioxide, CO_2, combines with water, H_2O, to form carbonic acid, H_2CO_3. It is this acid that is primarily responsible for dissolving limestone, and hence of vital importance in forming caves within the limestone. The solubility of carbon dioxide increases with an increase in pressure and with a decrease in temperature. By volume, the atmosphere contains approximately 0.03 percent carbon dioxide. Rain falling through the air takes into solution some carbon dioxide before reaching the earth's surface, but this produces only a very weak acid, capable of dissolving approximately 70 parts per million (ppm) of calcium carbonate. Carbon dioxide is

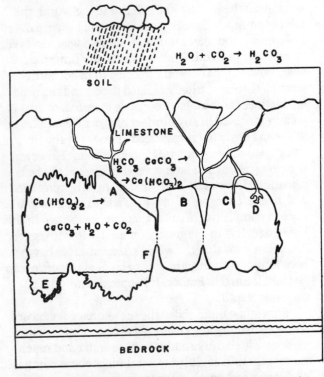

Limestone cave development. *In the atmosphere rainwater combines with carbon dioxide, causing the formation of carbonic acid ($H_2O + CO_2 = H_2CO_3$). As the carbonic acid and water soak downward through the soil additional carbon dioxide is combined with it. The carbonic acid dissolves limestone with which it comes into contact ($H_2CO_3 + CaCO_3 = Ca[HCO_3]_2$). As this water enters an air-filled cave cavity, carbon dioxide is lost to the air, the water becomes supersaturated, and calcite is deposited in the form of various speleothems ($Ca[HCO_3]_2 = CaCO_3 + H_2O + CO_2$).*

A. *Drapery;* B. *Stalactite;* C. *Soda-straw stalactite;* D. *Helictite;* E. *Pool deposits;* F. *Stalagmite.*

produced by a variety of means: as a by-product of metabolism, for example, being given off in the breathing of animals; through combustion; and through the decomposition of animal and vegetable matter. Because of organic decomposition, soils contain greatly increased amounts of carbon dioxide, which constitutes approximately 10 percent of the soil air. Thus water, once it soaks into the soil, varies as to the amount of carbon dioxide it will be able to take into solution, but has a vastly increased supply available to it. A stronger concentration of carbonic acid is thereby formed, and the acid-charged water's ability to dissolve limestone is greatly enhanced to an upper limit of approximately 400 to 500 ppm.

Water may wash the surface of exposed limestone, or it may soak through upper soil levels and reach lower limestone beds. Limestones vary in their permeability, or the degree to which water can penetrate the rock directly. Permeability through the pores of the rock is known as primary permeability, and this varies from one type of limestone to another. However, primary permeability of limestones is usually very limited. Permeability through joints, faults, and solution cavities is termed secondary permeability, and it is in this regard that the various fractures within the limestone assume major importance. Water enters the diaclases, joints, and faults, if present, and in these locations deep within the limestone begins the very long, slow process of dissolving the surfaces with which it is in contact. This is called *speleogenesis*, the birth of a cave system. It is apparent that the form a developing cave takes is strongly influenced by the fractures found in the limestone, as well as the bedding planes present.

As far as water and its limestone-dissolving abilities are concerned, bedding planes may present zones of either strength or weakness in the limestone. Depending upon the makeup of the rocks to either side of the bedding plane, some provide avenues of increased permeability and others provide decreased permeability. Some, such as those where shale is present, may be less permeable but are mechanically weak and therefore subject to breakdown by the water's force. Iron pyrite is often found in bedding planes and in the adjacent limestone; when oxidized, iron pyrite produces sulphuric acid, which also attacks the limestone. A bed of porous limestone adjacent to a fine-grained bed will provide greater permeability. Thus bedding planes exert a strong influence on the underground route water may take, deflecting its path through adjacent limestone beds or providing it with a preferred pathway.

Movement of water through small fissures in the limestone is dependent on a hydraulic gradient, and eventually much of the water reaches the water table, that level beneath which the pores of the rocks are water-saturated. Here, too, at the upper surface of the water table, this dissolving of the limestone, or *corrosion*, continues as a portion of the water gradually moves laterally. Lateral movement occurs because of discharge from major springs, a characteristic of limestone terrain; from seepages; or from streams flowing into surface rivers. Movement of the groundwater occurs primarily in its upper levels; J. Thrailkill has postulated that water movement in this zone is concentrated in the upper 100 meters, but primarily in the upper 10 meters.

The water's pathways through fissures and along bedding planes are slowly enlarged by corrosion. Initially certain of the fissures are naturally larger than others, and some of these will also have a greater hydraulic gradient than others. These will gradually appropriate more and more of the water, thereby continuing to enlarge exponentially, while the smaller pathways, their water totally or partially pirated by the larger, more favored ones, remain approximately the same size. Thus it is from the larger solutional cavities that caves are eventually developed.

Theoretically, it would appear that the water within the limestone would become saturated with calcium carbonate in solution very rapidly—perhaps within the first few inches of its travels—and therefore be incapable of further corrosion. Scientists long pondered the immensity of some underground chambers and gigantic cave systems and found difficulty in reconciling these great voids with water's limited corrosive power. It was not until 1964 that the theory of "mixed water corrosion" was proposed. It has been shown that a mixture of two waters, each saturated with calcium carbonate but each containing different amounts of it in solution, is capable of further solution of limestone. Within the network of fissures and larger cavities in limestone there is ample opportunity for water mixing and hence greatly enhanced possibilities for corrosion. This is particularly true at the water table and the zone immediately below it, for it is into this groundwater that the many disparate drainages of water from the surface, traveling through fissures, eventually find their way, and certainly a great amount of water mixing occurs in this location.

It was long thought that caves were simply formed by underground rivers in a manner similar to the cutting of river valleys aboveground. However, studies of cave characteristics over the past half century have altered this view. It is now generally accepted that many limestone caves, at least in their initial phase, were formed in the zone immediately below the water table or in other water-saturated zones. The zone below the water table where water flows under hydrostatic pressure is called the *phreatic zone*, and the water movement, *phreatic flow.*

One characteristic type of cave passage formed under phreatic or forced water flow is that of a circular or elliptical tube similar in form at both top and bottom, the entire tube having been subjected equally to the water and its action. Also, because the water flows under pressure, it is possible for the passage to form on an uphill gradient or even for the water to be forced directly upward for some distance, hollowing out a vertical chimney—usually a narrow, vertical shaft that may be of considerable height.

Once initial speleogenesis has occured, the water routes initiated may remain in the phreatic or water-filled zone. Many changes occur, however, both above and below ground, that profoundly affect solutional cavities or fully formed caves once they have developed in the phreatic zone. One of these changes may be the lowering of the water table in the general drainage area in which the cave is located. When this occurs, the cave passages are completely or partially drained of their water and filled with air. These may remain dry; often, however, the cave continues to serve as an underground drainage system. Water percolating from above by means of joints and bedding planes may accumulate to form a stream, but more often surface streams enter and flow through the caves. The lowest levels of the cave stream may in some cases correspond with the current water table. Below the cave itself, in the phreatic zone, further cave development may be continuing. Eventually the water table may again drop, leaving behind a second level of cave passages that originated in the phreatic zone. Conversely, water tables may also rise, and thus some caves that were once air-filled are today water-filled, or may have undergone these changes more than once. Some of the blue holes off the coast of Bermuda are examples of once air-filled caves that have been reinvaded by water —in this case as a result of rising sea levels.

Once air enters a cave, any water present flows through its passages under the pull of gravity, unlike the hydrostatic flow of phreatic water. This free, unconfined water movement is termed *vadose flow,* and an underground area subject to freely draining water is termed the *vadose zone.* The boundary between the vadose zone and the phreatic zone is the water table. Occasionally water flow may be of an intermediate type, at times under pressure, other times free-flowing; this is known as *paraphreatic flow.*

A vadose stream behaves much like its counterparts aboveground and greatly modifies and enlarges the cave through which it flows. This water not only corrodes but also mechanically wears away the limestone, for the stream carries sand, gravel, and rocks picked up from within the cave and from the outside. These abrade, gouge, scrape, and otherwise mechanically wear away at the stream's limestone bed; this process is called *corrasion.*

Initially the vadose stream exploits the preformed

phreatic passages; eventually it may develop additional vadose passages through its erosive powers. In contrast to the phreatic flow, when a vadose stream flows through an older phreatic tube or cavity, it does not normally wash the roof and upper portions of the phreatic tube, and these areas are less directly affected by the vadose flow. However, in the areas where the vadose flow does wash, changes are very pronounced. Where the stream flows along the cave floor it may cut deeply but narrowly downward, forming a gorge in the floor of the formerly rounded phreatic tube. In cross section these passages then assume the shape of an old-fashioned keyhole and are referred to as keyhole passages. Rather than a distinct gorge being cut along the cave floor, the stream's erosive power may be directed laterally, and a formerly circular phreatic tube through which the stream now travels will become broader at the bottom where the stream erodes and undercuts the cave walls.

As a surface stream may develop cutoffs, streambed potholes, meanders, and similar features, vadose flow will also do so underground when the proper conditions are present. The vadose flow, being pulled by gravity, continually seeks and where possible develops and adopts lower hydraulic routes. In time, upper cave levels may be abandoned by their stream as lower passages are invaded by the water. The eventual result is often cave development based upon a preexisting network of phreatic solutional cavities, and also through new hydraulic routes corroded and corraded out by the vadose stream. In generally horizontal limestone beds the passages formed often develop along a stairstep pattern. The water flows down a solutional cavity formed along a joint. This water reaches a bedding plane or an impermeable layer of rock and is diverted through voids corroded in the limestone until reaching a point where another joint-developed cavity or other weakness in the rock allows water to flow downward again. As a result of the stream's gravity flow along certain geological features and the development of numerous stairstep systems, a map of a mature vadose cave system located in generally horizontal limestone beds often has the appearance of a maze of city streets, the cave passages meeting or intersecting one another at approximately right angles. Vadose caves formed in inclined, rather than horizontal, beds of limestone often may have a more sloping profile.

Where solutional cavities have formed along master joints or faults the vadose stream may plunge downward with tremendous force for impressive distances. Such a vertical shaft descending from a horizontal passage is called a *pit*. When large waterfalls are present they stir strong air currents in the pits and water is splashed and sprayed against the walls, flowing downward and corroding them until the voids often assume a cylindrical form, often with a notch worn at the location where the water flows over the edge. Deep pits many yards in diameter with massive waterfalls present spectacular cave scenery and demanding and dangerous challenges for the caver who seeks to descend and ascend them.

Surface water seeping downward in the vadose cave from a surface inlet may corrode out a vertical, usually somewhat oval or circular opening called a *dome* in the ceiling of a cave passage. The walls of this cavity are marked with vertical grooves by the action of the corroding water flowing downward over their surfaces. In some cases this vertical solutional void may extend into a pit below the passage floor called a *domepit*. The term dome is also used for a rounded opening, closed at the top, that is located in the ceiling of a cave passage and has been corroded out under phreatic flow.

As noted earlier, uphill sections of cave passages may be formed during a phreatic phase. Later, during a vadose phase, a U-shaped tube is formed where the lower portion of the cave passage meets the uphill gradient; this may be permanently flooded. Thus a phreatic or water-filled section may occur within an otherwise vadose cave passage. A section of cave that is obstructed in this way is termed a *siphon*.

The breaking away of blocks, slabs, or smaller pieces of rock from the cave ceiling or walls, which is known as *cavern breakdown,* may strongly affect the shape of a cave. Block breakdown is a term often used to denote massive breakdown in which the rock derived from more than one bed remains as a coherent unit. Slab breakdown refers to that derived from a single bed. Chip breakdown refers to rock fragments of a smaller size. In its phreatic phase, the water within the cave helps to support the weight of the cave roof. When the phreatic flow is drained this support is lost, and breakdown may occur. Factors influencing roof breakdown include such variables as the weight of overlying beds above the cave, the shape of the cave passage, the thickness of the limestone bed that forms the cave roof, and the distribution of joints within that bed. Thus a thin limestone bed with numerous joints would be expected to be more prone to breakdown than would a massive bed with relatively fewer joints.

Erosion and undercutting of cave walls by vadose streams promotes breakdown from the walls. Major breakdown from a cave ceiling has seldom been observed, but cavers should take loosened wall rock susceptible to breakdown into consideration when climbing.

In colder climates some breakdown at or very near cave entrances is caused by ice. Water within the limestone fractures freezes, exerting pressure against the rock. Repeated freezing and thawing may eventually cause portions of the rock to shatter, and rock fragments may break away.

Breakdown from ceiling and walls is evidenced by mounds of rock fragments ranging in size from small to massive that often litter or cover portions of a cave floor and may be large enough to require scrambling by cavers, or to block a passage completely.

Another distinctive physical feature of caves is the sediments they contain. These can be classified as *endogenetic,* or derived from processes operating within the cave, and *exogenetic,* or derived from external sources and transported into the cave by such forces as water, wind, ice, and animals—including man. These two types of sediments, of course, are often mixed within a cave.

Endogenetic sediments include insoluble residues freed from the dissolved limestone, such as sand, silt, mud, and quartz. Blocks or smaller-sized pieces of limestone broken from ceiling and walls as well as other gravels and sands may be carried along by water in the cave. Deep in the earth's crust, fractures in limestone may occasionally be invaded by fluids that fill the voids with minerals as they cool. Eventually these minerals may be freed from the limestone to become a part of the sediment.

Exogenetic sediments tend to be varied and plentiful, dependent upon many variables, such as the transport agent; the portion of the cave being examined, for example, the entrance or the deep interior; the immediate environment outside the cave; and others. Some of the materials that are carried into the caves, fall through surface openings, or enter through other means include dust, glacial till, loess, clay, mud, peat, silt, sand, gravel, rocks, plant debris, bones and other animal remains, materials (including burials) from man's occupancy, and bat and bird guano.

Caves may act as traps for sedimentary materials, and deposits several feet deep may form in vadose caves. As moving water slows, losing some of its force, it drops the heaviest materials it is carrying first; therefore water-deposited sediments within a cave often tend to become finer the deeper they are deposited. Occasionally a flood of unusual magnitude may wash through a cave, flushing before it sediments that had been collecting over a long period of time. During such a flood, water may overflow into cave passages that ordinarily do not cary vadose flow; sediments will be deposited in these passages as the waters recede.

Caves that are dry or receive only very limited quantities of water are commonly known as *dead* or *inactive* caves. Those with streams are known as *active* or *wet* caves. The latter can be further subdivided. Some are known as *influent* or *inlet* caves, which means that they have streams entering them. *Effluent* or *outlet* caves have streams flowing out of them, often as a spring, sometimes as a stream with a free air surface above it. Occasionally a caver can both enter and depart from a cave by following its stream; this type is known as a *through* or *tunnel* cave. Effluent, influent, and through caves may at a later date lose their streamflow, with a lowering of the water tables, so dry equivalents of these types also occur.

Many vadose streams, while still within the cave, disappear by sinking into rocky debris, flowing into a pool, disappearing into small passages, or feeding into the phreatic level. This "lost" water may eventually reappear somewhere on the surface, such as through springs, but its route of travel is not always readily apparent. In studying water supplies and flows, hydrologists sometimes add a harmless but potent coloring agent known as fluorescein dye to cave streams, then watch for the brightly colored water to appear at resurgences on the surface. Another method often used is that of placing dyed spores of club moss, *Lycopodium clavatum*, in the water. These very small spores are then collected where they reemerge by means of fine plankton nets. One advantage of the spores is that they can be dyed various colors. Spores of one color can be released from one location, those of a different color from a second location, and so on. Thus several experiments or tracings can be conducted in the same general area simultaneously. A *resurgence* is the reemergence at the surface as a stream or spring of a watercourse that originally was a surface stream before entering the limestone. An *exsurgence* is the re-emergence at the surface of water that simply fell upon limestone and percolated downward through it. In common usage little distinction is made regarding the origin of the water, and the term resurgence is the one most often used referring, as an overall term, to the point where water exits a cave through a spring or stream.

The formation of caves in limestone by the action of water would appear to follow a simple formula that could be expected to produce many similar-appearing cavities in rock. But limestone caves, although often sharing many characteristics, are infinite in their variety. As we have noted, the geological structure, including joints, faults, bedding planes, and the depth and orientation of the limestone beds are of vital significance in determining the form a cave will assume. Most limestone caves are formed in a typical massive, fissured, fine-grained limestone; however, in some parts of the world caves have formed in quite porous limestone and these have distinctive features.

Other types of rock in the immediate area will often influence cave development. Limestone beds may be overlaid by other kinds of sedimentary rock. These may be impermeable and prevent the downward percolation of rainwater to limestone; or runoff from these may gather at their perimeters, and in these areas large amounts of runoff may reach limestone beds directly below. Conversely, if the upper layers of rock are porous they will allow water to percolate through them to reach the limestone. Strata underlying limestone beds may assume importance also; for example, these may be impermeable, thereby having an absolute effect upon the depth at which cave formation can occur in that location.

Climate exercises a tremendous influence on cave formation. The amount of water available is of importance; limestone areas with high rainfall or snowfall have greater cave potential than those with limited moisture. However, temperature is also an influence, for in very cold, high mountain or arctic land, even though moisture is present, it may be frozen most or all of the year, in which case its potential for cave development is limited or nonexistent. Carbon dioxide is more soluble in colder than in warmer waters; hence colder climates may offer a greater possibility for limestone corrosion. This advantage is offset, however, if temperatures are low enough for the water to be frozen for part of the year. In the world's mid-latitudes temperatures vary widely on a seasonal basis, and this is reflected in the temperatures of the upper layers of the earth. These variations result in water of varying temperatures and therefore with varying amounts of carbon dioxide held in solution. Such variations offer enhanced opportunities for mixture corrosion and consequent cave development. It is in the mid-latitudes that the longest, largest, and deepest caves are currently known to occur. However, many areas of the world are relatively unexplored insofar as caves are concerned, and the tropics may well contain interesting record-setting cave systems waiting to be discovered.

Climate may also strongly affect the interiors of caves, particularly in the formation of stalactites and stalagmites and other speleothems. And while not directly related to cave development, temperatures greatly affect the biota (that is, the living things) inhabiting caves. Cave temperatures, obviously, may range from those that result in permanent ice in caves to year-round warm temperatures in tropical caves that are conducive to large cave animal populations.

Climatic history has a strong bearing on the caves we see today. Thus caves may occur in environments that are currently arid or semiarid. For example, world famous Carlsbad Caverns is located in semiarid New Mexico, yet contains vast rooms. These are considered to have been formed in pluvial climatic periods—that is, during prolonged periods of wet climate. Certainly the ice ages with their attendant glaciers had profound effects upon cave development over large portions of the Northern Hemisphere. Variations in temperature and streamflow between glacial periods were tremendous influences, at one extreme inhibiting and at the other extreme promoting cave development. Also, the glaciers scoured out deep river valleys in mountainous limestone, which, after the withdrawal of the ice, drastically lowered water table levels. As a result, water within the mountain masses cut downward toward the river valleys, causing the formation of steeply descending, frequently stepped caves. The weight of masses of ice above some caves caused massive changes, ranging from rock breakdown to cave destruction. Great quantities of water were released during the interglacial periods, causing numerous changes on and under the earth's surface.

Cave development may also be influenced by the amount of, or changes in, the vegetational cover on the surface. Tropical regions with lush vegetational cover provide rich sources of carbon dioxide. The Arctic presents the opposite extreme. Where man has removed forests, or where in past times climatic changes producing increasing aridity have reduced vegetation, cave development doubtlessly has been slowed.

We have focused in this chapter on limestone caves, voids lying beneath the earth's surface. It is important to understand that these often constitute a part of a larger whole—a very distinct type of limestone landform known as *karst*. We tend to think of a "normal" landscape as one in which rainfall drains into organized streams and rivers. These flow through valleys that they create. In such areas breakdown of surface rock mixes with organic matter and soil is formed. Depressions or cavities on the ground surface eventually tend to be filled with soil and other material.

This does not occur in karst lands, which are marked by solutional activity. Karst is a solution-controlled landform developed in calcareous rock, and many of its features are subsurface ones. Karst occurs where there are massive, surface-exposed limestone beds. Because of the solutional nature of limestone, rainfall flows into its fractures and cracks and these grow progressively larger by solution. The limestone surface also is marked by the water's dissolving power. Water enters the available openings in the limestone, flows or percolates downward, and often forms and enlarges caves, where it is gathered in stream form; these then flow through underground drainage systems. Thus in classic karst lands drainage is vertical, then underground; there are no, or very few, surface waterways. Because the bedrock is dissolved and carried away in solution, relatively little soil is formed, vegetation is likely to be sparse, and the terrain tends to be rocky and sometimes desolate. Where water finds its way into the limestone a depression is often formed. This grows larger through the water's dissolving power, rather than being filled in. Sufficient quantities of water, usually at least 10 or more inches of annual rainfall, are a prerequisite for karst to form. Thus desert areas often do not develop typical karst landscapes.

Many additional landforms are often associated

with karst. These include limestone springs, or streams with air above them, which serve as resurgences for phreatic or vadose water in limestone. Blind valleys, half-blind valleys, pocket valleys, and dry valleys may be present. A normal stream may flow onto a massive limestone area and sink into it at one point. Where this valley "dead-ends," a blind valley is formed. A half-blind valley is one in which a stream normally flows into the limestone at one point, but may, under unusually high water conditions, have a portion of its water flow beyond that point along the surface. Pocket valleys are those formed where water emerges from, rather than enters, the limestone. Thus large limestone springs often cause a U-shaped valley to develop, the resurgence at the bottom of the U, that is, at the head of the valley. Dry valleys may occur in some karst areas; these may be related to local rainfall patterns, to past drainage systems that once occurred above the limestone, or to other factors.

Perhaps the most characteristic feature of karst, and certainly one of importance to cavers, is the circular or nearly circular closed depressions in the surface of the limestone. Much of the water drains underground though these depressions. These drains are located where a joint or fracture allows water to enter the bedrock; solution enlarges the area into a circular depression that in cross section would appear funnel- or bowl-shaped. These features are known as *dolines*, or more commonly in the United States as *sinks* or *sinkholes.* They may vary from a meter or less in width to tens of miles in some of the classic European karst (the latter are known as *poljes*). Often sinks are very dense in occurrence, up to several hundred per square mile , and their edges may touch or actually overlap. A depression formed of coalescent dolines is known as an *uvala.* Dense groups of dolines or sinks are often referred to as sinkhole plains in the United States. Sinks may be developed due to solution; they may also result from the collapse of portions of the roof of underlying cave passages, and some may be the result of a combination of the two. To the caver sinks indicate a strong possibility of caves below, and often entry into a cave is provided through a sink.

Dolines, sinks, or sinkhole plains as described above are features of generally temperate to colder karst landscapes. In the tropics the rather circular doline is replaced by star-shaped, irregular hollows. These are known as *cockpits* and are separated by rather regular, conical hills. Yet another form is the tower or pinnacle karst. Classic examples of tower karst are present in southern China. Here plains are studded with steep, isolated, vertical-sided limestone towers that often contain caves within them. Still other distinctive karst terrains exist in other parts of the world.

It is obvious that any particular limestone cave is the total product of a vast number of factors, which, in combination, have caused its genesis and subsequent development. No two caves are exactly alike. What made each the way we find it today poses intriguing questions. Some of the answers are readily discernible; others, not at all. Exploring the differences, posing the questions, and seeking the answers are strong motivators luring cavers inward, onward, and downward.

3

CAVE MINERALS AND SPELEOTHEMS

LIMESTONE IS NOT THE only type of rock in which caves formed by solution may occur, although it is the most common one. Caves may be formed, for example, in salt and gypsum.

Salt, NaCl, has a solubility in water of approximately 26,000 parts per million (ppm). Gypsum, $CaSO_4 \cdot 2H_2O$, has a solubility of approximately 2,000 ppm. The solution of salt and gypsum, unlike that of limestone, is straightforward and not dependent upon the addition of carbonic acid. We noted earlier that the solubility of limestone, even when corroded by water charged with carbon dioxide, is at a maximum only 400 to 500 ppm. Thus both salt and gypsum have very high rates of solubility, and caves may form in them; however, salt is so soluble that the mineral deposit itself may break down almost as rapidly as the cave is formed within it. For this reason, and also because large deposits of salt and gypsum are not numerous, caves formed within these minerals are much less common than those formed in limestone.

There are other rocks in which solutional caves may be formed that are closely related to limestone. One of these is marble, which is simply metamorphosed limestone. A second is dolomite, $CaMg(CO_3)_2$, a carbonate in which much of the soluble calcium carbonate has been replaced by magnesium carbonate. The latter dissolves somewhat less readily than calcite, hence cave formation in dolomite, although very similar to that in calcite, may be slower. Thus in speaking of limestone caves and all their features we are actually using an umbrella term that includes all caves formed in carbonate rocks. However, we are not including caves formed in salt or gypsum unless specifically stated.

Distinctive physical features of limestone caves may be divided into four general groups: clastic fills, speleogens, petromorphs, and speleothems.

CLASTIC FILLS

The term *clastic fill* refers to rocks and materials derived from rocks, such as sand and silt, as well as other particulate matter, such as bones. We discussed these materials in terms of sediments and cave breakdown in the previous chapter. Clastic fills may be of significant depth and breadth, occasionally completely blocking or filling a cave passage. In some cases calcite may be deposited upon the fills, thereby crusting, cementing, or otherwise stabilizing them. These accumulations are often scientifically valuable. They may contain important sequences of bones of extinct animals; materials related to human cultures, important to archaeologists; or pollens that, when analyzed, provide important information regarding climatic history over thousands of years. Weathering, in the usual sense of the term, is reduced or practically nonexistent underground, and erosion of many such cave deposits is negligible. Therefore deposits in caves are often far less disturbed than surface materials, which are vulnerable to many destructive forces.

Clastic fills should never be disturbed except by scientists equipped to study them correctly. Even these individuals should excavate only when a real justification can be presented. Scientists today tend to excavate as sparingly as is feasible, when possible leaving a portion of the deposit intact. There is good reason for this. New scientific techniques are constantly being developed. If a portion of a deposit is left *in situ*, further study of it in twenty, fifty, or a hundred years may reveal a great deal of additional information due to future advancements in equipment, techniques, and knowledge.

SPELEOGENS

Speleogens are those features that result from removal of the bedrock through corrasion or corrosion. Dome-pits and other vertical shafts are often considered to be speleogens, as are vadose-sculpted stream canyons; narrow streambed floor slots; incised meanders and cutoffs; grooves cut into the cave walls by the vadose flow; and streambed potholes—generally circular, bowl-shaped depressions worn in the bed by the grinding action of stones or gravel whirled around by the water. Where films or small flows of water descend vertical walls, as in domepits, irregular solution of the limestone may cause the development of vertical grooves known as *ribbing*. Partial, irregular solution of the bedrock may at times cause a jagged and unpatterned sculpting of the limestone; this is often referred to as *hackling*.

Speleogens formed under phreatic conditions include solutional pockets or other cavities formed in the ceiling and in and on the cave walls. *Spongework* or *honeycombing* is a particular type of solutional feature consisting of many interconnected, rounded, minor cavities separated by irregular partitions of remaining bedrock, resulting from the differential solubility of the limestone. *Pockets* are cavities larger than those of spongework, and the individual pockets are separated by areas of unaffected wall. *Joint-determined cavities* in the ceiling and walls are often narrow, deep slots that have been dissolved out along a joint. *Anastomoses* are small, tubelike solutional cavities that twist, branch, and intersect, forming an irregular, intricate network. These tubes lie in one plane and occur in both joint and bedding planes, most often in the latter.

Scallops are small, asymmetric, concave hollows occuring in groups, and are sculpted by flowing water on the surface of bedrock. Scallops may also be formed on other types of rock, and in ice, mud, and clay. When formed in limestone, scallops have rounded edges on their upstream side, are more pointed at their downstream end, and in cross section display a steeper slope at their upstream end. Scallops thus serve as indicators of the direction of water flow. They may also serve as indicators of the velocity of the flow that formed them. Scallops vary in size, as measured from crest to crest, from a few millimeters to a meter or occasionally more. The distance between the crests is considered to be inversely proportional to the flow velocity; thus the smaller the scallops, the faster the water flow. Scallops are associated with some phreatic flow and with some vadose streams, past or present, and are shaped in the limestone forming the streambed or the portion of the cave walls washed by the water. Abrasion destroys scallops; therefore streams carrying significant amounts of abrasive material will not produce them, or may destroy them when present.

PETROMORPHS

Petromorphs are secondary mineral deposits within the limestone bedrock that became exposed in the course of the cave's development. A well-known example is that of *boxwork*, which is composed of mineral blades projecting from cave ceilings and walls, forming an irregular, intersecting pattern resembling a honeycomb. In the case of boxwork, veins within the limestone were originally filled with a mineral; common examples are calcite, gypsum, or quartz. When the vein fillings do not dissolve as readily as the limestone about them, they remain projecting from the bedrock, following the solutional breakdown of the enclosing limestone. Boxwork may also occur in gypsum caves. In this case cracks in gypsum bedrock have become filled with selenite, which is a less soluble variety of gypsum. As the gypsum bedrock is dissolved, the selenite fillings are left exposed.

A second example of petromorphs is that of mineral-lined *vugs*. Vugs are small (usually less than man-size) cavities in rocks or veins which are often crystal-lined or filled and are exposed during cave development.

SPELEOTHEMS

The fourth group of cave features includes the distinctive formations that provide great beauty in many caves. These are the *speleothems* (a word derived from the Greek *spelaion*, meaning "cave," and *thema*, meaning "deposit"), which are secondary mineral deposits formed in the caves themselves. Secondary minerals are formed through chemical action from primary minerals in the bedrock or material carried into the cave, such as sediments. Included in this category are the familiar stalagmites and stalactites, as well as a vast array of lesser-known speleothem types. Water percolating downward through soil, rock, and fissures takes into solution various substances derived from the matrix through which it has moved. When this water enters the stable cave environment, conditions are ideal for the deposition in the cave of minerals carried in the water. Over eighty minerals have been recognized from solution caves. Of these only twenty are at all common; the remaining sixty are rare in caves and are the result of unusual circumstances or conditions. The carbonate minerals are by far the most common of the cave deposits.

As noted earlier, water charged with carbon dioxide corrodes limestone, forming caves within it. Conversely, such water entering an air-filled cave often partially fills in the space previously created with secondary mineral deposits such as calcite. Water entering a cave by percolation downward through soil and limestone bedrock often has a carbon dioxide content 25 to 250 times higher than that of the atmosphere and is therefore capable of carrying quantities of calcium carbonate in solution. The carbon dioxide content of cave air is ordinarily not a great deal higher than that of the atmosphere. As the water reaches the air-filled space, it begins to lose carbon dioxide to the cave air until equilibrium is reached. As the carbon dioxide is lost, the amount of carbonate mineral the water can continue to hold in solution is proportionately lowered; hence calcite or another carbonate mineral is precipitated.

Minerals can also be deposited in caves by means of evaporation. When cave water evaporates, deposition of minerals may occur. A majority of caves, however, have a high level of humidity, and evaporation in these locations is a minor factor in speleothem formation.

Speleothems can be grouped according to mineral class, origin, or morphology (form). The latter category includes the following three groups. The *dripstone* and *flowstone* forms, also known as *gravitomorphic* forms, are developed as a result of vadose water moving under the influence of gravity. The second group consists of the *erratic* or *nongravitomorphic* forms. The third group consists of *subaqueous* forms, speleothems formed in cave lakes or pools.

Names of speleothems are confusingly varied. Some names, such as flowstone, denote origin; others, such as cave pearl or draperies, describe the form of the speleothem. Some are combinations of words that provide more than a single bit of information, often about both the type of mineral and the form; for example, selenite needles. Still other names are more fanciful and colloquial, such as fried eggs or cave cauliflower.

Carbonates

Carbonate minerals found in caves include calcite, aragonite, dolomite, huntite, hydrocalcite, hydromagnesite, magnesite, and nesquehonite. Calcite and aragonite have the same chemical composition but have contrasting crystal structures. Aragonite may at times revert to calcite. It has long been thought that aragonite tends to be formed in warmer caves, and calcite in cooler ones; however, this statement is challenged by some speleologists. Additional factors also have a bearing on which of the two minerals will be deposited. Calcite is by far the most common mineral deposited in limestone caves. Let us survey some of the speleothem types that are commonly formed by carbonate minerals, beginning with the dripstone and flowstone forms.

A *stalactite* is a speleothem that hangs vertically from a cave ceiling or ledge and is formed by dripping water. A water drop hangs from the ceiling, carbon dioxide is lost to the air, the water becomes super-saturated, and a thin film of calcite forms over it. As the water drop breaks away, the calcite ring remains attached to the ceiling or to the calcite deposits of previous drops. More drops follow, hanging then falling from the hollow center of the gradually length-ening calcite tube. These long, hollow tubes, their diameter approximately that of a single drop, are often referred to as soda straws or tubular stalactites. Under stable conditions with a constant water supply, soda straws may be one-fourth to one-half inch in diameter and grow to be several yards in length. They are extremely delicate and easily broken.

There are many factors that may cause a change in the growth pattern of these hollow tubes. The water supply may increase or decrease, thus changing the drip rate. The hollow central canal may become partially or wholly clogged. The wall may rupture. Water may percolate from the hollow canal to the outer surface. An increase in the amount of water may cause the water to flow both externally and internally. An increase in water entering the cave may cause additional drip sites to form adjacent to the tubular stalactite, enlarging it. There may be seasonal variations in growth. The calcite may become stained with mineral impurities. The end result is that the relatively simple tube shape is often greatly changed and the stalactite may gradually assume an icicle or conical shape. Even large stalactites may have at least a remnant of the central canal, but the vast amount of their bulk ultimately derives from water moving over their outer surface. In a cross section such a stalactite often displays growth rings reminiscent of a tree's growth rings in appearance. The ultimate size a stalactite may reach is limited by the weight that it can support.

As water drops from the tip of a stalactite it hits the cave floor. The force of impact may cause further loss of carbon dioxide with consequent deposition of carbonate. A *stalagmite*, defined as a convex deposit formed by dripping water, gradually develops. As this deposit increases in size, water runs down its sides and additional carbonate is deposited. The stalagmite, unlike the stalactite, has no central canal. The diameter of a stalagmite fed by a single drip point is limited, for the water spreads out radially from its point of contact. Precipitation of the mineral is greatest at this central point and decreases toward its outer limits. Therefore stalagmites formed under constant conditions from a steady, unvarying drip often assume a tall, cylindrical shape with a rounded top, the whole made up of convex or caplike layers. As with the stalactites, however, many factors may influence the ultimate shape of a stalagmite. These include humidity, temperature, the amount of water, its solution concentration, the height from which the water drops, changes in drip rates, impurities, and other factors. Also, more than one drip point may ultimately feed a stalagmite, and this results in stalagmite forms that may resemble pillars, stools, mushrooms, cones, cauliflower, or even fried eggs. The latter term is used for the top of a stalagmite that has a round center stained yellow, surrounded by a white calcite rim. The size of stalagmites is not limited by weight considerations, as it is for stalactites, and they may reach very large sizes. Some exceptionally tall ones, over 120 feet in height, exist. In cases where a stalactite and stalagmite meet and join, the formation is called a *column*. The term pillar is sometimes incorrectly used for this speleothem. In cave terminology a *pillar* is a supporting piece of bedrock that remains when all the bedrock around it has been removed due to solution or other causes.

Dripping water may also create smaller and less common formations than the familiar stalactites and stalagmites. Among these are *conulite* or *mud cups*. In this case water drips into mud, drilling and splashing, causing a circular or cone-shaped cavity. Thin carbonate coatings gradually cover the mud walls of the cavity, forming cup shapes. In some cases the surrounding mud may later be partially eroded away, leaving the cups exposed.

Thin films or sheets of water flowing over the cave surfaces, such as floors, walls, and ledges, may produce the large sheetlike speleothems known as *flowstone.* These deposits may be massive, becoming large enough to block cave passages. Where the water flows over ledges, the carbonate may build up huge deposits known as frozen waterfalls or cascades. Flowstone may form over the tops of clastic fills; if the fills are later eroded away, the largely unsupported flowstone may still remain, forming what is known as a canopy. In some cases a canopylike flowstone formation may form without the clastic fill support; these assume a bell shape, and the formation is known as a bell canopy.

Draperies are sheetlike, often curving and folded speleothems that hang from cave ceilings, walls, or ledges; they often resemble undulating curtains. Draperies are formed where water flows downward along an inclined ceiling or ledge surface, leaving an elongated streak of deposited mineral. The draperies are often less than an inch in thickness, may be several feet in height and length, and may be translucent. In some cases impurities may be present in certain bands of the deposit. Draperies with stained bands running through them are popularly known as cave bacon.

Erratic speleothems are varied, and in some cases their means of formation is not completely understood. Some are formed due to seeping water. Crusts or erratic coatings of calcite may occur due to water seeping out of cracks in a cave wall. In some ways the end result is similar to flowstone, except that flowstone is formed by flowing water. Erratic speleothems formed by seepage may intergrade with flowstone in some cases.

The terms *coralloidal* or *botryoidal* are used to

describe a variety of distinctive speleothems, including those popularly known as cave cauliflower, grapefruit, popcorn, grapes, coral, and clouds. Basically, most of these are globular formations composed of concentric layers of carbonate. The individual nodules range in size from less than an inch in diameter for cave popcorn and grapes to a yard or more in diameter for masses of cave clouds. The origin of this type of speleothem remains open to debate, although one possible source is a film of water derived from seepage that bathes the outside of the speleothem; some are thought to be of splash origin.

Helictites, of all the speleothems included in this category, seem to fit most aptly the classification of erratic. These are delicate, twisted, hairlike to wormlike forms that appear to grow up, down, and sideways with no relationship to gravity. Their name is derived from the word *helix*, meaning "spiral." Their twisted forms may rise from cave walls and ceilings. When they arise from the cave floor or from the surfaces of other speleothems they are called *heligmites*. In general the diameter of these twisted, tubelike speleothems is limited, and within each is a central canal of extremely small size. Helictites are usually small speleothems, although one exceptional specimen has been reported to be approximately 4 meters in length.

Helictites are formed by seeping water. A very small amount of water is forced by hydrostatic pressure through a minute opening in a cave surface. The water evaporates and a thin, cone-shaped crystal is deposited about the opening. As more water is forced through the opening and the precipitated material, it too evaporates at the outer reaches of the precipitate, and the formation continues to grow. Thus helictites grow from their tips. There is some conjecture regarding the matter, but it appears that the twisted growth of the speleothem may be due to a variety of factors. The erratic, nongravitational form suggests that the forces having to do with crystal growth, aided by the extremely slow seepage of water that never attains drop size, are dominant over the gravitational forces of faster-moving water that forms specific drops. It is thought that the eccentric growth pattern may be due to the fact that each of the tiny cone-shaped layers making up the whole does not fit perfectly with the previous one; hence growth is tilted. Heligmites may also form on the sides of stalactites; these may be caused by seepage from a stalactite whose central canal is partially or completely blocked, although this explanation does not explain all such occurrences.

Shields, or *palettes* as they are sometimes known, are semicircular speleothems that are attached by their straight edge to the cave ceiling, wall, or floor, and project outward at random angles from their attachment. Shields may be several feet in diameter and are often approximately an inch in thickness. Each is composed of two parallel plates separated by a medial fracture. Water is pushed by hydrostatic pressure through a small joint or fracture in a cave wall. Deposition of carbonate occurs. As more water is forced through the opening, it moves outward by capillary action through the small central fracture, which serves as a continuation of the bedrock fracture. Mineral deposition in layers occurs at the expanding, hemispherical outer edge of the deposit. Thus the central void is maintained between the two discs, transporting water and the carbonate it carries to the ever-expanding outer edges of the discs. Because the water is under hydrostatic pressure, the shields may form at any angle. In some cases, if the supply of water is increased, water will form drops at the outer edge of the medial crack, and stalactites or draperies will form along the outer edge of the bottom half of the shield. A decrease in the amount of water may cause the central void to fill with calcite; a later increase in hydrostatic pressure may then cause a breakthrough in one area of the shield, causing the development of a new shield.

Anthodites (from the Greek *anthos*, meaning "flower") are flowerlike speleothems composed of clusters of quill-like crystals of aragonite, or very occasionally of calcite. One type, known as frostwork, consists of radiating clusters made up of masses of icy-looking, short aragonite crystals. Frostwork is normally found in conjunction with botryoidal speleo-thems. Another type, known as quill anthodites, has a heavier, less delicate, more branched appearance than frostwork.

Moonmilk is one of the strangest carbonate de-posits in the cave world. This formless deposit is soft, pasty, and cheeselike when wet, and powdery and somewhat sticky when dry. Most commonly it is com-posed of calcite, but may be made up of any of several other carbonate minerals. Moonmilk has been found frequently in alpine caves, yet also occurs in other locations, including caves in arid areas. Its means of formation is open to debate. It is theorized that moonmilk formation may be due to the disintegration of limestone through the action of microorganisms.

The third large category of speleothems is the subaqueous forms. Water in cave pools and lakes may become supersaturated with calcite as carbon dioxide is lost from the water's surface to the cave atmosphere. Calcite may then be deposited in a variety of forms. *Cave bubbles* are thin-walled, round, hollow speleothems of calcite up to $\frac{3}{16}$ inch (5 millimeters) in diameter. They are formed when calcite is deposited around gas bubbles in the water. Initially the cave bubbles float in the water; eventually, as more calcite is deposited on them, they become heavier and sink to the bottom of the pool.

Cave rafts are free-floating, exceedingly thin crusts of calcite or aragonite that form on the water surface in quiet cave pools. Layers of sunken rafts may collect on the pool bottoms.

Shelfstone is somewhat similar to cave rafts, except that it is attached to the cave wall and grows outward from it at and just below the water surface. It may also form outward from objects such as stalag-mites that have been submerged in a pool. Shelfstone may reach substantial size and thickness. Later, if the water in the pool is drained or evaporated, the shelf-stone often remains as projections from the cave wall.

Rimstone dams, sometimes called *gours*, are dams composed of calcite or aragonite and are formed by mineral deposition where water flows over floor irregularities, on steep flowstone slopes, or often in cave streams at the overflowing edges of pools. These dams may vary from a few centimeters to several meters in height and may be many meters in length. They often become very large in tropical caves. Frequently each dam encloses a pool of water behind it, and some of these pools may be of very large size. It is thought that dam formation commonly occurs at the shallowest point of a pool, where water overflows the pool edge. The turbulence caused by the overflow increases carbon dioxide loss, causing carbonate deposition. As any particular shallow point is filled with the mineral, the overflow then occurs at a new shallow location; the dam continues to build, achieving and maintaining a rather uniform height during its growth. Often a series of many such dams is formed along a stream or slope and a stairstep or terraced pattern results.

Concretions are spherical or slightly more irregularly shaped deposits of calcium carbonate that have been built up in concentric mineral layers formed about a nucleus of material such as gravel, sand, or similar small objects. Cave pearls are the best known concretions; they usually occur in groups lying in "nests," that is, shallow depressions in cave floors. These concretions are formed where the dripping of water produces sufficient agitation and rotation of the pearls to prevent them from being cemented in place. Concretions other than pearls may also be formed in locations where they are covered by water for long periods.

The term *spar* is used for distinctive large calcite crystals that have been formed in still, undisturbed cave pools or water-filled cavities. Two well-known types are dogtooth spar and nailhead spar. Both resemble their namesakes in shape. The individual dogtooth crystals are often approximately the size of a dog's tooth, although crystals 6 inches (15 centimeters) in length have been reported; they occur commonly in clumps or large masses. Dogtooth spar is more commonly found than is the nailhead. In some instances crystals may line the walls of a pool; later, if the water is drained, the crystal-lined cavity remains. Occasionally caves may be mineralized while filled with water; when drained their walls and ceiling may be lined with crystal. Certain caves in the Black Hills of South Dakota have resplendent passages that are lined or adorned with spar.

In their pure form the carbonate minerals we have been discussing have no color, and the speleothems formed of them may be transparent or more often translucent. However, impurities are usually present, and these color the speleothems to varying degrees. Yellows and tans may be caused by iron; brown by silt; black, blue, and bluish-gray from manganese; green from copper; some yellows from nickel. Some other colors are as yet unexplained, although it is conjectured that red coloration, in some cases, may be due to microbial activity. Indeed there is much debate regarding the role microorganisms may possibly play, not only on the coloration of some speleothems, but also in their actual formation. Microorganisms have been cultured from various speleothems. Their presence in these locations, however, does not necessarily prove causation of coloration or formation.

Some speleothems composed of carbonate or sulfate minerals exhibit luminescence after being illuminated by a light such as a photographer's strobe light. The luminescence can occur in a wide variety of colors, and its duration ranges from seconds to a few minutes. It is caused by small amounts of impurities included in the carbonate or sulfate crystal.

The presence of speleothems in a cave is dependent upon a variety of factors, some of which are similar or identical to those that cause the cave to form originally. Thus carbonate deposits tend to be more numerous and more massive in tropical or near-tropical than in temperate or cold regions. Reasons for this include more vegetation and a longer growing season in the tropics, hence larger amounts of carbon dioxide in the soil. Also, the tropics receive more precipitation than temperate areas, and no freezing of the soil takes place, thereby allowing year-round percolation of quantities of water through the ground.

In general, calcite speleothems are exceedingly slow growing. Studies of some stalactites reveal that the rate of growth is never much over 2 millimeters per year and that annual growth may average only a little more than one-tenth of a millimeter (Moore and Sullivan, 1978). It is difficult to determine the exact ages of speleothems, although various means, including radioactive isotope methods, are being employed in an attempt to do so. One of these, the thorium-230 method, is considered by many speleologists to provide accurate dating of some calcite stalagmites, up to an age of approximately 300,000 years. Scientists using measurements of thorium isotopes reported the age of one stalagmite as 90,000 to 270,000 years, the younger age derived from dating its outer portions, the older from its more central portions (Warwick, 1976). Studies regarding speleothem dating, and the information that can be derived from analysis of the calcite of which speleothems are composed, are gaining momentum. The calcite studies are providing scientists with a record of past temperature and precipitation changes, thereby providing important information regarding paleoclimates.

The age of the limestone caves themselves, as we see them today, is a matter of some conjecture. The age of the limestone beds in which they lie varies. For example, the approximate age for the limestone in which Carlsbad Caverns is located is judged to be 250 million years, while that of Lehman Caves in Nevada is 550 million years. It is thought that the caves are much younger than the limestone in which they are found. It is estimated that large limestone caves are at least 1 million years old, but less than 10 million years in age (Moore and Sullivan, 1978).

Sulfates

It is estimated that the second most common mineral in caves is gypsum, a sulfate mineral. (The most common cave mineral is calcite; some authorities consider aragonite to be the third most common, while others place ice in third place.) The primary means of deposition of sulfates in caves is by the simple evaporation of water carrying the mineral. Water percolating through rock that contains sulfates dissolves some of the mineral and carries it in solution. When that water enters the cave environment the water may be evaporated, providing the cave atmosphere is not prohibitively humid, and the sulfate is then deposited. Also, chemical reactions within limestone bedrock may cause deposition of gypsum. For example, water may percolate downward through sandstone that contains pyrite, that is, iron sulphide. Some of the sulfate is carried in solution by the water into a limestone cave where the mineral reacts with the limestone to form gypsum, which is then deposited in the cave. Sulphate minerals may also be present in veins in limestone, causing formation of gypsum when exposed to the air of the cave. In addition to gypsum, other sulfates found in caves include epsomite (Epsom salt's), and mirabilite (Glauber salts); these two are not particularly common. Even rarer are celestite, thenardite, hexahydrite, and bloedite.

Speleothems formed by sulfates are often known as *evaporite* speleothems. Due to differences in the way in which they are deposited, and more importantly, due to basic differences in crystal growth habits, speleothems formed of sulfates are often much different from those formed by the carbonates. In sulfate deposition, water is usually not common in large amounts. The water often merely seeps through cave walls, and therefore the mineral often tends to be deposited as coatings rather than as single isolated speleothems formed by dripping water.

Stalactites composed of gypsum do occasionally occur, and at times gypsum may be deposited over or within calcite stalactites. Mirabilite stalactites are small and glasslike or icelike in appearance. Epsomite stalactites, or at least portions of them, are also often clear and transparent.

Stalagmites may also be formed of the sulfate minerals where sufficient water is present to drip from a stalactite above. Their formation is caused by evaporation of the dripping water as it hits the surface. Not only are stalactites and stalagmites formed of the sulfate minerals less common than those formed of the carbonates, they do not attain the large sizes of the calcite speleothems. Gypsum stalactites and stalagmites have been reported in length or height as 3 meters and 2.5 meters respectively; maximum sizes for those of epsomite and mirabilite are even smaller. Where sufficient water carrying sulfates in solution is present, flowstone may be deposited by the water as it flows over bedrock.

Sulfate crusts are deposits that may coat cave walls, ceilings, and occasionally floors. They are produced by water seeping through small openings, evaporating, and leaving the mineral at the site. These deposits may grow to a thickness that causes portions of them to break away and fall to the cave floor. Uneven growth may cause buckling or bulging of the crusts.

Spectacular among the evaporite speleothems are the monocrystalline speleothems. Gypsum growth habits often tend to produce long fibrous or bladelike crystals. *Gypsum needles,* or *selenite needles* as they are often known, are basically straight, long, thin, clear, needlelike crystals that grow upward from cave soil, sulfate solutions having moved through the soil to its surface by capillary action. The base of the individual needles extends only a very limited distance into the soil. Growth is from the base, pushing the needle upward, usually approximately perpendicular to the soil. These needles may range in length from a few centimeters to several meters and in diameter from a fraction of a millimeter to a few millimeters. The needles often grow in dense masses.

Monocrystalline speleothems include the *fibrous sulfates.* These crystals of gypsum, epsomite, or mirabilite are similar in form to the needles just discussed, but are more elongated, although much smaller; all have a diameter of less than a half millimeter. The fibrous sulfates grow on cave walls and ceilings in addition to growing in cave soil. Included in this group of speleothems is cave cotton, formed of masses of usually short crystals matted together. Cave hair consists of single, long strands that may reach 2 meters in length and less than a half millimeter in diameter. Each "hair" is a single crystal. These grow downward from their point of attachment in cave ceilings or ledges. Cave hair is extremely fragile. The maximum length an individual crystal can attain is limited, at least in part, by weight considerations.

Included in the category of fibrous sulfates are *oulopholites*, or as they are more commonly known, cave flowers. These are composed of curving and branching bundles of crystals. The individual "petals" radiate outward from a common central point and display various degrees of curvature. Curvature is caused by more rapid growth on the side of the petal nearest the center of the flower, for this is the point where the sulfate solution emerges from the bedrock. Flowers are most often composed of gypsum, but may also be formed by epsomite and mirabilite.

Starburst gypsum consists of faceted gypsum crystals that radiate from a common point, grow parallel to the cave wall, and terminate in pointed projections, assuming a starburst design on the wall. Starbursts do not grow perpendicular to the cave wall and thus have a more two-dimensional aspect than most speleothems. Where growth of starbursts is profuse, they may grow into one another, forming completely covered portions of walls.

Tabular gypsum, consisting of flat, platelike gypsum crystals, may grow clustered in groups, producing small speleothems that resemble roses.

Phosphates

A variety of minerals of the phosphate group occurs in caves. For the most part these are associated with animal excrement, primarily that of bats, and also with animal remains. Where bats are numerous in caves, thick layers of guano cover the floor. Water drains downward through these layers, and the nitrogen in the guano is dissolved and leached away. Phosphorus remains and interacts with inorganic sediments and the limestone of the walls and floor of the cave. Several phosphate minerals may be formed in this way in the altered bat guano, and often these are stratified within the deposit. Phosphates reported from caves include whitlockite, hydroxylapatite, monetite,

brushite, crandallite, taranakite, ardealite, biphos-
phammite, carbonate-apatite, fluorapatite, tinticite,
and variscite. Phosphates are often present in large
quantities in tropical caves due to the large amount of
organic debris often occurring in these caves.

Nitrates

Nitrates are among the most widely known and least
understood of cave minerals. Three nitrates—niter,
nitrocalcite, and soda niter—are all commonly known
as saltpeter and were mined in the eastern and southeastern United States in the nineteenth century, particularly during the War of 1812 and the Civil War, for
use in the production of gunpowder. The saltpeter was
obtained by digging up cave soil. The leached solution
was then passed through vats of wood ashes to produce
potash niter, which was then further purified.

The formation and presence of saltpeter in caves,
as yet, has not been satisfactorily explained. Soils
containing nitrate minerals are dry, aerated, and
located in fairly dry caves in temperate climates, as in
the southeastern United States. Cave nitrates, however, do not necessarily occur in all caves fulfilling
these conditions. Interestingly, it is reported that if
leached saltpeter soil is returned to the cave and left
for several years, its saltpeter content will regenerate
and the soil can again be leached and the desired
mineral obtained.

Many theories have been proposed in an attempt to
explain the presence of nitrates in cave soil. None have
been proven. One interesting possibility is that
nitrogen-fixing bacteria in the soil are responsible.
Unlike the phosphates, saltpeter is not associated with
bat guano or animal remains.

Halides

Speleothems formed of halite, or common salt, are
similar in many ways to sulfate speleothems. Deposits
of halite in limestone or lava caves result from evaporation of dripping or seeping water that carried salt in
solution. The speleothems formed by salt include

stalactites, stalagmites, columns, crusts, flowers, and individual large crystals.

Oxides

Manganese oxides are rather commonly found in caves. These usually occur as thin, black coatings of material on walls, floors, and even on speleothems. Manganese has occasionally been reported in massive quantities, more than a yard deep, for example, in Jewel Cave in South Dakota.

Ice

Ice is present in many caves located in limestone and lava, and it, too, forms speleothems. This ice may be ephemeral, that is, forming near cave entrances during cold periods and later melting under warmer conditions. Or, it may be perennial ice, maintained by average annual cave temperatures below the freezing point.

Freezing of dripping, seeping, or flowing water may form stalactites, stalagmites, columns, flowstone, draperies, and occasionally other forms. These resemble calcite speleothems in form, and in some respects in means of formation. However, in the case of the stalactites, there is usually no central canal. Water films move over the outer surface of the stalactite and freeze there.

Spectacular speleothems may occasionally be formed from freezing water vapor. These consist of large masses of complex, transparent ice crystals.

Silicates

Included in the silicate group are various clay minerals, cristobolite, quartz, and chalcedony. Cristobolite, commonly known as opal, may be found as encrustations or may form portions of speleothems in conjunction with calcite. In lava caves opal may form speleothems such as stalactites, stalagmites, helictites, and flowstone.

Other Cave Minerals

Where caves are formed in a location adjacent to

bodies of ore, or where special conditions prevail, occasionally less common or rare minerals may be deposited in caves, or may occur in veins or vugs exposed by cave formation.

SPELEOTHEMS AND THE CAVER

Never take, break, destroy, deface, or otherwise damage any cave minerals or speleothems. These are an important scientific record of the cave's history and a source of beauty and pleasure for all spelunkers who will visit the cave in the future. Don't even remove those speleothems that are already broken and lying on the cave floor. The sight of speleothems outside a cave, however innocuously obtained, may serve to motivate others to collect speleothems through cave defacement. The only excuse for removal of a speleothem from a cave is for scientific study by a qualified scientist undertaking a valid project, and very few should be removed even by these individuals.

Be particularly aware of how easily speleothems may be damaged by those who enter caves. Do not touch speleothems. Body oil on the hands is capable of staining a speleothem, as is, of course, the mud or dust usually present on a caver's hands. Some speleothems are so extremely fragile that such simple air movements as those created by cavers' movements or by the heat from a caver's lamp will cause them to break. Walk carefully in caves so as to avoid damaging speleothems. If a path has been established previously, use it; do not contribute to a proliferation of new trails.

Dedicated cave enthusiasts and conservationists must rank very high on the list of the world's best secret-keepers. Seldom do they reveal the location of a cave except to their most trusted and respected fellow speleologists. Rightly so. In the past the beauty of many caves has been completely destroyed by collectors who have blatantly removed speleothems for their own collections or for sale. Vandals, too, have entered caves and systematically destroyed, within a matter of hours, speleothems that required many thousands of years to form. There is absolutely no place in today's cave world for the collector, the entrepreneur, or the ignorant destroyer. The National Speleological Society states it succinctly: "Take nothing but pictures. Leave nothing but footprints [to which we add, leave these very carefully]. Kill nothing but time." If you cannot heed this admonition, do not enter caves.

4

LAVA, GLACIER, AND OTHER TYPES OF CAVES

DESPITE SOME CAVERS'
protestations to the
contrary, limestone
caves are not the only type of cave worthy
of exploration. Man has been exploring the numerous
limestone caverns and admiring their beauty in both
the Old and New Worlds for so long that a strong tradition and rather exclusive mystique has attached itself
to them. It has been only relatively recently, with the
strong upsurge in the numbers of cavers, that an increased interest in other types of caves has developed.

LAVA CAVES

In some ways lava caves may resemble those in limestone. Both types may be extensive, may serve or have
served as natural conduits, may have stalactites and
stalagmites, may be entered through collapse openings, and, through their shape and markings on walls,
floors, and ceilings, provide clues to their means of
formation. The resemblances between the two types,
however, are superficial rather than actual.

In contrast to limestone caves, those in lava
usually lie close to the earth's surface. In this location
they are subject to more extensive deterioration than
are limestone caverns. Hence lava caves are relatively
short-lived, and the ones we see are among the young-

est of existing caves. Caves are created in lava as the enclosing rock is formed, rather than through corrosion and corrasion of the rock itself. Lava formations resembling speleothems are developed by a different means than limestone speleothems. And the material originally carried in the lava conduits was molten magma, not water, as is the case in limestone.

The major type of cave formed in rocks of volcanic origin is that formed of lava tubes, which we will consider in detail. However, lesser-known caves of volcanic origin do exist; we will survey these briefly at this point.

Caves in volcanic rocks may occur in lavas or in *pyroclastic rocks*, which are rocks of various types blown from a volcanic vent with tremendous discharges of gas. Pyroclastic rocks include volcanic bombs (solidified lava), blocks of rock, ash, and similar materials. Wood (1976) divides caves in rocks of volcanic origin into exogenetic and endogenetic types. *Exogenetic* caves include those formed in pyroclastic deposits. Those deposits consisting of large chunks of material are often known as agglomerates; those of finer material such as ash, when indurated or hardened, are known as tuff. Caves formed in pyroclastic rocks are not nearly as common as those formed in lava, and the means of their formation is considerably different than the formation of lava caves; in some ways their formation more closely resembles the formation of limestone caves, since water and erosion play an important role. These agents attack the more easily destroyed material, such as the layers of ash, thereby forming voids in the pyroclastic materials.

It is with the much more common caves formed by molten lava that we are primarily concerned, and these are classified as *endogenetic*. Not all types of lava possess the characteristics necessary for cave formation. Basaltic lava is the primary type in which lava caves may be formed, and it is divided into several types. Foremost of the basaltic lava varieties for cave formation is that known by its Hawaiian name, *pahoehoe* (pronounced pah-hoey-hoey). Other varieties of basaltic lava include *aa* (also an Hawaiian name, pronounced ah-ah) and *block lava*. Pahoehoe is more fluid than the others, but as it cools it sometimes assumes the aa or block form.

Molten basaltic lava—flowing, creeping, pushing, being pushed, erratically moving like a giant fiery tide—is one of nature's most awesome sights. The irregular, bare landscape that remains after the lava has solidified can also be impressive. Because of pressures, gases, and the flow of lava beneath cooled outer crusts, voids, which in some cases are large enough to be classified as caves, are often found within solidified lava flows. Wood includes among these cavities beneath pressure ridges, fissure caves, blister caves caused by gases trapped within the flow, and others. The foregoing are minor types, however, in comparison to the most numerous, extensive, and interesting of the lava caves, those formed by lava tubes.

The basic principle involved in lava tube formation, stated in a simplified manner, is as follows. Molten lava flows outward from a volcanic vent, rift, fissure, or similar opening and becomes channeled into streamlike or riverlike flows. The surfaces of the magma flow begin to cool from the outer portions inward. Crusts of cooling material may form along the flow's sides and upper surface, pieces of crust may break loose and be jammed against one another, and a levee may be built up along the edges of the flow due to spatter and other means. Eventually a roof composed of the solidified lava may form over the flow. The mass of molten magma beneath this roof, however, remains very hot, hence liquid, and flows onward, leaving behind it a solidified hollow tube. The end result is a linear conduit formed by a single flow of molten basaltic rock. (In reality, of course, formation of most lava tubes is considerably more complex than this description suggests.)

The surface topography and gradient exert a strong influence on the flow, the form it takes, and whether or not it is possible for a tube to be formed. The lava flow may divide into two or more molten streams; it may spread out in a delta effect; lesser tributaries may flow into it. An area may be subject to repeated flows over a period of time. One tube may form atop another, or a later flow may break into an older, previously formed tube, producing a lava falls or cascade. Molten magma may melt its way downward into the bed over which it flows, forming a passage similar to a vadose canyon. In some cases the flow of lava from the tube may proceed spasmodically, and a crust may form over the lava remaining in the tube; the lava below it then drains out. This results in what is called a false floor, and more than one of these floors may be formed in a tube. Rather than developing a complete floor, some crust formation may occur only laterally along the edges of the tube, thus forming what are termed lateral benches.

The interior of the tube is often marked by various features, such as gouges in the walls caused by solid

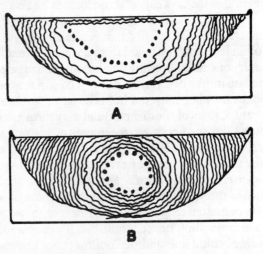

Lava tube cave speleogenesis.

A. *Molten lava forms a streamlike flow moving away from its source. The magma flow gradually cools and solidifies from its outer portions inward. Gradually a roof may form over the actively flowing molten magma, represented in the illustration by the clear, central area.*

B. *Here the outer portions and roof have solidified (irregular lines) and the center tube, which once carried molten material, has become emptied. The remaining magma has drained away. Thus there is a hollow tube (clear area) formed in the lava. With access by a point of roof breakdown or other means the tube can be entered.*

rocks carried by the lava and splash marks on the floor where pieces of crust have fallen from the ceiling to the partially solidified floor. The phenomenal heat within the tunnel often causes the formation of a black or blue-black glaze on the tunnel ceiling and walls as the magma flow gradually recedes. Stalactites and stalagmites composed of lava often decorate tubes. These are formed due to molten material dripping from ceilings or ledges, from lava being splashed upward from the flow and then dripping, or may be derived from the glaze material. These "speleothems" are therefore formed in a different manner than those in limestone caves.

Actually, according to our earlier definition of a speleothem as a secondary mineral deposit formed within the cave itself, these lava formations are not speleothems in the strict sense. The term speleothem, however, is often used to embrace them. In addition to stalactites and stalagmites, other lava speleothem-related forms reported from lava caves include draperies, flowstone, columns, helictites, and coral types. Even tubular stalactites may form where dripping lava cools on its outer surfaces and the interior, liquid lava drains out, leaving a hollow tube. Lava tubes may also occasionally contain secondary mineral deposits left behind when groundwater has percolated through the basalt of the lava caves.

Lava tubes are formed near the surface, and their roofs are often relatively thin and fragile. It is ordinarily through a point of roof collapse that human entry into the tubes is possible. Also, due to frequent roof collapse, long, totally complete tubes are less common than their shorter, segmented counterparts, many of the tubes having undergone some roof collapse at one or more points along their length. Because of their proximity to the surface, lava tube caves are also subject to other destructive, erosive agents.

Today lava caves are found in many parts of the world where volcanic activity has occurred in the not too distant past. These include Africa, Australia, New Zealand, Japan, Korea, Iceland, the Mediterranean area, and the Middle East. The lava caves of the western United States, and particularly the Hawaiian Islands, are best known to Americans.

An outstanding study of lava tube formation has been conducted in the Hawaiian Islands. Peterson and Swanson (1974) reported on their observations of tubes formed in 1970 – 71 on the island of Hawaii due to the action of a volcano known as Kilauea. During that time numerous very large flows of pahoehoe occurred, including lava fountains several hundred meters in height erupting from the volcano and producing, as one example, up to 12 million cubic meters of lava in nine hours or less.

Flows soon organized into distinct channels, averaging 2 to 5 meters in width, and the flows gradually deepened their channels. Banks built up along their edges, crusts formed on the surface of the lava, and eventually roofs formed across them; in one observed case, roof formation occurred over a period of two to three days. Eventually the pahoehoe flow developed numerous tubes, flowed through them, and the molten lava ultimately reached the sea, 12 kilometers from its volcanic source.

The scientists observed the interiors of these active lava tubes through skylights, that is, occasional holes where the roof failed to form or collapsed over the tubes. They reported that lava flowed almost noiselessly within the tubes with only a soft sticky sound, moving at a velocity of approximately 1 to 6 kilometers per hour. The heat was intense, the view "a glimpse of the ultimate inferno." The walls and ceiling of the tube took on fantastic shapes. Colors were varied within the tube—the molten lava bright yellow, the walls a darker yellow or orange, and the area near the skylight, which allowed the entrance of oxygen, was orange to red. A smooth, shiny glaze formed on the walls. Stalactites of lava and of the glaze formed. Lava falls up to 10 meters in height were observed where lava broke through into lower-level tubes.

Such observations of lava caves in the making are not for amateurs or the fainthearted. It can be dangerous work, for these scientists reported that it was difficult at times to determine whether or not the solidifying lava crusts were strong enough to hold their weight. One individual in their group stepped on a deceptive crust that collapsed, plunging his foot and leg into molten lava at an approximate temperature of 1150° C; he was extremely fortunate to survive the accident.

For the would-be explorer of established, cooled, solidified lava tubes, we can characterize certain distinctive features of these caves that have a bearing on their exploration. They tend to be near the surface. Most lack the degree of vertical relief often found in solution caves. The walls are very dark in color; they do not reflect light as do many limestone walls; hence stronger light sources are often required in lava caves. For the most part these caves lack streams; however, a rare few may at times be subject to flash floods. For reasons we will be noting later, some ice formation in lava caves is not uncommon. In many lava tubes humidity is relatively low and the presence of dust and dry guano should be taken into consideration in the planning stage. Lava tubes, especially near their entrances, are often used as homes or retreats by animals; this seems to be particularly true in some desert areas, where more than one startled explorer has discovered rattlesnakes in residence.

Compass readings tend to be unpredictable and irregular in lava caves; both foresights and backsights should be taken by compass during lava cave exploration. One of the characteristics of foremost importance to lava tube cavers is the abrasive, jagged, often unstable nature of the rock of which the tubes are composed. The rock can be destructive to skin, boots, and clothing, and the explorer may wish to increase knee padding and wear rugged clothing for extra protection. Also, in a good many instances, surface approaches to lava caves are over very rough lava terrain. One final, obvious point regarding exploration of lava caves: never cave in areas where active volcanic or earthquake activity is occurring or threatening to occur. Certainly the recent volcanic activity on Mount St. Helens presents a case in point.

The study of caves in rocks of volcanic origin is known as *vulcanospeleology.* It is a relatively new field

of exploration that received impetus, along with the
study of surface volcanic features, as man prepared to
land on the moon and as man continues his study of
other planets. Whether approached as a sport, a scientific pursuit, or both, vulcanospeleology certainly
offers a fertile, relatively untouched field for exploration and scientific discovery in a highly distinctive,
challenging terrain.

GLACIER CAVES

Caves formed by molten lava and those hollowed out
of ice surely represent two extremes in speleology.
Even newer than vulcanospeleology in attracting
cavers' interest is the field of *glaciospeleology*, the
study of caves formed within glaciers. Glaciospeleology has received special attention since the late 1960s in
the northwestern United States, where explorations
first centered largely on Paradise Ice Caves. Here,
within and under the Paradise-Stevens Glacier, located
on Mount Rainier in the state of Washington, glacio-
speleologists found a complex series of passages, many
reported as averaging approximately 10 feet in height
and 20 feet in width; also discovered were several large
chambers, one reported to be 250 feet long, 90 feet
wide, and 25 feet high (Halliday and Anderson, 1970).

A definition of terms is in order at this point.
Following Halliday and Anderson, we use the term
glacier cave to designate a natural cavern that occurs
within a glacier or lies between the glacier and its bed.
An *ice cave* is a natural cavern, occurring in rock,
containing ice in some form that persists most or all of
the year. In the past it has been fairly common for a
French word, glacière, to be used when referring to ice
caves. The similarity of the word glacière to the word
glacier has often caused confusion, since some people
have incorrectly assumed that the word glacière
referred to what we designate as a glacier cave. Therefore we will not use the French term, but call it to the
attention of the reader who may find the term in
speleological literature.

Most glacier caves are initiated by water running

beneath the glacier, eroding its bed and melting the ice above it. Further streamflow continues to enlarge the cave, but a great deal of the enlargement is caused by *ablation*—that is, a decrease in the volume of ice as a result of melting and evaporation caused by the entry of warm summer air into the developing cave passages. Ablation causes the development on glacier cave walls and ceilings of giant scallops, similar in shape to stream scallops or flutes but much larger in size, some more than a meter in width. Glacier caves may change rather rapidly, particularly as compared to limestone caves, for the form and duration of both the glacier and its cave are entirely subject to fluctuating climatic conditions.

The interiors of glacier caves are strikingly beautiful, their milky-white or blue-white ice often adorned with speleothems of ice, and in some locations with filtered bluish light. Floors of these caves may consist of the rock or soil beneath the glacier, or may be composed of the glacial ice. In some cases domelike openings occur in the ceiling; water may descend through these, building huge ice deposits at the bases.

Studies of glacier caves in other locations have determined that glaciospeleogenesis also may be initiated by less common means than we have described. Thompson and McKenzie (1979), studying glacier caves in Peru, found obstruction caves, formed where the glacier ice flowed around an obstruction such as a huge boulder, leaving a void on the opposite side of the obstruction. In some instances such caves may have no entrances, or may have one only briefly during summer months. Another type of glacier cave they described was that formed by the roofing over of a crevasse. In their study of glacier caves they observed ice speleothems, including stalactites, stalagmites, columns, coral, flowstone, and other forms.

Exploration of glacier caves is a very specialized undertaking, really more akin to mountaineering than speleology, and specific details regarding it are beyond the scope of this more general caving book. Special clothing, equipment, techniques, and experience gained aboveground in snow and ice are vital to any glacier cave exploration. There are a number of dangers inherent in glaciospeleology, even for well-prepared individuals. Low air temperatures and cold water pose a constant threat of hypothermia. A danger reported within glacier caves is the fall from the roof of huge flakes of ice weighing many tons. Such flakes may develop where scallops coalesce; they are extremely unstable and are often not readily discerned until after the caver has passed under them.

During the summer months the amount of water flowing from the glacier may be extreme and preclude exploration, or occasionally water levels may unexpectedly rise rapidly while exploration is in progress. In some cases exploration is undertaken during the winter months when streamflow presents no problem. At this time, however, low temperatures may reach extreme levels. Since many glacier caves are at elevated altitudes, reaching a glacier cave in winter can involve problems such as snow, fog, and unexpected winter storms.

SEA CAVES

Sea caves, more properly called littoral caves, are those that occur in cliffs along ocean shores. Erosion, primarily through the sea's action, and weathering cause their formation in cliff faces, which contain zones of weakness that are more easily destroyed than the surrounding rock. Many factors in addition to weaknesses in the rock and direct contact with wave action play a part in sea cave development and the form and size they gradually assume. These include the size and frequency of the incident waves, the size and amount of abrasive material carried by the water, tidal range, currents, the nature of the sea bottom topography in that location, the type of rock surrounding the weak zone, the degree of exposure to storm waves, the solution of soluble rock, weathering, intrusion by percolating groundwater, and the actions of organisms.

Sea caves are relatively abundant in many parts of the world, and a few can even be found inland today where large bodies of water washed ancient shores.

The majority of sea caves are relatively shallow in depth, but large sea-washed voids that are true caves do exist.

Any exploration of sea caves is largely dependent upon local conditions. Tides, currents, and wave patterns must be conscientiously studied before entry is attempted. Boats are often required, and the use of scuba gear is not uncommon. Animal life is often rich, distinctively different than that encountered in any other cave environment, and ranges from small organisms to large mammals, all of which should be respected, and some of which should be avoided for the explorers' safety.

Here again, as in glacier caving, skills and knowledge needed for exploration of many sea caves should be perfected before use in caves. Respect for the sea cave environment and the power of its natural forces is a prerequisite to its exploration.

BLUE HOLES

Blue holes are not a distinct type of cave, but represent an unusual condition of solution caves. They are mentioned here as a very special type of cave environment. Blue holes are portions of limestone caves that have been invaded by seawater following their formation. They occur offshore in Latin America, the best-known and most studied being those off the Bahamas, specifically Andros Island. The Bahama Islands consist of the tops of limestone mountains. Cave systems were formed in these mountains over vast periods of time. As glaciers formed and melted, sea levels varied. When the last glacial period ended, sea levels rose and inundated portions of these caves. The submerged cave portions received their popular name due to the fact that the underwater cave entrances, as seen from the air, are dark blue in contrast to the greener waters of the lagoons in which they lie.

Some blue holes are characterized by very strong reversing ocean currents. At low tide fresh water derived from the cave systems' landward portions exits from the blue holes into the sea; as the tide rises, water from the sea is sucked into them with great force. Entrance by divers into the blue holes that experience these profound current changes must be timed very carefully in relationship to the tides. These ocean-invaded caves surely represent one of the most challenging of spelunking and scuba pursuits, and expertise in both areas is a vital requirement for any who would enter them.

TALUS CAVES

Talus caves consist of voids formed within piles and jumbles of rocks, such as those that sometimes occur at the base of cliffs or masses of rock filling a ravine or gorge. Over 3000 feet of passage have been surveyed in several talus caves in the eastern United States. In a few cases speleothems have been found. The random pattern with which the boulders collect results in a mazelike cave system, with frequent skylights. Exploration of talus caves should be undertaken with caution, due to the frequent instability of the enclosing rocks.

SANDSTONE CAVES

Sandstone caves usually consist of shallow recesses in sandstone cliffs, caused by differential erosion of the cliff face. To speleologists they seldom rank as true caves, for although their height and width may reach truly impressive sizes, their depth ordinarily does not.

These are referred to by a variety of names, including sandstone shelters, sandstone caves, shelter caves, and similar terms, many of which highlight their importance to early man. Shallow shelter caves may exist in other rocks in addition to sandstone. Such caves have long been used by man as sites of shelters and homes. They were neither dank nor dark, as are many limestone caves, yet they offered a measure of protection from inclement weather and often, due to their elevated location in towering cliff faces, also afforded a location defensible against enemy attack.

The sandstone shelters of the southwestern United

States, such as those at Mesa Verde National Park and nearby sites, provide outstanding examples of human use of sandstone caves. These caves are not without interest to the speleologist, even though their limits are not so extreme as those of caves in limestone. Such shelters are of great importance to archaeologists. Often containing ancient ruins of buildings and middens and adorned with paintings, many of these beautiful shelter caves in the United States and in other parts of the world are rich depositories of man's history.

Under no circumstances should any archaeological material be disturbed, dug up, or carried off from shelter caves or any other type of cave, except by qualified scientists with prior permission for an approved study.

5
CAVE METEOROLOGY

THE CAVE ENVIRON-
ment is remarkably
constant. The sun
never warms it directly nor provides light
within its confines. Rivers may flow through it, underground water usually drips from its roof, drops of water
condense on its walls, ice may freeze within it, and
occasionally giant ice crystals may form when water
vapor in the atmosphere condenses at below-freezing
temperatures, yet it never rains nor snows directly
within the cave. And the air currents that move
through the passages are rather constant in direction
and velocity; even when changes do occur, they are
often predictable.

In this chapter we will be considering only certain
meteorological aspects of this environment; that is,
the atmospheric variables of caves, including temperature, humidity, and air movements. We will be
describing these meteorological conditions as found
primarily in limestone caves in temperate regions, for
these caves are numerous, have been explored and
studied more than tropical limestone caves or other
types of caves, and exhibit what are currently considered the most typical cave conditions. In many cases,
of course, some of the same or closely related
conditions also exist in other types of caves and in
limestone caves located in nontemperate regions.

TEMPERATURE

Within the depths of a cave the air temperature ordinarily remains essentially constant throughout the year. It is controlled to a large extent by the temperature of the walls. Deep within a cave these wall temperatures, and hence air temperatures, are approximately equal to the mean annual temperature outside the cave in that particular location. Daily and seasonal temperature fluctuations aboveground are damped or diminished as they move downward from the surface through soil and rock. Moore and Sullivan (1978) state that an abovegound temperature fluctuation "throughout the year of 30°C is reduced to 1°C at a depth of 11 meters." Therefore most caves in their inner, deeper portions have a narrow annual temperature fluctuation of 1°C or less.

As mean aboveground temperatures vary greatly from place to place depending upon a number of factors, so, too, do cave temperatures. Thus both the latitude and altitude at which a cave occurs are important determining factors regarding its inner air temperature. A map plotting cave temperatures of the United States reveals a cave temperature differential from north to south of approximately 15 Centigrade degrees. "The average temperature of caves near the southern border of the United States is about 20°C, and that near the northern border is about 5°C" (Moore and Sullivan, 1978). Insofar as altitude differentials are concerned, the same authors cite "a gradient of about 6°C per thousand meters." Therefore a general rule is that the higher the elevation or the latitude at which a cave occurs, the lower the deep cave temperature. Thus caves located at high altitudes and/or latitudes may contain permanent ice where moisture is (or once was) available and the mean annual temperature of the area is below 0°C.

Cave temperatures are influenced by other factors. As air and water move into a cave, they exert some temperature influence on the rock walls and are gradually cooled or warmed by the rock until an equilibrium is reached. Water is a much more efficient conductor than air, and by its very nature—often quickly flowing from cave entrance to deep cave interior—may exert considerable influence on cave temperature. For example, the waters of a stream entering a cave may be derived from melting snow and ice at certain times of the year. Eventually flowing deep within the cave, this cold water is efficient in reducing cave temperatures to a lower level than would be the case for a similar, dry cave at the same altitude and latitude. Conversely, water that is warmer than the cave walls may also have some warming influence on the cave temperature.

HUMIDITY

In the majority of limestone caves, water seeps through walls, ceilings, and floors and occurs frequently as streams, pools, or lakes; thus the air of these caves is ordinarily saturated with water vapor. Relative humidity is the ratio of water vapor actually present in air at a particular temperature as compared to the total amount of water vapor needed to saturate the air at that temperature. Cave air, then, in active or wet caves, is ordinarily at or very close to 100 percent relative humidity. However, this is often not the case near a cave entrance, where unsaturated air may be entering the cave from outside. The temperature of the entering air will gradually change as it is cooled or warmed by contact with the cave walls.

Cold air is not capable of holding as much water vapor as warm air. Thus if air is entering a cave and is cooled, its relative humidity increases; if it is warmed instead, its relative humidity decreases. In summer, warm air entering a cave soon reaches 100 percent relative humidity as the cooler cave walls lower its temperature. In winter, entering cold air that has a temperature lower than the cave rock will be slowly warmed by the rock and may not attain 100 percent relative humidity for some time. Eventually, as this air moves backward into the deeper cave portions, water is absorbed by the air and the humidity rises. Relative humidity near cave entrances may thus vary to some degree from that of the intermediate and deeper cave portions. Depending upon whether the cave walls are cooler or warmer than the dew point temperature of the air, moisture will either be evaporated from or will condense on the walls where this temperature differential exists.

AIR MOVEMENT

While water and humidity are important contributing factors regarding cave temperatures, air movements are undoubtedly, overall, the single most important atmospheric variable influencing the temperature of the majority of caves. The greater the amount of air exchange between a cave and the outside, the greater the variations in temperature and humidity within the cave. Air movements into and through caves are governed by a variety of factors.

Changes in surface barometric pressure outside caves often affect air movements within them, particularly near the entrances of both single and multiple cave entrances. Air moves into or out of the cave entrance in the process of maintaining a pressure balance between the cave air and the external air. During the day, air outside the cave is ordinarily warmed. Warm air being less dense than cold air, the barometric pressure falls. At night the outside air is cooled and barometric pressure rises. Thus there are continual adjustments taking place between the cave air near the entrances and the outside air in order to maintain a pressure balance, resulting in some air movement into a cave at night and out during the day. More profound barometric pressure changes occur irregularly in conjunction with major weather changes, and these also influence air flow near cave entrances.

Single Entrance Caves

Warm air is less dense than cold air, hence cold air is heavier than warm. Caves with a single entrance and without vadose streamflow are therefore often subject to gravitational air drainage. In a downward-trending, single entrance cave, entering cold air sinks and flows along the floor to the bottom of the cave. It displaces any warmer air in the cave, which in turn flows along the cave roof and eventually out the upper portion of the single entrance.

Gravitational drainage in single entrance caves is important in producing one type of ice cave in which permanent ice is maintained in the cave's lower portions despite the fact that the mean annual temperature aboveground is higher than 0°C. In areas with cold winters, cold air may enter the single entrance cave, sink to the cave's lowest levels, and cause ice to form if water is present. The summer's warm to hot air is largely incapable of displacing the heavier cold air in the cave, and low deep cave temperatures are generally maintained. Such ice caves are wellknown from various lava areas. It is not uncommon for lava caves to have but a single entrance, and to be well-insulated, rocky, and downward-trending. A single entrance cave that trends upward, will display the opposite phenomenon, with the cool, heavier air flowing out of the cave entrance during the summer months, being replaced with the warmer, lighter, rising outside air.

In some cases a single entrance cave may have a stream flowing with considerable force through the entrance and on into the cave passage. The stream drags air along above it by friction with the surface of the water. The result is air movement at low levels in the cave passage. A return air flow is necessary; therefore air movement also occurs at a higher level in the stream cave passage, and/or may also occur through other adjacent connecting passages. The pulling along of air by the stream is referred to as entrainment.

In a single entrance cave with a stream, strong outward-flowing air movements may occur if the cave undergoes rapid flooding, the water displacing the air, forcing its movement out the entrance.

Multiple Entrance Caves

Caves with multiple entrances occurring at different levels may exhibit what is known as the chimney effect in response to temperature differentials between the outside and inside air. These variations in

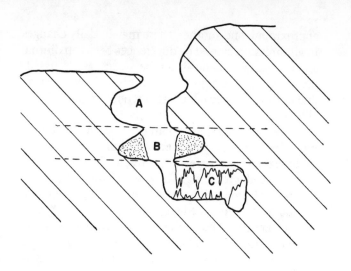

Ice cave. *Single entrance caves may have ice year-round in their lower portions. The cold winter air sinks into the cave and is not displaced by warmer summer air.*

A. *Cold air reservoir.*
B. *Snow and ice present, temperature approximately 0°C.*
C. *Accumulation of ice, often in the form of stalactites and stalagmites; air temperature below 0°C.*

---

temperature cause an air pressure difference at the lower cave entrances, and air flows either into or out of the cave to restore the balance. Cold air will flow out of a cave's lower entrances when the cave air is colder than the air outside the entrances. As the cold air flows out the lower entrances, warmer air will be flowing into the cave at its higher orifices. Conversely, air movement will be into the lower entrances when the cave air is warmer than the outside air. The warm cave air will then flow out of the upper entrances, and the colder air into the lower entrances.

Thus caves displaying the chimney effect exhibit seasonal changes in the direction of air movements at their entrances, the persistent air movement in winter being into the lower entrances, and in summer being out of the lower entrances. In spring and fall, when cave and external air temperatures more closely approximate one another, there may be daily changes in air direction caused by differences between diurnal and nocturnal outside air temperatures, as discussed previously. Caves exhibiting rather persistent winds due to the chimney effect are often referred to as "blowing caves."

A very few caves are popularly known as "breathing caves." In these the direction of air flow reverses quite regularly every few minutes, as though the cave were, indeed, breathing. The cause of these movements has been attributed to a resonance phenomenon similar to that produced when one blows across the neck of a bottle. The air in the bottle compresses and expands with a particular frequency; the result is vibrations that can be heard. In the case of breathing caves, it is thought that turbulent winds blowing across the entrance initiate the oscillations of the air mass within the cave. A cave chamber, however, contains much more air than does a bottle, and oscillations of the cave air are much slower, due to mass, than is the case with air in a bottle. In the latter, the oscillations are observed as sound waves. In the case of a cave, the oscillations are too slow to produce a sound audible to the human ear, but are instead observed as regular reversals in air flow at the opening to the resonating cave chamber.

THE CAVER AND CAVE METEOROLOGY

Air movements within a cave are often caused by a combination of factors and conditions, and these in conjunction with temperature and humidity variables produce distinctive underground atmospheres that may vary appreciably from one cave to another. It is important for the cave explorer to understand and respect the power of the atmospheric variables within a cave. For example, due to the fact that cold outside air can generally be expected to move into the lower entrances of a cave in winter, the entrances and adjacent areas can be expected at that time of year to be the coldest portions of the cave; breezes, water, and waterfalls in these areas will be colder than in the deeper cave portions where water and air temperatures have reached an equilibrium with the cave walls. In midsummer the entry areas are warmer, and by comparison the coldest cave conditions are to be expected in the deeper cave portions.

Caves tend to feel pleasantly cool in summer and warm in winter, as compared to outside temperatures. This can be deceptive, for, in general, temperate cave temperatures tend to be cool to cold. Often breezes or lesser air movements seem to be lacking within a cave; yet in most caves there is some air movement occurring, even though it may be largely imperceptible. Air movements in conjunction with cool to cold temperatures produce a wind chill factor, intensifying the cold for the caver. Water is an excellent conductor of heat or cold, far more efficient than air. Water in conjunction with low temperatures and air movement can produce water chill that greatly stresses the caver who is wading, swimming, or has inadvertently become damp or wet, unless he is prepared with proper equipment and clothing such as a wet suit.

Certainly the cave explorer who combines extremes of temperature, wind, and water in his cave exploration must be knowledgeable and prepared—or preferably sufficiently astute to forgo the exploration until more favorable conditions prevail. For example, a caver entering a cave in winter via descent through a roaring waterfall is exposing himself (and others) to extreme stress—cold winter temperatures in the cave entrance, the coldness of the air intensified by strong air movements generated by the falling water, and the cold intensified to an extreme point due to water chill. Such an undertaking is not to be recommended.

Respect the power of the cave's atmosphere. Low temperatures, air movements, and cold water can be killers, but should never prove to be so for the properly prepared, cautious, and intelligent caver.

6
CAVE BIOTA

THE MOST FAMOUS highly adapted cave animal, the European blind, long-legged, long-snouted, depigmented salamander, *Proteus anguinus*, long ago was tentatively identified as a baby dragon. In the mid-sixteenth century a European author described a cave from which ancient bones were removed and sold as those of unicorns. Thus has man over the ages creatively explained life, past or present, within caves. The truth as we know it scientifically today may be less spectacular but no less interesting. A wide variety of plants and animals live in caves, often by means of rather remarkable adaptations that may be behavioral, physiological, and/or morphological (of body form).

In considering cave biota (animal and plant life) it is helpful to divide a cave into three basic parts. The first portion is known as the twilight zone. This extends from the entrance to the farthest point to which light ever penetrates; in this area certain types of green plants capable of growing in low light levels will be found. The second zone, the variable-temperature area, is beyond the limits of outside light, but the temperature and humidity levels are affected by seasonal or weather variations outside the entrance. This zone is colder in winter and warmer in summer than the deep cave. The third area is the constant-temperature zone, which is the cave's deeper, inner portion. Each of the three zones is normally inhabited by various species of animals that find the particular conditions of one or another appropriate to their needs. Ordinarily, in both numbers of species and individual animals, the twilight zone ranks first, the variable-temperature area second, and the constant-temperature zone third; this ranking may change, however, when colonies of bats are present in the cave.

Animals that live in or visit caves regularly are divided into three general classifications according to their degree of dependency on the cave environment. *Trogloxenes* (from the Greek *troglos*, meaning "cave," and *xenos*, meaning "guest") are animals that occur in caves, either accidentally or habitually, but do not complete their entire life cycle there. Common examples include many species of bats and pack rats. *Troglophiles* (*phileo* means "love" in Greek) are facultative cavernicoles (cavern-inhabiting); that is, they are found living permanently in caves, successfully completing their life cycle there; however, they are also found living in suitable habitats outside the caves. *Troglobites* (*bios* means "life" in Greek) are obligatory cavernicoles, unable to survive except in caves or similar underground habitats.

In discussing the biota of caves we will be primarily considering temperate rather than tropical caves, with some comparisons between the two types being drawn later. At this point, however, we should point out that a primary difference between temperate and most tropical caves is the amount of food available within each. Food is a determining factor regarding types and numbers of animals that can live in a cave. And the matter of food ultimately goes back to green plants.

In the sunlit world it is only green plants that can use the sun's radiant energy to produce food, a process known as photosynthesis. A plant takes carbon dioxide from the air, water from the soil, and in the presence of light, through complex chemical reactions involving the plant's green coloring matter known as chlorophyll, produces glucose. This basic food may then be changed through other chemical reactions in a plant or animal body to more complex carbohydrates, proteins, and fats.

Green plants thus form the base of the food pyramid for animal life on earth. Green plants cannot grow in the absence of light. And the absence of light is the cave's basic condition. Hence all food present within a cave (with few exceptions) must originate outside the cave, and by one means or another be transported into it. The two primary cave food sources are guano and organic debris washed into the cave during floods. Of course, cave animals themselves may die and thus become food, but this is simply food one or more steps removed from its origin outside the cave.

Although green plants do not grow beyond the twilight zone, certain types of plant life do exist in a cave. These are the bacteria, fungi, and actinomycetes, which are organisms intermediate in character between the previous two. Basically these three types of organisms grow on, break down, and consume organic debris. Thus they fill the role of decomposers, and serve as the first step in making nutrients available to animals within the cave or for return to the cave soil or water.

The bacteria can be divided into two basic forms—heterotrophic and autotrophic. *Heterotrophic* bacteria require food in the form of organic substances. Certain *autotrophic* bacteria, known as chemoautotrophs, found in caves and also often in soil, actually produce organic molecules using energy produced by reactions of inorganic chemicals rather than radiant energy. For example, iron bacteria get their energy from the simple oxidation of iron compounds. Sulphur bacteria do the same with sulphur. Still others metabolize nitrogen compounds. The chemoautotrophs constitute one exception to the rule that only green plants can produce food from inorganic materials. Heterotrophic and autotrophic bacteria are not ordinarily found together, and the heterotrophic bacteria and fungi are quantitatively much more important in the cave food chain than are the chemoautotrophic bacteria. Overall, the vast majority of the food present in a cave is exogenous in origin.

In any community of living things energy and nutrients are constantly being passed from one trophic (that is, feeding) level to the next. However, all along the food chain energy is constantly being lost, degraded to heat. Energy thus cannot be recycled in a community; however, chemical elements can be. These are returned to the community by various means: oxygen and carbon are released back to the atmosphere during animal respiration, and minerals are returned to the environment (with the help of decomposers) through excreta and the bodies of dead animals.

Because large amounts of energy are lost at each trophic level, an illustration of a community food pattern forms a pyramid shape. Its broad base is composed of plant life. Certain animals feed on this and in turn they are fed on by other animals; however the number of organisms supported at each level grows progressively smaller; the food pyramid thus tapers to a point at the final trophic level.

Aboveground there may be several trophic levels, with herbivores eating green plants, the herbivores being eaten by carnivores or omnivores, and these being eaten by other animals in turn until several levels have been sustained. Food chains in caves are simpler and trophic levels are fewer than many of those aboveground. Herbivores are lacking, and cave animals tend to be less specialized with regard to food than surface forms. Thus, in a cave food chain fungi and bacteria, which have grown on organic debris, may be consumed by protozoans, which are eaten by isopods or similar creatures, which are consumed in turn by crayfish, fish, salamanders, or other species. The waste materials produced by these animals, and upon their deaths their bodies, serve as food for the bacteria and fungi, bringing the cycle full circle.

Caves are remarkably stable, in temperature and humidity. The latter in wet caves is high, hence desiccation of the animal's body is not a problem. Wet caves support more life than dry. But while stability may be a positive environmental factor, this is counterbalanced by two factors that constitute a negative quality for many types of animals—darkness and a general shortage of food. As a result of these factors, temperate caves usually display low population densities of troglobites, and the species in them, although belonging to a rather wide range of invertebrate and vertebrate groups, come from the lower evolutionary stages. The majority of them belong to the phylum Arthropoda (consisting of articulated invertebrate animals with jointed limbs and bodies generally covered with a chitinous shell; the phylum includes crustaceans, insects, spiders, and others). Of all vertebrate groups, only the fish and the amphibians have troglobitic representatives. There are no reptile, bird, or mammal troglobites, although two types of birds, not found in the United States, that nest in the dark areas of caves, and certainly some mammals, primarily bats, are strongly dependent on the dark cave environment for an important part of their life.

Troglobitic species often display distinguishing characteristics. Insects may have thinner chitinous shells and longer appendages than their related non-troglobitic relatives. Certain other species may also display a long, thin body form or longer legs than related aboveground forms. This is seen to varying degrees in certain troglobitic salamanders. Some animal species display very long antennae. Two of the most obvious and striking characteristics displayed by some troglobites are reduced or totally lacking skin pigment and degenerate or total loss of eyes. White, blind fish, crayfish, and salamanders, due to their striking appearance and extreme adaptation to cave life, are probably the best-known troglobites to the general public.

Troglobitic species are extremely efficient in their use of energy, display low metabolic rates, are able to subsist over periods of time on small amounts of food or none at all, and have behavioral adaptations that aid them in surviving with limited and irregular food supplies. They often produce only a few eggs, but these are very large, providing the young with a distinct advantage at birth. Also, troglobitic species often have a smaller number of larval stages or have almost completely bypassed the larval stages. This, too, provides a distinct advantage for the species, for in a food-poor environment, the more normal, relatively helpless, often fairly immobile larval stages would be at a distinct disadvantage in obtaining food and in escaping from predators. Many troglobitic species display an expanded life span. Reproduction in these species is closely timed to coincide with the periods of greatest food availability, often an annual flooding of the cave or at least increased water flow during the rainy season. Populations of cave animals are also closely regulated according to the amounts of food available.

In summary, then, the environment of temperate, wet caves is one in which food supplies are generally severely restricted, but utilized with strict efficiency by specialized animal life. The animals present are for the most part small or microscopic, including one-celled protozoans, planarians or flatworms, snails, crustaceans, millipedes, beetles, crickets, spiders, crayfish, fish, and salamanders.

Troglobitic species have evolved from former troglophiles that were preadapted for cave life and long ago became isolated in caves. As long as a troglophilic species exists both within and outside a cave, genetic transfer between the two is possible. However, if the species population outside the cave is destroyed or removed, the cave-inhabiting members of that species are then in genetic isolation. Providing they continue to live and breed in the cave, genetically this isolated population will move toward troglobitic status over vast periods of time.

The glaciation that occurred during the Ice Ages was probably a major factor in the isolation of species that became the troglobites we find in caves today. Lowered temperatures and ice effectively made it impossible for many species to live on portions of the earth's surface where they formerly occurred; at the same time, at least on the peripheries of the areas affected by ice, the same animal species could continue to exist in the more protected cave environment. Thus troglobites are best known from portions of Europe and the United States that were not actually covered by ice, but whose climates were severely affected by the proximity of glaciers.

A great deal of research is being conducted in regard to Mexican caves. Speleologists are discovering increasing numbers of troglobites in these previously largely unknown caves, which were not affected by glaciation in the same way as caves that were located farther to the north. Life in these Mexican caves is an exciting area of study, and important findings will undoubtedly continue to be made there.

Once isolated in a cave, some animal species, primarily small aquatic ones, may move through tiny joints, along bedding planes, or through similar small pathways and achieve a rather wide underground distribution. Larger species, however, are more confined and have fewer opportunities for colonization. In general, terrestrial troglobitic species are more restricted in their distribution than aquatic ones, and small species are more widely distributed than larger ones. As a result some of the larger troglobitic species may only be found in a single cave or in a series of several interconnected caves.

Many of the genetic changes that have occurred in the troglobites are degenerative. Aboveground the environment is more variable, predators may be more numerous and varied, and the environment is in other ways more unpredictable. Animals that lack pigment and are thereby extremely apparent to predators, or that lack sight, would not last long and thus would have difficulty passing genes for these traits to future generations. In the cave situation lack of pigment and sight do not work against the individual animal with these traits. Due to the fact that the population is isolated, the gene pool is limited. Such isolation of populations leads to divergence, as is so often obvious on islands; eventually, divergence results in the development of distinct new species. This may occur in the isolation of a cave as readily as in the isolation of an island. Changes may transpire in caves that eventually cause the species to become an obligatory cavernicole, unable to live even as a troglophile. Poulson and White (1969) state in this regard that "degeneration and decreased genetic variability are associated with adaptation to an unvarying environment," which, of course, is the general case with the dark, inner cave zone.

Where food within caves is plentiful, a somewhat different picture emerges. In these caves rich food is ordinarily supplied by vast numbers of bats, which leave quantities of guano below their resting places in caves. Guano is a rich food source, and life in guano caves is abundant, seething with insects feeding on it, dead bats, and other debris. In some southern temperate caves bat colonies exist in sufficient numbers to support a rich cave biota. It is primarily in tropical caves, however, where large bat colonies exist year-round, that a veritable profusion of cave life exists. Animals in these caves for the most part are troglo-xenes and troglophiles, able to spend a large part of their lives within these caves due to the availability of generous food supplies. Visiting a tropical bat cave can be a startling experience; there are great numbers of bats, a fetid, ammoniac guano odor, masses of cockroaches, and myriad other creatures—the food base of all largely dependent on guano.

Lengthy volumes have been written regarding the trogloxenes, troglophiles, and troglobites of our North American caves. Certainly the subject can merely be skimmed in a chapter such as this.

We conclude this chapter with an urgent message. Caver, spelunker, speleologist—whatever you may call yourself when you enter caves—respect and do all within your ability to preserve cave biota. Only relatively slight modifications in a cave environment may spell doom for cave species, and the status of numerous of these species ranges from endangered to tenuous. Increased numbers of visitors to caves, decimation of bat populations by insecticides and other factors, pollution of cave waters, and many other conditions or actions are placing severe stresses on certain animal life found in caves. As a concerned caver, do not add to this pressure unnecessarily. For example, if entering a cave will disturb a hibernating bat colony, do not enter the cave at that time. Return later when hibernation is over; mortality is high among hibernating bats that are disturbed and forced to fly when food is unavailable to them. Never collect cave life. Notify a scientist if you discover something of interest; leave the animal where you find it.

7

CAVE EXPLORATION: GETTING STARTED

ABALL OF STRING, a candle, a cave, and enthusiasm will not a caver make. Whereas preparation, practice, a cave, and enthusiasm may well do so. But what preparation? What practice? How does the would-be caver become a caver?

Start by visiting the commercial caves that are available to you. True, these are lit by electricity, have neat negotiable stairs or even elevators, and provide a guide to take you in tow. Several such visits should either convince you that perhaps your enthusiasm for the world beneath was misplaced, or conversely that you are increasingly anxious to explore wild caves. There is an excellent, comprehensive, recently revised (1980) publication that pinpoints major U.S., commercial caves and provides interesting information about each. This is the *Gurnee Guide to American Caves: A Comprehensive Guide to the Caves in the United States Open to the Public*, written by Russell and Jeanne Gurnee, and published by Zephyrus Press, Inc.

Before beginning cave exploration, take into consideration whether or not you have any tendency toward claustrophobia, the abnormal fear of enclosed or narrow places; acrophobia, the abnormal dread of being at a great height; or abnormal uneasiness at being in darkness.

As an introduction to caving, seek out competent local cavers who are willing to take you with them into a cave or caves suitable for a novice. The ideal place to find such individuals is in your local caving club. Ordinarily this will be a grotto (local chapter) of the National Speleological Society. It is strongly urged that all cavers join the National Speleological Society and their local grotto of this organization.

The NSS, as it is usually termed, was formally organized in 1941. It is affiliated with the American Association for the Advancement of Science, and is dedicated to the exploration, study, and conservation of caves. Membership in the society is open to any individual interested in caves, and consists of cave scientists, conservationists, cave owners, and those who simply enjoy visiting and exploring caves.

There are many advantages to be gained from membership, not least of which is the opportunity to become acquainted with the cavers in your immediate area, and throughout the United States and the world as the opportunities are available. The NSS publishes the *NSS News* monthly. This informs members about activities in the caving community throughout the United States and publishes articles of interest, reviews of books, and other information. The *NSS Bulletin* is a quarterly publication that reports on original speleological research. Special publications relating to caving and cave studies are also produced. Included in this group is *The Caving Information Series*, which provides down-to-earth information about many aspects of caving, such as mapping, photography, clothing, and so on. The NSS maintains an extensive library of works pertaining to caves and caving, portions of which circulate to members upon request. The Society sells cave-related publications at a discount to its members; sponsors expeditions to U.S. and foreign caves; and tests, evaluates, and reports to the membership on the merits of new techniques and equipment. The NSS is also very active in promoting cave conservation and environmentally responsible caving. Your membership in the organization lends support to this cause. Letters of inquiry to the organization should be directed to:

National Speleological Society
Cave Avenue
Huntsville, Alabama 35810

Currently there are 200 grottos of the NSS in the United States. If there are none in your vicinity, you may be able to locate a local organization of cavers at a nearby college, or a group of interested individuals within another recreation or conservation organization, such as the Sierra Club. Contact your local chapter or write to:

Sierra Club
530 Bush Street
San Francisco, California 94108

A few rubrics on the craft of caving:

The beginning caver should seek instruction in caving techniques. Most NSS grottos provide such instruction to novices and get them started participating in actual caving trips. Classes in vertical techniques presented by climbing clubs or shops specializing in climbing and caving gear are beneficial, also, for gaining experience and expertise.

Read the literature available regarding cave exploration techniques and equipment. Reading is an introduction, but cannot replace actual practice and experience. Practice aboveground the techniques you need to master for exploration underground. Maintain your body in good physical condition by exercising.

For your introductory cave trips you may be able to rent or borrow any special equipment necessary that you do not own, such as carbide or electric lamps. However, if you continue caving, study the options available regarding personal equipment such as caving helmet, lights, pack, and similar items. Make your decisions and purchase what you will need. As you gain experience and decide to move into the area of vertical caving, you will again need to evaluate equipment options seriously and make decisions regarding your needs.

Caving should be regarded as *potentially* dangerous. It is a sport to be treated with respect. There are a good many rules that must be heeded for your own benefit, for that of other individuals, and for that of the cave itself.

The most basic rule of caving is *never cave alone*. The individual who disregards this rule and has an accident, becomes lost, or otherwise encounters serious problems while caving alone will require the assistance of rescuers. Not only does the lone caver unnecessarily endanger his life, but to varying degrees he may place the lives of those who come to his aid in jeopardy. At the very least he requires the expenditure of the rescue team's time, energy, and usually money in an effort that should never have become necessary.

There should be at least three members on any caving trip; an optimum minimum number is considered to be four. At least two, and preferably three members of the four-member group should be competent, experienced cavers. Normally the most competent should lead the single-file cavers, and the second most competent should be the last in line of progression, with the novice and least experienced holding the intermediate positions.

Four cavers are considered the minimum number required to deal with emergencies. For example, if one caver is injured and cannot leave the cave, one member of the group remains with the injured party caring for him, while the other two make their way back out of the cave to arrange for a rescue party. By having a total of four team members, two are free to negotiate the trip back to the entrance together, thus continuing to observe the never-cave-alone rule as a precaution against further problems.

Caving requires team effort and individual responsibility within that team. Essentially, any caving group is only as strong as its weakest member. Know your own capabilities and never exceed them. You will be endangering yourself and your companions if you do so. If you feel you need a belay (safety) rope or other aid, tell your companions. There is no room in caving for false bravado.

Never go caving when ill or with similar problems

that may make you a burden to your companions. And be aware of the condition of your companions. Never demand more from a team member than his common sense tells him he is capable of delivering, and never belittle another caver who requests some safety or similar aid.

Never needlessly waste energy in caving; you may need all your energy reserves later in the trip. Gauge your energy and that of the party members and act accordingly. Fatigue leads to carelessness, accidents, and can be a factor in hypothermia. Do not push yourself or your companions beyond their endurance level, and remember that the way out of a cave is at least as hard as the way in; often it is much more strenuous.

Be prepared for possible emergencies. For example, it is wise for caving, as well as for normal living, to take first aid and CPR classes before being faced with the need for proficiency in these areas.

As a part of a team, you need to realize that a leader is necessary. Usually the leader is the most experienced caver in the group. Oftentimes leadership is simply by means of tacit understanding. However, it is important that in an emergency situation a leader does assume command and that all members recognize his position and authority.

Take proper care of your equipment. Check it regularly, clean and maintain it, and retire any pieces that become suspect.

Before any caving expedition, always notify a responsible individual what cave you are entering, what portions you plan to explore, where it is, any changes in plans that might occur due to weather or other conditions, and when you plan to return. Be explicit in your information in order that time and effort need not be wasted if rescue operations are necessary. This information is given with the understanding that the contact will alert authorities or other individuals who will initiate search and rescue operations if you do not return when stated. Allow yourself a margin for error in your planned return time. At least one member of the caving party should have a watch along in order that the party will not be late in leaving the cave. Underground, time often seems somewhat distorted to the caver who is busy with his activities and has no external clues, such as sunlight, to guide him. Once you have returned, be sure to notify your contact that you have done so.

Obtain permission of the landowner, government agency, or other overseer before entering caves. It may be beneficial or necessary to write or call ahead to make these arrangements. When you arrive, check in with the owner. Be polite. Be considerate. Follow the owner's rules and requests. The owner is extending a favor to you when he allows you to cross his land and explore beneath it. A single rude, inconsiderate caver may be the cause of a private landowner denying access to a cave on his land to all other cavers thereafter.

Leave everything inside and outside the cave in the condition in which you found it—or in an improved state. Leave gates as you encountered them. If the cave entrance is barricaded to prevent animals from entering or falling in, replace these barriers when leaving. Leave no trash behind and take out someone else's, if present. Park your vehicles where requested. Check out with the landowner when leaving. If it is late at night or the owner is away, leave a note letting him know you have left the cave. In person or by note, be sure to thank him for his permission and help. It doesn't hurt to send the owner a photo or series of photos taken inside his cave, or a copy of the map you have produced from your visits, or to offer to take him into parts of the cave he has never seen.

Learn as much as you can about a cave before entering it. Study a map of it if one is available. Talk to other cavers who have visited it in order to learn about any special conditions present and what equipment and techniques may be needed for its exploration.

Carry at least three sources of light and spare parts, and power sources for at least twice the expected stay. Wear a proper helmet with secure chin strap. Dress for the conditions to be encountered in the cave. Eat a nutritious meal before entering the cave. Carry some high energy snack foods with you into the cave. Carry sufficient water for the length of your visit, unless you are certain there is sufficient potable water within the cave. Cave waters are increasingly contaminated, making them unfit for human consumption.

Never drink alcohol or use hallucinogenic drugs before or during a cave trip. They adversely affect your judgment, concentration, coordination, reflexes, emotional stability, and stamina—all qualities of vital importance to both yourself and your companions in caving. Nor should alcohol ever be given to an injured caver.

You have a major responsibility to protect the cave environment, both while visiting the cave and while absent from it. Do not reveal the exact location of an unprotected cave to anyone except conservationists who can be trusted not to be indiscriminate with the information. This may sound extreme, but over the years many cavers have learned to their sorrow and consternation that the beautiful formations of a favorite cave have been destroyed by vandals, idiots, collectors, or souvenir hunters who by one means or another have learned the cave's location. At other times the damage is wrought not by destructive individuals but the uninformed.

This is another good reason to become a member of a responsible local caving club. It is the chapter members who know the locations of local caves. They share that information with other members who have proven themselves trustworthy and responsible, but with very few nonmembers, unless the cave in question is well protected. The NSS Policy for Cave Conservation states, "Where there is reason to believe that publication of cave locations will lead to vandalism before adequate protection can be established, the Society will oppose such publication."

Take nothing from a cave except your trash (and anyone else's you may find there). Take your garbage home to your own garbage can; never abandon it outside the cave entrance. Never bury spent carbide in a cave or outside it. Spent carbide kills animals—take it home along with the rest of your trash.

Never remove formations, even broken ones.

Leave bones, artifacts, and animals where you find them. Notify a scientist if you think your find is important, but remember that it is necessary to study such finds in place; much information is lost to the scientist if the caver collects the items to deliver to him. The NSS advises, "All contents of a cave—formations, life, and loose deposits—are significant for its enjoyment and interpretation. Therefore, caving parties should leave a cave as they find it. . . . Scientific collection is professional, selective and minimal. The collecting of mineral or biological material for display purposes, including previously broken or dead specimens, is never justified, as it encourages others to collect and destroys the interest of the cave."

Never mark the walls of a cave. It once was common for cavers to use smoke from their carbide lamps to mark arrows on walls indicating the route out. This is no longer acceptable. Today's cavers who find it necessary to mark their route should use reflective tape or other temporary markings, which should be removed as they exit the cave.

In answer to some sort of ego drive, over the centuries a good many cavers have smoked, carved, or painted their names on cave walls. While it may be exciting to some individuals today—although probably not to hard-core conservationist cavers—to see the original signature of George Washington written in a cave he once explored, it is no thrill to see your name or that of other contemporary cavers marring cave walls. Washington's cave signature may be classified as historical; yours, ours, and anyone else's are simply disfiguring graffiti.

Be alert moving through a cave. Single file is often the best means of moving with the least destruction to the cave. Stay on established paths where possible in order to avoid cave disfiguration by a proliferation of trails. Do not step on delicate speleothems, bone deposits, and similar fragile and/or significant items.

Do not touch speleothems with muddy hands; permanent staining will result. Be careful to avoid brushing against delicate speleothems on ceilings and walls. A mere touch or even breathing on them may provide sufficient force to break very delicate soda straws and similar speleothems.

On your inward journey, in order to facilitate your later exit from the cave, turn around regularly as you move through the cave in order to view your route from that perspective. Note junctions, passage configurations, slope of roof, distinctive speleothems, other formations and deposits, and similar keys to help you remember the route you will be following on your exit.

Stay with your companions; do not wander off alone.

Never use ladders, ropes, or mechanical climbing aids left in a cave unless you have personal knowledge of their reliability. Ladders and ropes deteriorate rapidly in the cave environment. Do not risk your life or that of others by using these found items. Conversely, remove any potentially dangerous equipment you may have placed in a cave when you have finished using it.

Never light a fire underground. Fires may endanger your life by consuming available oxygen in the cave, replacing it with deadly carbon monoxide. Bat guano is flammable and has been known to explode. Also, fires smoke and disfigure cave walls and ceilings, and the smoke may be damaging to animal life in the cave. If cooking or heating of water is to be done underground, a backpacker's stove should be packed into the cave. These are small, lightweight, compact, safe, and useful.

If your party is fortunate enough to discover a new cave or new passage in a known cave, explore any new cave area in a responsible manner. The path you establish will be followed by others. Determine the most ecologically sound route for it. Be alert and aware of your surroundings. Move cautiously for your own safety as well as that of the cave.

If your passage through newly discovered or previously known caves or cave passages will cause serious or irreparable damage to the cave or its biota, do not attempt it. For example, as noted earlier, some caves should not be visited when entry will disturb hibernating bats. Or, in cases where the floors of cave passages cannot be traversed without destroying previously untouched speleothems, resist the temptation and do not enter.

If an emergency occurs, do not panic. Maintain a calm, level head. After all, your brain is the best thing you have going for you. Use it.

When alternatives present themselves in caving, as in choosing a route or in deciding upon a means of accomplishing a particular move, always choose the safest alternative. The sport of caving is not one in which to display individual bravado, daring, or self-aggrandizement. Rather it is a team effort, with all members equally responsible for one another. Risks should be minimized as much as possible where choices are to be made.

Speleologists of all degrees, from scientists to cavers, have a moral and ethical responsibility to educate the public in appreciation and conservation of caves and the cave environment. The NSS states, "It is the duty of every Society member to take personal responsibility for spreading a consciousness of the cave conservation problem to each potential user of caves. Without this, the beauty and value of our caves will not long remain with us."

Take it beyond that. Be politically conscious and actively work for conservation measures regarding caves and cave environments. The NSS states, "The responsibility for protecting caves must be assumed by those who study and enjoy them." Both underground and aboveground, for concerned cavers (and there should be no other kind), conservation must be not only a state of mind, but an active way of life.

8

PERSONAL EQUIPMENT FOR GENERAL CAVING

THE NUMBER OF INDI-
viduals entering caves
for sport continues to
increase dramatically   every year. Speleological studies are also expanding annually in number,
scope, and variety. In order to enjoy caving in safety,
anyone who plans to enter a cave should realize that
he will need specific skills and equipment. This
chapter describes some of the basic personal equipment a caver should carry with him.

CLOTHING

Proper clothing selection is important; it can mean the
difference between life and death. Clothing serves
several purposes. It must protect the body from jagged
rocks, rough crawls, and other potentially abrasive
contacts with the cave. Clothing must also assist in
maintaining an equilibrium between heat gain and
heat loss in the caver's body.

The human body must maintain a specific core
temperature. If this fluctuates more than a few
degrees, serious bodily harm will result. The body sus-
tains this core temperature by metabolically generat-
ing heat and by dissipating heat through sweating and
other means such as convection, or the transfer of heat

by air molecules, and conduction, or the transfer of heat through body contact with surface areas or with water.

Similarly, the body may gain heat through convection and conduction as well as, when above-ground, through direct radiation from the sun or reflected radiation from the ground and sky. If, as often happens in caving, the body must deliver bursts of energy, the metabolic rate will increase, thereby increasing heat production. If heat production is not approximately equaled by heat loss, overheating of the body and subsequent heat exhaustion are very real possibilities. *Hyperthermia* is the medical term that refers to the physiological state of greatly elevated body temperature.

If the core temperature of the caver's body is approaching the upper limit of heat tolerance, it is extremely important that prolonged bursts of energy be minimized and sufficient resting time be allowed in order for the body to cool. Cavers wearing heavy coats and other warm clothing in cooler caves have been known to contract heat exhaustion while ascending a rope out of the cave. The atmosphere may have felt cool while they were exploring at the bottom of the cave, but upon producing the energy needed to propel the body up a rope, they generate a large amount of body heat. With heavy clothing the heat is difficult to dissipate and the body may overheat. Thus it is impor-tant for cavers to select clothing that will permit venting. Further, rather than wearing a single heavy coat to keep one warm in a cave, it is much more efficient to wear several layers of clothing that can be easily added or removed as required.

In caving, hyperthermia occurs only occasionally; it is not as common as *hypothermia*, or a state of greatly decreased body temperature. Certainly, proper clothing in sufficient amounts plays an important role in the prevention of hypothermia, as we will be noting in this chapter. (For a discussion of symptoms and first aid for hyperthermia and hypothermia, consult Chapter 17.)

Now, to the clothes themselves. Wear woolen longjohns over regular underclothing. Some cavers use woolen net underwear. Dead air provides fine insulation because it is a poor conductor; hence the dead air pockets developed by net underwear become very efficient insulators. Woolen underclothing is preferred because it insulates better than cotton, particularly when wet. Wet, cotton garments often cause more harm than good; they are little better than wearing nothing.

Blue denim jeans are often worn over the underclothing. Blue jeans are fairly rugged; however, they are relatively thin, offering little cushioning to the legs during crawling, and offer little insulation, since they are composed of cotton fiber. Also, they tend to fit the caver's body rather snugly and to restrict movements when scrambling and climbing. Woolen pants are considered best by many cavers and should be considered mandatory when caving in wet, cold caves.

The shirt should fit loosely enough to allow ease of movement and should also be made of wool for cold, wet caves.

The third most common layer used, especially in cold, wet caves, is a pair of coveralls. These help to maintain warmth and hence are sometimes omitted in warm caves. In any type of cave, however, separate items of clothing tend to get caught and snagged on rock protrusions when the caver is negotiating a tight squeeze. Coveralls serve as the name implies; they efficiently cover all loose clothing and pockets, and this is often their most important purpose in caving. Caving is very hard on clothing. This is particularly true of cave mud, which often penetrates all layers of clothing worn. Coveralls with buttons are recommended over those with zippers, for zippers are often penetrated and ruined by mud.

For cavers who do a great deal of crawling on their knees, or who find themselves sitting for periods of time while surveying or photographing, it will add to their comfort, and in many cases prevent undue heat loss from conduction, to have butt and knee patches added to their clothing. These patches may be composed of ⅛-inch Ensolite pieces cut to the proper size and inserted in pockets sewed into the clothing, thus allowing easy insertion and removal of the pads as needed for laundering purposes.

When exploring caves with water passages where the caver will be wet constantly, it is suggested that the caver replace the outer two layers of clothing with a wet or dry suit (see below). Caving in water with temperatures below 80°F can be extremely heat-exhausting. Water conducts heat approximately twenty-five times more efficiently than does air; so the potential for development of hypothermia while caving in cold water poses a very grave danger. When exploring caves that require extensive wading or swimming, it is all but mandatory that a wet suit be used.

Wet suits are body suits made of neoprene rubber. The rubber is impregnated with millions of air bubbles that provide excellent insulation. An extremely thin layer of water is allowed to seep between the caver's skin and the wet suit. This water is quickly heated and maintained by the body at its temperature; hence the wearer has a protective buffer zone about his body. Wet suits are made in various thicknesses. The most common is $\frac{3}{16}$-inch, which provides for fairly free movement; $\frac{1}{4}$- and $\frac{1}{8}$-inch are sometimes used. Many options are available on these suits. Some of the recommended options for cavers are knee pads, elbow pads, butt patches, rolled seams, and spine pad. In cool caves one may want a "farmer-john" style, in which the pants also cover the stomach and the vital organs to provide for double insulation. Be sure the suit's neoprene is lined on both sides with nylon and that all seams are sewed as well as glued.

Until recently dry suits for caving were not recommended. They were known to tear and rip quite easily, and, in order for a dry suit to work, one needed to remain dry underneath the suit. The major weakness of these suits was the fact that they were constructed of rubber-impregnated cloth. Most dry suits are now made from $\frac{3}{16}$- or $\frac{1}{4}$-inch neoprene, and these work quite efficiently in keeping the caver dry. Modern dry suits stand little chance of ripping, and when custom fitted they work as a wet suit if torn. Both wet and dry suits can be purchased at diving shops.

It is extremely important that cavers keep their feet warm and cushioned. Use a two-sock combination: a light, inner pair and a heavier, outer one. By using two pairs you insulate and protect the feet more than with a single pair of socks, but more importantly you provide a second interface, so that the two socks shift and rub against each other, rather than your foot rubbing against the sock and developing blisters. The socks should be made of wool, except in extremely cold, wet caving conditions, where the caver should wear thin, wet-suit neoprene socks. These neoprene socks keep your feet warm, even when you've been wading in cold water for hours.

Today one sees cavers using a variety of types of shoes, from tennis shoes to leather work boots. Tennis shoes are lightweight and inexpensive, but they give virtually no support to the ankle, which is constantly experiencing twisting in active caving. Also, tennis shoes give little insulation to the foot, do not protect it from jagged rocks, and often have slick soles that can prove dangerous in caves. Low-topped shoes have a tendency to become stuck in the mud and to be pulled from the feet. Nailed climbing boots, once the favorite mountaineering types, work well on slick clay traverses; however, in caving they should not be worn as they may damage cave formations and have the potential to damage climbing rope and cable ladders. A favorite boot among many cavers is mostly canvas. It has a good rubber lug sole, canvas top, and provides fairly decent support for the lower ankle. These boots were used in Viet Nam and until recently were easily available from surplus stores and were fairly inexpensive. However, at present they are becoming more difficult to find and inferior copies are cropping up.

The best footwear for caving is leather lug-soled boots. The lug-patterned sole should be composed of a hard rubber such as those marketed under the trade name Vibram and should be cut close to the welt. The boots should have sturdy leather uppers to ankle height to provide insulation and support. Higher uppers provide few advantages and reduce foot flexibility needed for climbing and traversing. The boot toes should be hard for protection; this is especially important when pushing off in tight crawlways.

When you are fitting a pair of boots for caving, make sure they fit looser than the extremely tight fit of rock shoes and a bit snugger than looser-fitting hiking boots. Your toes should not jam against the front of the boot when walking normally, but if kicked solidly at the toe a few times, the foot should move forward to the end of the boot. It is also important that you wear two pairs of socks of the weight you intend to use in caving when you are fitting boots.

The cave environment is hard on boots, which must be cared for if you expect them to last. Wet, muddy boots need to be dried and cleaned. The most common method of drying boots is to wipe them inside and out, then stuff them with newspaper to absorb the moisture. The newspaper should be changed periodically as it becomes saturated. Putting the boots on a boot tree will help retain their shape. The leather should be treated with the proper leather conditioner or waterproofing agent. Sno-Seal and Bee Seal work effectively. As the Vibram soles wear and become rounded they provide no better traction than a smooth-soled boot and should be replaced. Be sure to inform the shoe repairman to trim the new sole very closely, which is necessary for climbing.

HELMET

Helmets are absolutely necessary in caving. No experienced caver would ever enter a cave without one. The helmet serves three major functions. First and foremost, the helmet protects the caver's head when he inadvertently stands up under overhanging formations or low ceilings. It is surprising how many times during a single cave trip you will be grateful for it as you feel the cushioned impact of your helmet coming into contact with rock. The helmet also serves to protect the head against damage from falling rocks. And, finally, the helmet provides a mounting bracket for the caver's light source.

It has been common in the past for cavers to use

helmets made of metal, fiberglass, or plastic and manufactured to meet state and federal standards for use by the mining and construction industries. These helmets are primarily designed to protect the wearer's head in the event of short falls or from injuries caused by objects falling a few feet. It has gradually become apparent that for serious caving, where the risk of falling rock is not uncommon, these types of helmets do not suffice. Serious cavers are now beginning to use helmets designed to withstand higher impact than the older types of helmets.

These preferred helmets consist of an inner high-density polyethylene liner covered with a high-impact

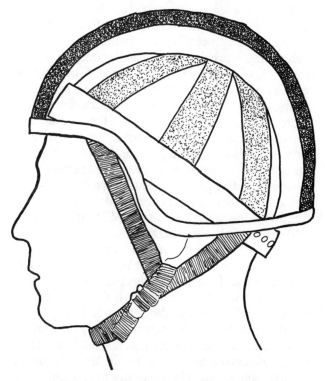

Helmet. *A quality climber's helmet used for caving purposes should contain a high density, impact-absorbing, foam lining inside a fiber-glass plastic shell. The caver's head is safely suspended away from the shell by means of a nylon strap suspension system. The helmet is securely held in place by means of a four-point attachment system.*

fiberglass shell. Two of the most popular are the Joe Brown and Ultimate helmets, which are designed for mountaineering. The foam liner in these helmets will absorb an incredible amount of impact force, giving the caver greatly increased protection in comparison to older types of helmets. This mountaineering type of close-fitting helmet also gives increased protection against falls or blows to the side of the head.

It is important that whatever helmet you use has an approved suspension system with all inner edges rounded. All cavers' helmets must have a well-designed chin strap with four points of attachment to the helmet—that is, two points on each side of the helmet—in order to prevent it from pivoting on the head. A helmet without a chin strap often provides about as much protection as no helmet at all. Without a chin strap, the helmet will usually come off at the beginning of an impact, leaving the caver unprotected.

An important function of the helmet is that of providing a mounting bracket for the caver's primary light source, thus leaving both hands free for climbing and negotiating the cave. Some of the miner-type hard hats have brackets for attaching a light. However, the mountaineering helmets, such as the Joe Brown and Ultimate, will require the addition of a mounting bracket. The best brackets I have found are manufactured by Mine Safety Appliances (MSA) and will mate to the newer contoured helmets.

Yet another good reason to have a chin strap is that the lamp will sometimes cause your helmet to become front-heavy, and the helmet may tend to fall off more easily. If the weight of the light is bothersome and the helmet continually rides down in front, it may be worth your while to counterbalance it by the addition of some lead to the helmet's rear. It should be noted that any bolts or screws placed or drilled in the helmet for attaching the light bracket carry the possibility of causing damage to the skull if the helmet is subject to high impact. Flush or very shallow rivets or similar mounting devices should be used for attaching brackets; in some cases attachment using an epoxy may suffice.

LIGHTS

The choice of the type of light source for caving is the subject of major debates among cavers. There are essentially two basic types: the carbide lamp and the electric lamp. Until fairly recently the majority of cavers used carbide lamps, but over the years the continuous improvement of the electric lamp has increased its popularity until now there are almost equal numbers of enthusiasts on each side of the issue.

Carbide lamps tend to possess their own personalities and are often temperamental. For this reason many cavers prefer to use electric lamps, which are more straightforward to operate. However, most carbide lamp malfunctions are due to poor maintenance. If you know your lamp as you should and carry the proper spare parts, almost all problems can be avoided or remedied.

Carbides do have one unique quality not shared by electric lamps—the flame itself. The carbide delivers heat and has the ability to arrest caver hypothermia. A space blanket over a cold caver used in conjunction with a carbide lamp has saved cavers' lives. A carbide can also be used for fusing rope ends together to arrest unraveling, for cooking, and for heating water for drinks. Conversely, the flame may also pose problems, having the potential to cause fires or damage ropes.

There is a weight factor to be considered as well. As most cavers will agree, carrying sufficient batteries to provide light becomes an increasing burden, and for some long trips electric lights become an unreasonable choice. Carbide will weigh approximately half that of the equivalent electric batteries. The carbide will occupy a greatly reduced volume, and even when water for the carbide must be carried, the volume is still less than that required for batteries. Oftentimes, of course, water need not be carried for the carbide lamp as water can be obtained in the cave.

Regardless of what you decide on as your primary light source—electric or carbide—it is essential that you know the unit inside and out, and that you are capable of repairing and adjusting it. You should always carry spare parts and know their function.

Carbide Lamps

In the past, three separate manufacturing firms competed with one another in the United States in the production of quality brass carbide lamps. Then Autolite and Guys Dropper discontinued their production, leaving the Justrite Company as the only U.S. manufacturer. Soon thereafter Justrite stopped producing brass lamps and began manufacturing a new plastic lamp. These lamps proved to be a step backward rather than an advancement in the field. They were often extremely troublesome and were too brittle, very easy to break, shatter, and mutilate. Some were recorded as exploding, and in many the entire front end of the lamp melted.

There are certain modifications that can be carried out to improve these plastic carbide lamps slightly, but it is our belief that plastic carbides should be bypassed for a used brass lamp, if available, or one of the quality

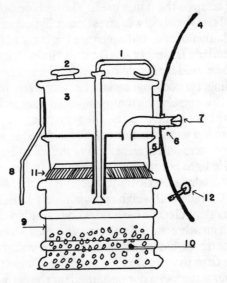

Cross section of a carbide lamp.

1. *Water-adjusting valve;* 2. *Water filler cap;* 3. *Water reservoir;* 4. *Reflector;* 5. *Reflector-backing plate;* 6. *Reflector retaining nut;* 7. *Tip;* 8. *Mounting blade;* 9. *Lamp bottom;* 10. *Carbide chips;* 11. *Gasket;* 12. *Flint and striker.*

brass lamps still produced in England by the Premier Company. Many of the parts of the Premier will interchange with those on the Justrites. There is a carbide lamp made in Japan called the butterfly, but it is generally considered to be too flimsy by most American cavers.

The principle behind a carbide lamp is quite simple. There is one portion of the lamp that acts as a reservoir for water, and another that holds calcium carbide, a solid chemical. A regulating tube routes the water in controlled drips into the carbide reservoir. When water and carbide mix, acetylene gas is produced. The quantity of water that is allowed to pass into the carbide is directly proportional to the amount of gas produced. The gas is then routed through a felt filter into a tube that ends in a tip with an extremely fine hole. Here the acetylene gas mixes with air and is ignited by a striker. The flame is long and thin, the size dependent upon the amount of water dripping onto the carbide. Behind the flame is a reflector that focuses the light ahead of the caver, illuminating his path.

It is important that you become very familiar with the carbide lamp if you plan to use it as a primary light source. A very obvious component of the lamp is the reflector, the shiny, curved collector of light. Reflectors are available in various sizes; the most common is the Justrite reflector, which is 4 inches in diameter. The reflector is held against a backing plate by a retaining nut. This nut is threaded around the end portion of the acetylene collecting tube. At the end of the tube is the tip seat, where the brass and porcelain tip is seated. The lamp may also have a wind guard seated in the retaining nut to shelter the flame. A wind guard is a most beneficial accessory. Not only does it prevent the flame from blowing out under windy conditions, but also prevents the tip from falling to the ground if it becomes unseated. Located on the reflector is a flint striker assembly used to ignite the acetylene gas.

On the top of the lamp you will find the water door, which permits access to the water reservoir. In the center, with a radial arm, is the water adjustment lever. On the rear of the lamp is the spring clip, the means of attachment. If you unscrew the bottom portion of the lamp, you will expose the carbide container. Note the rubber gasket around the top lip of this portion; the gasket insures an airtight pressure seal. Now, holding the upper portion of the lamp, look underneath this section and you can see the end of the water adjustment lever. Rotate the arm at the top and you will see the lower plug rotate, drop slightly, and permit the passing of water. Around this water adjustment assembly there is a brass felt retainer and a piece of felt that filters the acetylene gas as it is produced. By removing the retainer and filter you will be able to see the entrance to the acetylene collecting tube.

To operate a carbide lamp, the caver fills the bottom portion of the lamp one-half to two-thirds full with carbide rocks; these are small, each about ¼ inch in diameter. He checks to assure that the water reservoir is full, then turns the water adjustment lever a few clicks clockwise and watches the water begin dripping. At this point he may allow a few drops to fall directly on the carbide chips to begin the gas production process. He then screws the base to the top, making sure that the rubber gasket makes a positive seal.

Next the caver cups his hand over the reflector and the cavity it forms, covering it as completely as possible, then draws his hand across the reflector and strikes the spark. A spark is produced and the gas ignited. Many cavers assemble the lamp without priming the carbide. To light the lamp this way, open the water adjustment assembly completely clockwise for one or two seconds, then turn it approximately halfway off, and strike the flint.

It is very important to carry a repair parts kit for the carbide lamp. As a minimum, the following items should be included in this kit:

2 tips
2 felts
1 gasket
1 flint
1 flint assembly

1 tip cleaner (attached to helmet or lamp)
1 retainer nut
1 flame protector
1 felt holder

Fresh carbide should be carried in a sturdy, water-proof, plastic container, such as a Nalgene bottle or quality plastic baby bottle. Never carry carbide in glass containers. Spent carbide must always be carried out of a cave, as to leave it behind is to poison the animal life and water, as well as to deface the cave. Spent carbide should be carried in the same type of container as the unused carbide, or in sturdy plastic bags. *Caution: be sure your spent carbide is vented slightly until it is completely non-gas-producing,* for often-times spent carbide will continue to give off small amounts of acetylene for short periods of time. If placed in an airtight container, it may build up enough pressure to break the seal and may catch fire.

Do not bury or discard spent carbide after leaving the cave. It can be dangerous to cattle and other animals, produces litter, and is almost sure to enrage the landowner. Take it home with you and discard it in a proper manner.

Problems and Precautions. Carbide lamps, as noted, are temperamental. They often have one problem or another; however, virtually all problems can be traced back to a few easily repaired mal-functions.

Let us begin with the most serious of these prob-lems—a nonburning lamp. First determine whether the lamp is producing gas, and if so, whether the gas is being delivered to the tip. Check to see that acetylene is being emitted by sniffing the air near the tip. If there is gas being delivered, you will undoubtedly smell it. If you're not sure, place the tip of your tongue near the hole in the tip, and you should be able to feel the gas escaping.

If gas is being delivered but the lamp does not light, it may be due to the fact that the striker is not working correctly. Check whether it is delivering a spark. If it is, but the lamp is not lighting, then your lighting technique may be poor. Attempt to light the lamp with a match or another burning carbide lamp, and practice your lighting technique later. If the striker assembly is not producing a spark, the wheel and assembly may be contaminated by mud, the flint may be exhausted, or the tension may be too tight. Remedy any of these conditions that may be present.

If you determine that there is an insufficient amount of gas being delivered, start by assuring that there is carbide in the bottom of the lamp and water in the reservoir. Also check the water adjustment valve to be sure that water is passing down the tube. If it is not, clean and adjust the valve so that water can pass. If water does pass, try increasing the water flow. Clean the tip with the tip cleaner; a dirty tip is a common problem.

If no gas is being delivered, check the lamp bottom for holes. If there are any, replace it. Check the gasket, turn it over, and wet and reseal it, or replace it if necessary. Check the felt to be sure it is dry; if not, replace it. Check the vent hole in the water door; if clogged, clean it. The most common reasons for no gas delivery are a wet felt or a clogged tip orifice.

A clogged tip may also produce an angled, weak flame. To remedy this, clean the tip. If the flame is temporarily excessive and the lamp bottom is hot, the lamp is producing too much gas. Let this excess burn off and lower the quantity of water being delivered. If this condition is not controllable, the water delivery system is probably faulty. Try to repair it, if possible, or replace the lamp. If there is a flame around the tip, the tip seat is damaged or the tip is not seated well. At times the caver may hear a popping sound, a telltale sign that the tip base is igniting and that the caver should remove the lamp and check it. If there is a flame igniting around the gasket between top and bottom, gas is escaping. The gasket needs to be replaced; sometimes turning it over and setting it will suffice. If water squirts out of the water door vent hole, you probably have too much gas being produced; reduce water delivery. Or, you may have a wet or impregnated felt that needs to be replaced. If your lamp produces a good flame but the light output is poor, your reflector probably needs to be cleaned.

If your lamp burns poorly, the cause could be a combination of any of the problems described above. Clean the tip, replace the felt, clean the water delivery port, and make sure that both water and carbide are present. These steps will usually solve the problem. The caver's best bet in using a carbide lamp is to keep the lamp clean and to work with it until he knows it inside and out.

It should be noted that while carbide lamps possess some unique advantages over electric lamps, such as the use of the flame to produce heat in certain situations, that same flame has the potential to melt through ropes. Be careful when ascending a rope: watch that flame.

When caving in below-freezing temperatures you may need to mix the water in the carbide lamp half and half with vodka to keep the water from freezing. This is a suggestion of William Halliday, who states that such a mixture will not freeze until reaching approximately −20°F (Halliday, 1974).

Electric Lamps

A prime reason that electric caving has recently enjoyed tremendous growth in popularity is the fact that electric lighting systems have become increasingly efficient, safe, and reliable. There are dozens of commercial lights to choose from, and the options open to the ingenious home-mechanic caver are almost limitless. Most electrics are of basically similar design. They consist of a headpiece that is mounted on the caver's helmet and is connected to a power source or battery pack by an electric cord. The battery pack is generally carried on one's pants belt. The necessary connection between the headpiece and battery pack—that is, the cord—is one of the major drawbacks of electric caving lamps. The cord has the annoying habit of catching and snagging on just about everything, and it is sometimes very difficult, if not impossible, to back up in tight crawlways to free a caught cord. Some cavers run the cord under their clothing and this helps matters substantially. It is now fairly common caving practice to add screw terminals to the lamp or to add an inline plug. These can be disconnected and reconnected easily, allowing snagged wires to work their way loose.

Currently one of the most popular and easily modified electric lights for medium-duty spelunking is the standard Justrite four-cell headlamp. There are a few modifications recommended for this lamp. First, the serious caver should either replace the battery pack or insert tightening spacers, such as pieces of cardboard or masonite. If done correctly, this will remedy the common problem of poor battery contacts. Next, one should replace the clear lens with a honeycombed lens, which will help diffuse the light. Finally, it is recommended that some type of easy, quick disconnect plug be installed between the battery pack and headpiece to solve the snag problem. Some cavers also remove the light's elastic headband and bolt or solder a flat blade in its place to insure a solid attachment to the helmet light-mounting bracket.

If you are considering becoming a serious electric caver, it is important to understand the various possible combinations of light construction, bulbs, battery types, light output, and current draw, as well as life expectancy of the systems' various components. It is important that an electric caver understand the characteristic performance parameters of a variety of systems under operation in both ideal and less favorable situations. By selecting certain battery and bulb combinations, one can create the lighting system that will deliver the necessary qualities reliably.

Not long ago there were relatively few types of batteries for cavers to choose from. Today, however, possible choices are varied and increasingly complex. There are batteries of incredible variance in voltage, output, size, cost, and other factors. Dry cells and lantern batteries provide the power source for most of the lightweight industrial and sport headlamps.

Dry Cells. The standard battery is a carbon-zinc

power cell. These come in small, AAA, up to the larger D and lantern 6-volt sizes. The common D cell is manufactured by many companies; familiar brands like Eveready and Ray-O-Vac tend to be more reliable than some of the foreign brands. The standard D cell is rated to deliver 1.5 volts when new. However, if these deliver a voltage of over 1.1 volts they are considered passable. The carbon-zinc battery discharges fairly uniformly but declines steadily in output. This is noteworthy, as this battery will still possess usable reserve power even after the light has begun to dim. Some other batteries, as we will note, give constant output; then near the end of their life their output voltage suddenly drops off almost completely; this conceivably can cause a difficult situation in the cave environment. Usually D cells will work well for approximately four hours of constant use when combined with a 0.5-amp bulb of the proper voltage (that is, the sum of the batteries' combined voltages).

When stored, it is important that the batteries be kept cool. If stored in a hot or warm location, the batteries' potential will be greatly reduced. Batteries keep much more efficiently in cold storage, such as in a refrigerator. If they are stored in cold areas, be sure to warm them before use. They will deliver their peak performance at approximately 70°F, while their life will be reduced to about half if used at 35°F.

There are a number of different types of carbon-zinc batteries available today. Generally, the more expensive the battery, the better the performance characteristics. Alkaline batteries, familiar to photographers and electronics enthusiasts, are an excellent choice for cavers. They are more expensive than carbon-zinc cells but will last anywhere from four to ten times as long. They are heavier, but their efficiency is much greater as a result of their longer life. The alkaline batteries have about a threefold longer shelf life than carbon-zinc cells. They tend to work better for short, high-drain or long, low-drain operations. They will last much longer if the caver, when resting or when light is not necessary, turns his lamp off and allows the batteries to recharge themselves slightly.

Commonly referred to as a nicad, the rechargeable nickel-cadmium battery is one of the most efficient and reliable power sources used today. It costs considerably more than the carbon-zinc battery, but is engineered to be recharged over and over, making the cost per hour much less overall. Nicad batteries possess a much flatter discharge curve. They deliver slightly less initial voltage, about 1.25 volts, but maintain a 1.2-volt output right up until the end. This is usually an advantage; however, if unaware of how long they've been used, the caver can be left in the dark.

Recently two new types of batteries have been introduced: the mercury cell and the lithium cell. The mercury D cell is rated at 14 amp hours and has great potential; however, it must be kept very warm in order to obtain this output. This may prove to be the best choice in the future, after it has been evaluated thoroughly.

Wet Cells. For years the standard headlamp used by mining companies in Europe and the United States has been powered by some variety of rechargeable wet cell. The wet cell is reasonably efficient, quite reliable, and very rugged. Its voltage output is designed to last a bit longer than an ordinary eight-hour work shift.

Lead-acid lamps are manufactured by MSA and Kohler Manufacturing Company. MSA's Minespot and Kohler lamps are equipped with dual-filament bulbs. If the first filament fails, the caver can easily turn on the second. Currently the bulbs supplied by these companies are 4 volt, 1.2 amp. These are often replaced by cavers with 4 volt, 1.0 amp and .8 amp.

Recently wet cells using a nickel-cadmium power cell have become available. Used units are rare, but are reported to be quite reliable and durable.

The most common wet cell lamps available are the nickel-iron units. These have been in use for many years. Used units are common and are often in excellent leakproof condition. The units manufactured in the United States are the Edison units; however, it is not uncommon to run across British-made Nife units.

The Nife units use a 20 percent potassium hydroxide-lithium hydroxide electrolyte. When low, the electrolyte level should be brought to normal by the addition of distilled water. After each use the unit should be cleaned thoroughly and stored in a discharged state. When charging, the manufacturer's directions should be followed exactly. Generally, the cell should be recharged the same amount of time it was used at one-and-a-half times the amperage of the discharge; or, and this is often a better method, for each hour used, charge one-and-a-half hours at the same amperage drawn in the discharge cycle. Note that the seals tend to deteriorate in these lamps, and the stored corrosive electrolyte may leak out. The electrolyte can cause severe chemical burns and will destroy and damage ropes, as well as the caver's skin. In case of leakage, it is advisable to carry a weak neutralizing agent such as vinegar when using the Nife.

Lead-acid units also have the potential to leak and cause rope damage as well as burns. In this case

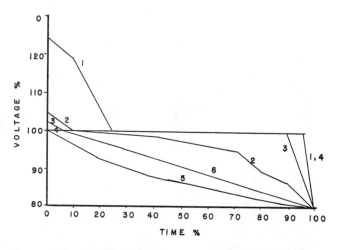

Battery discharge graph. *The graph shows voltage drop at a steady discharge rate over a period of time. Voltage is depicted as a percentage of the battery's rated voltage. A battery with 80 percent or less of rated voltage is considered a dead battery. Discharge graphs for individual types of batteries are illustrated:*

1. *Ag-Cd;* 2. *Ni-Cd;* 3. *Ag-Zn;* 4. *Hg;* 5. *Mn/C-Zn;* 6. *Pb.*

Chart 1. Bulb specifications

Bulb Number	Rated Voltage	Rated Current (amps)	Rated Bulb Life (hours)	Rated Candle Power
(FLANGE-BASED BULBS)				
PR 2	3	.5	15	.75
PR 3	4.5	.5	15	1.5
PR 7	4.5	.3	30	.88
PR 12	9	.5	15	4.5
PR 13	4.75	.5	15	2.1
PR 15	4.8	.5	30	1.9
PR 17	6.0	.3	30	1.0
PR 24	6.15	.3	15	2.0
(SCREW-BASED BULBS)				
13	3.7	.03	15	1.0
27	4.9	.03	30	1.4
31	6.15	.03	15	2.0
35	2.5	.8	150	1.3
50	7.5	.22	1000	1.0
153	5.8	1.1	50	7.9
157	5.8	1.1	50	7.9
248	2.5	.8	150	1.3
249	2.1	.9	3000	1.1
365	3.69	.5	15	1.6
403	4.0	.3	30	1.0
405	6.5	.5	500	1.9
419	8.0	.6	50	4.5
425	5.0	.5	15	2.3
426	8.0	.25	250	1.6
502	5.1	.15	100	.6
605	6.15	.5	15	3.4
965	9.84	.5	15	6.0
870	8.0	.9	50	9.0
993	9.83	.3	15	3.4

This chart summarizes the designed operating parameters of some of the more popular bulbs. When used in conjunction with chart #2, bulb performance can be closely estimated.

Chart 2. **Bulb parameters as a function of voltage variation, using design voltage as a base.**

Voltage Used	Current Required	Life Expectancy	Candle Power
70	88	7500	27
75	88	3200	36
80	93	1500	44
85	94.5	650	58
90	97	300	71
95	98.5	150	86
100	100	100	100
105	103	50	117
110	106	25	135
115	107.5	14	156
120	109	8	177
125	110	5	206
130	111	3	235
135	111.5	2	269
140	112	1	303

All figures are expressed as percent of design parameters. As noted bulbs used at higher than designed voltage produce higher candlepower but at the cost of shorter life expectancy.

It should also be noted that bulb life figures are somewhat imprecise and if protected from excessive jarring, the bulb may last much longer than indicated.

---

bicarbonate of soda should be carried as a neutralizing agent. Again, the electrolyte water level should be kept normal by the addition of distilled water. If the electrolyte level is decreased by spillage rather than by evaporation, the level must be maintained by the addition of electrolyte rather than distilled water. These lead-acid wet cells will become permanently damaged if allowed to remain completely discharged for any length of time.

Bulbs. There are so many bulbs available on the market today that it is impractical to list them all. A caver who knows what he wants and has time to experiment a bit can construct a battery pack that, when used with the proper bulb, will deliver precisely the needed light.

Lamp bulbs will increase their brilliance by 200 percent when used at 120 percent of their designated voltage, but at the cost of shortened life.

A question often asked is, at what candlepower is one comfortable caving? This depends on the size of the passage one is negotiating, which directly affects the amount of light reflected. Some dark-walled caves, notably lava tubes, seem to eat light. However, caving lights generally emit about 2 candlepower when fresh. One-half candlepower is necessary to do any serious exploration. It is generally possible to accomplish self-rescue with approximately $\frac{1}{8}$ candlepower.

Backup Light Sources

Thus far we have been discussing primary light sources. However, even the most knowledgeable caver with all the proper spare parts may find himself in the dark at some point. For reasons of safety then, it is important that each person entering a cave have three reliable lights. The most common second light source is some type of small flashlight using D or C cells. The Tekna Company manufactures reliable and efficient hand lights that are waterproof as well. When a hand light is carried, it is advisable to reverse one of the batteries until light is needed to avoid accidental actuation. When caving in wet caves that involve wading or swimming, you should place your light in a waterproof pouch. A standard D or C cell hand light may be tied securely in a condom to create a waterproof, sealed light.

The most common third light source underground consists of candles and matches. Matches should be kept in a waterproof container.

Chemical light sticks, commonly known as chem lights or cool lights, are now available. These are transparent tubes approximately $\frac{1}{2}$ to $\frac{3}{4}$ inch in diameter and approximately 8 to 10 inches in length. When bent they are actuated and begin to glow. They put out a surprising amount of light, lasting for approximately 8 to 16 hours depending on the type.

These are excellent for self-rescue or even for marking junctions as an aid to route finding. Another feature to be considered, however, is that they are not a source of ignition.

KNIFE

A good pocketknife is almost indispensable underground. It is used for cooking and eating as well as for cutting and trimming rope and setting up vertical systems. It may also be used as a surgical instrument for first aid purposes. The knife should have a can opener, and a screwdriver is extremely handy. It is inadvisable to carry a knife with a great many tools; such knives are cumbersome, and most of their gadgets will never be needed or used.

COMPASS, NOTEBOOK, AND PENCIL

A compass is very convenient, as well as comforting, to have in one's cave pack, especially when you realize you are turned around or are otherwise confused regarding your route. Brunton and other elaborate compasses are excellent for mapping caves (see Chapter 17), but are oftentimes more of a burden then a help to the amateur caver. A simple lensatic compass or other simply operated compass in the $6 to $20 price range will serve the purpose well.

When exploring an unknown cave, it is a good idea to put together a rough sketch of the cave as you progress through it. Sights, as well as back sights, should be noted by use of the compass. When entered in a small notebook with notes, these could prove to be your guide out of the cave.

It should be noted that occasionally compass readings may be thrown off due to magnetic bodies on one's person, or, particularly in lava tubes, by magnetic bodies located in the rock.

FIRST AID KITS

A basic first aid kit should accompany every caving party. An efficient, compact kit might include Band-

Aids, butterfly strips, cotton, a roll of inch-wide gauze, a roll of adhesive tape, needles, razor blade, aspirin, ammonia inhalant, small bar of soap, alcohol pads, Ace bandage, and a bandana. These items should be packed in some type of protective waterproof container. It is advisable to keep a more extensive kit in the car, along with drinking water and a wool blanket. (See Chapter 19.)

SURVIVAL OR BIVOUAC KITS

A bivouac kit stocked with survival items is very useful in cold, wet caves where prolonged exposure may be encountered. The most useful item is the bivouac sack, which can be purchased at backpacking stores. This item is an envelope or bag composed of nylon or similar fabric, in which the caver can place most of his body. It helps maintain body temperature and provides protection from the wind. The body will chill quite rapidly if exposed to cold breezes, especially if the body or clothing are wet from sweat or other sources.

Some cavers prefer to use space blankets rather than bivouac sacks. A space blanket is a durable, extremely thin blanket coated with a thin layer of Mylar on one side. Mylar is the material that was used on the astronauts' space suits. Used in a space blanket, it reflects the majority of body heat directly back to the body. A group of cold, tired cavers huddled under a space blanket, in conjunction with a heat tab or carbide lamp as a heat source, can maintain body temperatures quite effectively.

An Ensolite pad is very effective in reducing heat loss through conduction when sitting or lying down. Sleeping bags are usually impractical for bivouacking because of their bulk and weight and the transport problems involved. When they are used, however, wool or Polarguard bags are preferable to down-insulated bags, since down is worthless as an insulator when wet.

A knit stocking cap is very effective in conserving body heat when bivouacking. A large amount of heat is lost from the exposed head and neck of an individual subjected to cold temperatures; the exposure of your head to a cold breeze may determine whether your feet are cold.

Feet fare better inside a pack or other similar item than they do in wet boots, but remember: your feet will be warmer in wet wool socks than with no socks at all.

In many instances where equipment on hand is limited, conservation of heat will be greatly increased if the caving party huddles together.

PACKS

Some type of cave pack is necessary to carry the essential items on a caving trip. Some cavers prefer a pack carried on the back; however, most seasoned cavers prefer a pack with a good solid shoulder strap. This type of bag enables the caver to swing the pack around the body 360 degrees. The shoulder strap also permits the pack to be easily removed and pushed ahead or pulled behind in crawlways. Most packs used by cavers are some type of military surplus pack made from heavy duck canvas, which is quite resistant to the rigors of the cave environment. It is important that the pack can be opened and closed easily, even when infiltrated by cave mud. When purchasing a pack, check to see whether mud will prevent it from closing. Zippers are worthless in a cave pack, as are snaps. Buckles or drawstring closures work more efficiently under most cave conditions.

Large internal and external frame packs, although very useful for organizing caving gear and hauling it to cave entrances, should not be used inside caves except under special circumstances.

WATER

Water is ordinarily an essential item in the caving pack. Regrettably, the water available in most cave systems is contaminated, primarily due to the increasing pressure of human populations above-ground. Therefore, the caver must often pack his drinking water into the cave. Under certain circumstances, if you plan to drink cave water, it is wise to carry some type of water purification tablets; the purified water will taste more palatable with the addition of a drink mix, such as Kool-Aid, lemonade, Tang, or something similar.

In caving it is very important to drink water as needed rather than saving it. Water does the body no good in the canteen—physiologically the stomach is often a far better canteen. To be stingy with water can lead to dehydration, reducing physical performance and endangering the entire party. A caver may sometimes become dangerously dehydrated and not be aware of it, especially in colder cave environments. One good indication is a very dark-colored and strong-smelling urine.

An active caver can lose more than one quart of water per hour due to perspiration. It is therefore important to drink enough liquids, and sometimes it may also be necessary to consume sufficient salt to enable the body to maintain its electrolyte balance. Salt tablets work well, as do salty foods such as dried jerky and salted peanuts.

FOOD

Cavers generally carry an assortment of so-called nibble foods. Normally carried in a pocket in some type of protective container, the caver constantly nibbles on this food as a source of energy. The food carried should be tough and resistant to knocking and squeezing. Hard candies such as lemon drops and Life Savers, and toffees are popular choices. Chocolate tends to be unappetizing when mixed with body heat. A squeeze tube of honey is a good choice; the caver can easily obtain a squeeze of honey and some quick energy at any time. The tube has a tendency to get sticky, so many cavers carry it in a plastic bag.

Undoubtedly the most popular types of cave food in use today are combinations of cereals, nuts, dried fruits, raisins, M&Ms, coconut, and anything else of similar nature that tastes good and provides bulk in the caver's stomach. All these are mixed together and are generally eaten the same way, although there is always one caver who picks out his favorites.

Not only do nibble foods provide a refreshing energy source, but they also help to replace the dusty, sometimes guano taste in the mouth. They are a source of carbohydrates, which the body uses efficiently to provide quick energy, but are not a nutritionally balanced diet. The fact that they are not balanced is of little consequence on short caving trips. However, on extended trips, balanced meals become of importance. Cavers are now following the lead of mountaineers. Today a variety of lightweight, easily prepared, dehydrated foods ranging in variety from shrimp Creole to ice cream are available to sportsmen, and these are often prepared underground on longer trips.

For caving trips where cavers are exposed to chill factors, it is extremely important that hot food and drink be available to all present. At the slightest sign of hypothermia the entire caving group should consume as much hot food and drink as possible, short of causing indigestion or nausea. Hypothermia can kill the unprepared, and one poor decision by a member of the team in regard to the need for hot food or drink can endanger both that caver and others in the group. It is recommended that on any caving trip approaching eight hours duration, in any cave cooler than 60°F, at least one hot meal should be prepared, and eaten by all cavers. In colder caves it is wise to plan one hot meal for each six-hour period.

Caving is exhausting physical work, often under environmental conditions that submit the body to extreme stress. Food aids caver endurance—both food eaten in the cave and food consumed just prior to entering the underground. For this reason, most cavers eat a nutritious meal just before beginning their exploration, and this is a good practice to follow.

9

BASIC HORIZONTAL AND SEMI HORIZONTAL CAVING TECHNIQUES

THERE ARE A NUMBER OF techniques for negotiating passageways and rooms in caves; many of these techniques for cave travel, especially in horizontal cave sections, come naturally to the caver. In this section we will describe the more common techniques, point out their important features, and present information regarding when their use is generally indicated.

In the first section of this chapter we will be dealing with basically horizontal caves or horizontal sections of vertical cave systems. The majority of total cave passages traveled by most cavers tend to be of the horizontal or semihorizontal type, although in some cases these horizontal sections may be connected by pits and drops. We will then finish with information and techniques for use in more angled and sloping passages.

WALK OR CRAWL

When preparing to negotiate a cave passage, the caver

ordinarily studies the size of the passage and makes a decision as to what technique to employ. Passages 4 feet or more in height can be negotiated in some type of bipedal fashion. Although the caver may have to assume a stooped posture in passages approaching the 4-foot limit, walking is still the most efficient method of moving forward. Stooping posture, when required, does become tiring if the distance is great; the caver may find it less tiring if he rests his hands on his thighs or knees, thereby partially supporting his upper body. When the floor underfoot is solid, this technique of stooped travel is relatively easy; however, when the passage slopes and/or the floor surface becomes unstable, progress becomes more difficult and tiring. In this case you may need to use your hands against the wall or roof for support, but as always, be careful not to damage any delicate formations that may be present. As in any cave progression, the caver should always plan his path ahead, and when walking he should determine where each foot will be placed— both for his own benefit and for that of the cave.

If the passage narrows and decreases in height, the caver will need to change to another technique. In cases where the passage height is just under the limit where stoop-walking is possible, he may be able to squat with one leg extended slightly behind the other leg, under his body. Using the hands for balance and the hind foot for pushing, the caver makes headway in a semi-squat, semi-hopping duckwalk.

If the passage is too low for using the semi-squat position, the caver will need to resort to a crawl on all fours. The knees, although they work well for crawling short distances, are very vulnerable to injury. If you expect to be crawling for considerable distances, it is wise to use knee pads. The caver who finds himself crawling on hands and knees may want to switch periodically and crawl in a butt-up fashion, using toes and hands as his points of contact. This posture is extremely tiring but is effective for short distances. He can also switch to elbows, forearms, and toes. This position allows penetration in passages of even less height. At times it is easiest to crawl on one's side, using the forearm or hand or both, and sliding the bottom thigh forward. The action is similar to the side stroke in swimming.

When the passage becomes even tighter—that is, under 2 feet in height—the caver must resort to crawling on his stomach; this is required for many caves. Crawling is relatively simple where sufficient width of the cave passage allows the elbows to go out from and then return to the sides of the body. The caver makes his way propelled primarily by his toes and feet, pushing on nubbins and irregularities on the cave floor, and the hands also assist in pulling the caver forward. The majority of force should be exerted by the legs, which can exert the strongest force. Making headway will often be easier if the caver also wiggles his body back and forth.

Packs are taken off and pushed ahead of the caver during crawling. In some crawls the caver will need to remove his helmet and push it ahead as well. When the crawl is short, oftentimes the first caver completing it will pull the parties' packs through so that the remaining cavers negotiating the crawl will have it a bit easier. The caver preparing to pull the gear through can often work his way back down into the crawl feet first. At this point, packs can be looped over his foot and he can then pull them through.

SMALL SQUEEZES

How small a squeeze can a caver negotiate? This is a common question. Every caver has a slightly different physical build, so the answer varies. Most squeezes are narrow along one axis, either vertically or horizontally, whereas along the other axis the squeeze is generally wider. It is the narrow measurement that we will be discussing. The smallest size cavers normally can negotiate varies between 7 ½ to 12 inches. A statement often made is that if a helmet can fit through a squeeze, then so can the caver. This is not always true, however.

The caver must be examined to determine the largest, boniest portions of his body; these will set the limits of his penetration through a tight squeeze. It is not generally a beer belly or heavy thighs that stop progress, but the shoulders, chest, or pelvis. Body tissue conforms well to space available in a squeeze, but not so with bones. Depending upon their build, some cavers are stopped by their upper body, while others are held back by their lower body.

There are some tricks to getting through tight crawls. First study the squeeze and determine how your body will best fit through it. Then relax and enter the squeeze. Whenever attempting a squeeze, the caver should always attempt to relax as fully as possible to help his body conform to the passage more efficiently. If the shoulders are too large and inhibit progress, try putting one arm ahead and trailing the other one behind alongside the body. Many cavers negotiating squeezes find it necessary to exhale, thereby reducing the chest size by ½ to 1 inch. The caver then moves forward while his chest is con-tracted, and stops when he inhales.

In many crawls it is wise to empty your pockets of all their contents; it is surprising, but a few objects in a caver's pockets may make the difference between success and defeat in negotiating a crawl. In some squeezes, cavers may find it necessary to strip the outer clothing off the body, as it increases thickness and overall bulk on the body as well as providing an increased source of friction in certain situations.

GETTING UNSTUCK

Almost every caver who has caved for any length of time will at some point find himself stuck. Generally the situation is resolved very quickly and he manages to extricate himself. Being stuck often simply involves a loose piece of clothing, pack strap, or similar item that has become caught on a rock irregularity. After backing up slightly to unhook the offending piece, the caver can continue. Oftentimes a member of the party immediately behind the trapped caver can unhook the item causing the problem.

A caver who is more seriously stuck can usually

consciously relax; by doing this he becomes slightly more pliable and may work himself free. An anchored line with loops tied in it provides sound handholds for a victim to use in pulling himself free. If such a rope is run down next to his body to his feet, he can use a loop as a foothold. The use of fellow cavers to pull the victim free often works quite effectively. The above methods, singly or in combination, are almost always successful. However, if the victim is critically stuck, it is important to give him reassurance, keep him warm, and supply fluids and food while a rescue team is contacted.

Never investigate a tight, downward-sloping crawl headfirst. Always begin feet first. If the squeeze ends, it is much easier to retreat headfirst than it is to retreat feet first.

CLIMBING, SCRAMBLING, CHIMNEYING, AND TRAVERSING

Climbing, scrambling, chimneying, and traversing are techniques that need to be learned by any serious caver, for when a cave passage becomes too steep to simply walk up or down, the caver must employ one of these methods or resort to single-rope techniques.

The difference between climbing and scrambling is a fine one with no definite boundaries. Scrambling is used on less demanding slopes or pitches than those requiring climbing. Scrambling generally does not warrant a belay (safety) rope, whereas climbing does. A belay line should be used where there is a possibility of a fall that would result in serious injury. Both climbing and scrambling use many of the same techniques. Both generally use a three-point-contact climbing style. In scrambling these three points can be a number of body parts, such as hands, arms, head, back, stomach, seat, legs, feet, ankles, and so on. In climbing, the hands and feet are primary contact points. The caver strives to have three points of contact while the fourth searches for a new hold. Only after the fourth has been engaged does the caver remove one of the previous three. The support of body weight and upward or downward progress is accomplished primarily by the legs because they are the strongest of the body parts used. The arms and hands generally accomplish balance. In climbing situations the arms and hands are sometimes used more for support and progress than they are in scrambling.

Be careful. In caves the hand- and footholds are generally wet and muddy and at times quite slippery. Test your holds before applying full weight. Remember that it is usually easier to climb up than down; this is a point to remember when climbing up to check out a lead.

You will find it easier to climb up and down while facing the rock. Some novice cavers have a tendency to face outward when climbing down, which oftentimes makes the climb more difficult, although the outward-facing climb is more common in scrambling situations.

Traversing is a common mode of travel in many cave sections. This is horizontal progress around or along some feature that is to be avoided. For example, in a passage that drops severely and then proceeds upward again, the caving party may elect to traverse around its side at a higher level rather than descend and then ascend the drop, a procedure that would take much more time. Another example would be in the case of a caving party traveling a passage that changes into an active stream passage. The party may decide to traverse along one of the walls above the water until the water becomes shallow or disappears. In most traversing, where a narrow ledge or series of footholds is employed, the caver faces the wall, looking ahead and planning his path. He shuffles his feet, rather than crossing them one over the other, in order to prevent them from becoming entangled, causing him to lose balance.

When the traverse is difficult, the caver performing the traverse should be belayed from both sides to prevent a pendulum effect in case of a fall. The first caver to traverse will have only a single belay from one side; therefore he should be the most capable individual in the party. When a traverse is difficult and a number of persons must pass, a rigged line can be set from start to finish, anchored securely at both ends. As each caver approaches the traverse he clips into the line from his seat or chest harness.

Chimneying, or "back and footing," as the British call it, is used extensively to explore many cave systems. Generally it entails using two rock surfaces to apply opposite forces with the body, resulting in friction. Chimneying is used to move upward or downward and is usually used in narrow slots, fissures, pits, and similar locations. Applicable widths vary from 18 inches to under 4 feet, although some extremely experienced, fit cavers and climbers can chimney in widths of 5 to 6 feet. In narrow widths, the feet are placed as high up on one wall as is possible, with the back placed firmly against the opposite wall. Due to the narrowness of the cavity, the knees are restricted and not able to move upward to any great extent. For this reason the toes provide most of the holding power on the front wall. Generally one hand is on each wall as the caver squirms his way up. Going down is easier than going up because the caver need only provide sufficient friction to allow a controlled descent.

In wider chimneys of approximately 24 inches, one foot is placed in front as before, only much higher in this case, and the other foot is placed under the caver's rear on the wall behind. The caver still may place his back against the wall; however, the back foot takes up most of his weight. He then works his way up, one foot at a time, alternating movement in a scissors fashion. If the chimney continues to widen, the caver will position both feet on the front wall, pressing his back and seat into the wall behind.

Chimneying can be used to descend highly angled passages. To do this the caver lies down on the floor and places his feet over his head on the sloping ceiling. He can then work his way down. On slippery surfaces this may be the only feasible method to use, other than resorting to single rope technique (SRT).

HAND LINE

Hand lines are short pieces of rope, or sometimes

pieces of webbing, generally measuring 20 to 50 feet in length. These are used for assistance in ascending or descending. The operative word is *assistance*. The line lends some security and support, but is used mainly for balance. The caver should never put his entire weight on the rope. The feet and legs should support the climber.

It is extremely dangerous to attempt to go up a rope relying solely on one's hands and arms, as they are not as strong as they appear to be and their endurance is not anywhere near that of the caver's legs. Never climb up a vertical drop hand over hand.

BELAYING

Belaying refers to the use of a safety rope connected to a caver in situations where there is danger of his falling. This provides not only increased physical security, but also increased psychological security. In the event of a fall the safety rope should arrest the fall and catch the caver.

The general belay setup includes a climber and another individual who is the belayer. The belayer is tied into a secure anchor in such a way that the tie-in is directly in line with the belay rope to the climber. In other words, if a straight line were drawn from the anchor to the belayed caver, it would pass through the belayer. This is important; if there is an angle in the line between the anchor and the climber, in the event of a fall the belayer would be forced to a position that would eliminate the angle. This could lead to injury and the possibility of losing control as the belayer would be violently shifted to this position.

The climber must be tied in securely to the rope. The tie-in must be such that it distributes any possible impact over as much body area as possible, thereby reducing the impact on any one body area in a fall. This is generally accomplished in one of two ways. In the first, the climber ties a figure 8 in the end of the belay rope and clips it into his seat or chest harness via a locking carabiner. In an alternative means of attachment, the climber ties a bowline on a coil around his waist using a three- to five-wrap coil. The additional wraps, as compared to a standard bowline, aid in distributing the possible impact over an increased area.

Body Belay

The belayer should tie into the waist strap of his sling from the rear. This connecting sling should have no slack in it. The belayer positions himself so that the sling is taut. He then takes the rope, and positions it behind him so that both ends go away from him in front. The end of the rope going to the climber comes through the belayer's guide hand and around behind him to his control hand, positioned in front of his body. The guide hand does nothing more than simply

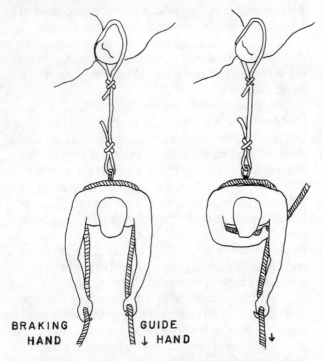

BRAKING HAND   GUIDE ↓ HAND

Body belay techniques. *In the use of a body belay, the belayer feeds or receives rope with a guide or feeling hand, and brakes with the hand on the opposite side of the body. The body is used as a friction device. The belayer must be securely anchored so as not to be displaced if he absorbs the force of the fall.*

guide the rope and keep it organized. The control hand, aided by the body's friction, controls how fast the rope is taken up or fed out. The control hand is always the hand *after* the point of friction. If the climber is below the belayer, the belay rope should pass over the top of the belayer's tie-in rope, for if a large force were exerted on the belay rope it might be pulled out under the belayer. If, however, the climber is above, and the suspected fall direction would result in an upward pull, the belay rope could be pulled over the belayer's head. In this case the belay rope should run underneath the belayer's tie-in.

If the belay rope is used to arrest a fall, the belayer brings his control hand and rope across his body, thereby increasing the frictional surface and hence friction.

It is important that the belayer strive never to remove his hands from the rope. When taking up slack the control hand slides up the rope next to the body, grasps it, pulls it out, and slaps it into the guide hand along with the other rope as it slides back to pick up more rope. The process is somewhat difficult at first, as the novice continually finds one of his hands has left the rope, which in the case of a simultaneous fall could prove disastrous. The belayer should wear gloves to prevent rope burns, which could also result in loss of control.

Practice these procedures aboveground to perfect them before going underground.

Dynamic versus Static Belay

As in aboveground climbing, in the event of a fall a controlled dynamic belay is much preferred to a static belay. The climber who takes a fall should be stopped in a gradual deceleration rather than in a sudden, complete stop. Too rapid a stop endangers the climber. Upon the initiation of the fall, the weight of the climber's mass increases its acceleration and hence its falling energy. If this energy is absorbed instantly, the force will be directed to the climber's body at the belay rope's point of attachment and has the potential to do much damage to the body, ranging from breaking of bones to rupture of internal organs.

In a dynamic belay the falling climber is slowed down over the space of a few seconds, and the energy of falling is thereby absorbed and distributed in a controlled fashion. This can be compared to an object connected to an elastic band and dropped. Because of the elastic properties, the falling object is slowed gradually. This is why belay systems almost never employ static rope; static rope has the same static qualities as a chain. Always use dynamic rope when belaying.

Mechanical Belays

Several mechanical devices used for belaying are available on the market. The two most common are the Sticht plate and the Edelrid-Bankl plate. In use, the belay rope is threaded through one of these plates in combination with an anchored carabiner. If a fall occurs, the belayer merely pulls the rope tight through the plate against the carabiner. This movement activates the plate, which increases friction, and the rope is held.

It is their efficiency that at times makes these mechanical devices dangerous. It is the tendency of the belayer to stop the rope slippage and hold the fall. When using these plates, it is often too easy for a belayer to lock up the rope completely. If the rope is locked up completely early in the fall, the total force will be absorbed instantly, putting extremely high stresses not only on the falling climber but also on the rigging. Tie-off anchors and other components in the system have been known to fail under these high stresses; whereas in a body belay the rope always manages to slip slightly, thereby adding to the dynamic qualities. Therefore, it is our opinion that the body belay should be the first choice when a belay is needed, unless the belayer has had sufficient practice with a plate to make safe use of it.

Self-Belay

The self-belay is an extremely important caving and climbing technique. The self-belay is essentially the use of an ascending device attached to a fixed rope or hand line. The most commonly used devices are the

Right: *Sticht belay plate with spring;* Left: *Standard Sticht belay plate.*

The Sticht belay plate is used as a mechanical belay device. The belayer simply pulls the two portions of the belay rope apart, forcing the belay plate toward the carabiner. The spring prevents the belay plate (right) from jamming up against the carabiner. The cord rigged into the belay plate (left) prevents the belay plate from migrating too far up the rope. Holes in the belay plate can also take cord.

Gibbs, the Jumar, or a prusik knot. The ascending device is connected to the climber via his seat harness. As he climbs, he moves the ascender upward. The Gibbs is often rigged to move up following the caver, requiring little attention. If the caver falls, the ascender holds the fall. The Jumar cannot sustain high stresses or loads, so it should be rigged to catch the fall before any acceleration occurs, as acceleration would increase potentially disastrous forces.

Belay Signals

The importance of the use of proper signals cannot be overstressed. All cavers should learn, practice and use proper belay signals. They are as follows:

On Belay: Called by the climber who is checking to make sure he is belayed.

Belay On: Called by the belayer, only when the belay is on and he is ready, not before.

Rappelling: Called by the climber as he prepares to descend.

Rappel: Called by the belayer, indicating he is ready for the climber to descend.

Climbing: Called by the climber as he prepares to climb.

Climb: Called by the belayer, indicating he is ready for the climb.

Falling: Called by the climber, indicating he is falling, or about to fall, so that the belayer can ready himself for the force.

Tension: Called by the climber, telling the belayer to take up slack in the rope. Never call "take up slack," for if the belayer hears only the word slack he may give you more rope.

Slack: Called by the climber, indicating he wants slack in the rope.

Off Belay: Called by the climber, indicating he no longer needs a belay and is off the belay rope.

Belay Off: Called by the belayer, indicating he is no longer belaying the climber.

It is important that these calls be used conscientiously and consistently; they ensure understanding and guard against confusion. The calls vary around the world, but parallel this format.

10
LADDERS, ROPES AND KNOTS

FOR THOUSANDS OF years man's explorations of caves have tended to be primarily in a horizontal direction. A great many cave systems, however, have considerable vertical relief as well as horizontal sections, and many caves have a greater vertical than horizontal extent. With the development of special equipment and techniques within the last twenty years, interest in vertical caving has increased much more quickly than interest in cave exploration as a whole, or more specifically the exploration of generally horizontal caverns.

Undoubtedly many individuals over the centuries have greatly desired to determine what lay at the bottom of vast underground pits, yet had no truly safe means of descending and ascending their precipitous walls. The appropriate technology did not exist. Yet what lay below and beyond them was always a challenge. Once equipment and techniques for using it were available for vertical caving, that challenge became intense and could be tested.

A unique aspect of the caving challenge was and is that its limits are unknown. What was once the dream of many adventurers, to climb the highest mountains in the world, or the ultimate dream of climbing Everest today seems almost routine. These mountains have been located and named. Their altitudes have often been recorded, and possible routes studied in detail by means of photography and observation, even before the first parties have successfully climbed them. Now, as additional parties ascend to the peaks each year, the mountains' challenges are, for man, psychologically diminished.

Cavers, on the other hand, point out that the reverse cannot be claimed. Caverns hide their sites and particularly their limits. No one yet knows where the deepest or longest cave systems lie on Earth. Thus, the challenge and exploration of deep and long cave systems attracts more interest each year; thousands of explorers work for the ultimate dream—that of bottoming the deepest cave in the world. This is an extreme challenge. Certainly locating a cave system is much more difficult than locating a mountain, for the cave entrance may be as small as, or smaller than the diameter of a caver's body. No observation from the air can tell the observer the depth of a cave, as it can tell him the height of a mountain. Nor can it provide him with photos of the route he must take. The cave system must be laboriously explored, foot by foot, to learn its limits—only painstaking and exhausting caving will determine the size, depth, and details of a cave.

Years of planning, preparation, and actual undertaking may be involved both in climbing the highest mountain or in bottoming the deepest pit. But here the comparison ends. The mountaineer knows which mountain to climb and the details of most of the extremes that face him. The caver does not know the depth of the unknown cave system he explores, nor all of its conditions. The caver's gamble is greater, for he may spend years determining that the cave system he has chosen, and to which he has devoted great amounts of his time and strength, does not reach the record depth he anticipated. The deep unknown, seeking the limits, testing the self, and the greater gamble—all are strong attractions of vertical caving.

Until the 1960's, vertical exploration of cave systems was very restricted due to the weight of equipment and related technical problems. In the 1960's climbers and mountaineers made many important advancements in the area of improved equipment, and they developed new vertical techniques using this equipment. Select groups of cavers quickly recognized the importance of these techniques to their own underground sport. Suddenly the feasibility of using single rope techniques, commonly referred to as SRT, became possible in caving. Previously the difficult and sometimes dangerous use of ladders of various types for ascending and descending drops had been the mainstay of vertical cave exploration, and the limited use of early SRT had been simply as an adjunct to the use of cable ladders. These older means of cave exploration definitely limited and, in fact, prevented serious prolonged vertical caving. Only with development of the full range of SRT could the sport of SRT caving begin.

This chapter is concerned with SRT equipment selection, care, and maintenance. Vertical caving is not for every caver or speleologist. Techniques employed in vertical cave exploration are strenuous, regardless of the knowledge and efficiency of the caver. That the caver be in good physical condition is a prerequisite for any serious exploration. Because of the rapidly advancing techniques and equipment involved, it is strongly recommended that anyone interested in this specialized area seek professional instruction.

CABLE LADDERS

At one point, cable ladders were the mainstay of vertical cave exploration. These are now being rapidly replaced by single rope techniques, though cable ladders do still have a limited place in cave exploration. They are very useful when a large group needs to move up or down a short drop. Cable ladders may also be a bit more efficient when exiting a body of water underground. In many parts of the world outside the United States, the cable ladder continues to be very popular; British cavers, particularly, employ it regularly.

For many years before the use of cable ladders, various types of rope ladders with rope, metal, or wood rungs were used in caving. The reasons for their abandonment are many. The rope ladders had poor abrasion characteristics; also the nylon rope, which in later periods was sometimes used for strength, was a dynamic type of rope that contributed to the stretching of the ladder as the caver climbed it. This meant that the climber had to climb the bottom 5 to 10 feet of the drop twice in order to take up the stretch in the ladder.

When the ladder is used today it is always a cable ladder, which has evolved to a fairly standardized construction in the last twenty years. The cable ladder is generally constructed of aircraft cable of good quality and aluminum rungs. The cables test to approximately 1,000 pounds. The rungs and their attachment brackets test to approximately 650 pounds. Brummel hooks, which are designed to attach to or around an anchor, are attached to the ends of the cable. The standard length of a cable ladder is 10 meters or 33 feet. The rungs are approximately 5 to 5½ inches wide and are spaced 12 to 15 inches apart. Some ladders may have closer-spaced rungs, which makes climbing a bit easier; however, this advantage is offset by the disadvantage of increased weight.

If a cable is employed, it should be used only in conjunction with a belay (safety) rope and a competent belayer. Cable ladders are not constructed with exceptional strength and they may break. If this does occur, it is indeed comforting to know you are attached to a belay rope four or five times stronger than the cable ladder.

There are techniques for climbing a cable ladder. It is recommended that the climber place his heels onto the rungs from the rear of the ladder, hands around the back of the ladder, and place his center of gravity as close to the plane of the ladder as possible. If a cable ladder is climbed in a normal manner, the climber may suddenly find his feet above his head as he swings back and upside down.

Be exceedingly cautious of older ladders and inspect them very carefully before using. In addition to normal deterioration problems that may occur, some ladders have had problems resulting from electrolysis between dissimilar metals, causing corrosion which can weaken metal components of the ladders—most notably the cable where the rungs and toe clips are connected. Never use old ladders of any type that you find abandoned in caves.

Treat cable ladders with respect and care. Your well-being, as well as that of your companions, may be seriously endangered if you do not.

When transporting cable ladders take care not to drag them in the mud and dirt. Do not walk on them when they are lying on the ground. Grinding grit into the ladder, especially the cable, is potentially hazardous and can weaken it. To transport a cable ladder, twist each successive rung in the opposite direction and fold it back over the first rung to form a compact bundle that can be placed in a pack or bag to protect it. When rigging a pitch, lower the unanchored end down; do not throw it. Wash the ladder between uses to prevent abrasion due to dirt ground into the cable. In order to store the cable ladder, untwist it and hang it loosely in a dark, cool, dry environment.

ROPE

The development of single rope technique (SRT) was possible only after the development of safe, strong, lightweight ropes. Until after World War II, the ropes being used in caving were composed of natural fibers such as hemp and sisal. Usually $7/16$ inch in diameter, this type of rope is vulnerable to rotting under prolonged caving conditions and possesses very poor abrasion characteristics. Such ropes are also dangerously affected by household chemicals. Another drawback is their poor handling characteristics. When nylon ropes finally hit the market, avid cavers and mountaineers accepted them enthusiastically despite their higher cost.

In SRT the main component in the system is rope, and therefore it is all-important that it not fail. When nylon ropes are compared with older ropes made of natural fibers for qualities such as strength, energy absorption, resistance to abrasion, and handling qualities, there is no comparison. Nylon ropes are far superior.

Nylon ropes are composed, obviously, of nylon, a general name given to a group of chemically similar substances (polyamides). There are basically two types of nylon used in climbing ropes: type 6 and type 66. There are two varieties of type 66, known as 707 and super 707. Although different nylons resemble one another in chemical makeup, their physical properties do differ.

Type 6 nylon melts at between 215°C and 220°C, but is not damaged to as great an extent as type 66 when exposed to elevated temperatures. Also, type 6 has greater resistance to abrasion and sunlight, with generally greater strength, and has increased elastic properties. It is used to manufacture mountaineering rope, where this quality is considered an advantage. Type 6 is also known as Perlon. Type 66 nylon melts at about 260°C and tends to be used in limited stretch ropes, since it is not as elastic as type 6.

There are other synthetic fiber ropes on the market and in use today. Polyester rope is one of these; a well-known brand is Terylene. Polyethylene rope is another type of synthetic fiber rope; a well-known brand is Courlene. Also available are various types of poly-propylene rope, including Tenstron and Ulstron, the former being more popular.

Terylene rope is widely used and does have some advantages over nylon. Terylene is stable at higher temperatures, with a melting point of around 250°C, and is not affected by moisture, as is nylon. Nylon's tensile strength exceeds that of Terylene; however, nylon is drastically affected by water, which is absorbed both between and directly into the nylon fibers. When a nylon rope becomes saturated it may lose more than 10 percent of its tensile strength. Because it swells slightly when wet, if at the same time it must absorb a force in which the rope is directed over an edge, it has a much greater tendency to rupture. This could mean failure under a much reduced load. Nylon, when dry, has better abrasion resistance then Terylene. Terylene may be a superior rope for wet caves, whereas nylon may be better for dry conditions.

Polypropylene and polyethylene ropes are inexpensive and lightweight. They float in water and are fairly strong. These qualities appear to be quite favorable; however, they also possess a few very poor features. These ropes have very low melting points and are extremely susceptible to abrasion. Several injuries and deaths have been attributed to these dangerous properties. Their use as a main rope is not recommended. They do have their place in climbing as ascending sling material.

Rope Strength

When choosing a rope on which your life is going to depend, you should compare many different aspects and qualities of that rope. First and foremost, strength must be considered. Strength, or more correctly tensile strength, is defined as the maximum weight the rope will hold; it will break if there is any increase in load. When selecting a rope one must calculate the maximum load that could conceivably be placed on the rope. In order to have a safety margin, the rope should be capable of holding five to six times this potential load, and the working load should not exceed 11 percent of the rope's tensile strength.

In order to understand potential forces, one must examine dynamic loads. It is commonly believed that if a 175-pound caver is climbing or descending a rope, he has the potential force of 175-pounds. This is simply not the case. A brief review of basic physics will tell you that if acceleration has a chance to work on the climber, a force far exceeding 175 pounds will be created.

For example, if the rope happens to be slightly detoured around a small obstruction, such as a fluke or nob, and finally works its way loose with the rope dropping the climber a few feet in straightening itself out, a force greater that the weight of the climber on the rope is generated.

In the field, the rope will never hold its manufacturer's stated strength, as its strength is reduced by many factors including knots, carabiners, pulleys, abrasion, and so on. It has been found that a rope passed around a bar by 180° (the bar being approximately the same diameter as the rope) will lose about half of its rated strength, but if the diameter of the turn is increased ten times, little strength is lost. A carabiner is essentially a small bar and can severely reduce the rope's strength.

For a rule of thumb it is wise to consider the useful strength of a rope to be approximately one-half the total strength. This is due to the fact that a rope can easily be weakened up to 50 percent through abrasion, knots, and similar factors. Thus a rope rated at 6,000 pounds on a testing machine now becomes rated to 3,000 pounds under actual field conditions, and if we follow our previous rule stating that a rope should hold five to six time the standard weight expected to be placed on the rope, you can see the safety margin narrows rapidly.

The strength of a rope is related directly to the amount of energy the rope can withstand. If a climber falls and is held by a rope he generates energy which must be absorbed. (Distance of fall × Weight of climber = Ft. lb. of energy.) When a climber is belayed and takes a fall, the generated energy is partially absorbed by the climber, partially by the rope and some of the energy will be converted to heat by the belayer who allows the rope to slide around his body, creating friction.

For simplicity, let's consider an object connected to a rope which is anchored to a static nonmoveable anchor. In this case where an object free falls and is held, the entire amount of energy is absorbed by the

A   B

Rope stress. *When rope is stressed over a sharp angle, as in figure A, stresses are dramatically increased, resulting in breakage, whereas the resultant forces are much reduced when rope is stressed over a less radical angle, as in figure B.*

rope in the form of mechanical energy, the cold stretching of the individual fibers.

The cold stretching characteristics of the individual nylon fibers in the rope can be measured in terms of the mechanical energy the rope can absorb. It has been found that regardless of whether the rope is dynamic or static, the amount of energy a rope can absorb is directly proportional to the weight of nylon involved and the rate at which stress is applied. A rope weighted slowly can absorb 12,000 foot-pounds of energy per pound of nylon, but this drops to approximately 4,000 foot-pounds if the energy is absorbed quickly, which we will term dynamic loading, as in arresting a fall.

Standard $7/16$ inch nylon rope weighs about .06 lb./ft. (.09kg/m). It can absorb approximately 250 foot pounds of energy per foot of rope with dynamic loading.

If we take our 175 pound caver and let him fall 10 feet on 10 feet of rope he generates (10 ft.) (175 lb.) = 1750 ft. lb. which must be absorbed by 10 feet of rope. This works out to 175 ft. lb. per foot of rope which the rope absorbs. But if we let him fall 20 feet on 10 feet of rope (the caver is 10 feet above anchor so falls the 10 feet to anchor and then 10 more feet below taking up the slack) he generates (20 ft.) (175 lb.) = 3500 ft. lb. of energy. This works out to 350 ft. lb./ft. rope which exceeds the limit and the rope breaks. These figures are simplistic as it is extremely difficult to incorporate all the variables, and testing methods and results differ.

It is important that the reader understand that the more dynamic qualities the rope possesses, the more the rope tends to absorb energy in a slower fashion. The more static the rope the quicker it will absorb the energy as it does not possess the stretching qualities, and the force's energy is exerted in a much reduced time.

If we compare static ropes, that is those of very low stretch characteristics, to dynamic ropes, those of higher stretch and more elasticity, it is found that a dynamic rope has a greatly increased ability to absorb a dynamic shock. For rock climbing and mountaineering purposes, where falls are commonplace, a dynamic rope is the natural choice. In caving, where in almost all cases the cavers are going either up or down the rope itself, rather than up or down the rock as in mountaineering, we must weigh the advantages of dynamic ropes carefully against the definite need to have low stretch ropes, a condition we get from the static rope.

In general, for caving, the desired properties of the static rope far outweigh those of the dynamic ropes. Cavers prefer to use a static rope for SRT because when they begin the climb out of a pit on a static rope, they will have less distance to travel twice as they take up the stretch. Most static ropes have approximately 2 percent stretch under body weight. If a caver is climbing out of a 300-foot pit on a static rope, he will need to take up only approximately 6 feet of stretch. On a dynamic rope he will need to take up perhaps as much as 20 feet. In other words, in the latter case he may be climbing up approximately 20 feet of rope before he even leaves the ground; also, once the caver becomes elevated on the rope he will bounce up and down as if tied to a rubber band as the rope illustrates it dynamic qualities. The motion of climbing the rope (prusiking) seems to have an up and down, yo-yo effect that increases not only the loading effect but also the chance of abrasion at any point where the rope touches the rock.

Rope Abrasion

Abrasion resistance is another important area of rope evaluation. A rope for caving must have high resistance to abrasion. The rope is most susceptible to abrasion where it lays over a lip or sharp edge or where it is rubbed back and forth on an abrasive surface. A rope with poor abrasion-resistant properties will weaken, and rope failure may well be the end result. Abrasion resistance partially depends upon the rope's construction.

There are basically two types of physical construction used for ropes available today: laid ropes and braided ropes. To understand the difference in construction, we must go back to the manufacture of nylon.

Nylon in a molten state is pushed through a plate with tiny holes. Long fibers come out the opposite side. These fibers are then bunched into yarns. In laid ropes these yarns are combined into three or more larger strands, which are twisted around themselves to form the rope. In braided ropes the yarns are plaited and braided around an inner core, forming an outer sheath.

Laid ropes have excellent abrasion-resistant properties and thus have been widely accepted. On the other hand, laid ropes have a few drawbacks relating directly to their construction. When weight is placed on the end of a laid rope, it has a tendency to begin unwinding, which in turn spins the climber around if he is located away from a wall. Again because of their construction, these laid ropes tend to be dynamic. As weight is placed upon the rope, it begins to untwist and to stretch.

Braided ropes do not initiate spinning, and they are readily available with static properties. As stated, a braided rope consists of an inner core and an outer sheath. The core is responsible for approximately 70 percent of the rope's tensile strength. The sheath is important in abrasion resistance. The tighter the sheath, the more abrasion-resistant the rope will be. Another plus for a tight sheath is that if the sheath is worn or cut through, the chances of it slipping any great distance down over the core are severely reduced over those of a looser sheath. The sheaths are very abrasion-resistant; however, the same cannot be claimed for the core, which is severely affected if it becomes vulnerable to abrasive forces.

Rope-Handling Characteristics

Another aspect of rope makeup that affects cavers is the handling characteristics of particular ropes. Sheathed rope is far superior to laid rope with regard to handling. Kernmantle ropes—that is, braided types—tend to be quite flexible, nonkinking, and limber, leading to easy coiling, carrying, and storage. Laid ropes tend to be stiffer and have a tendency to kink and to begin unwinding, and have in general are often quite difficult to work with. The laid ropes tend to kink more due to the fact that they are attempting to unwind. Once used, the laid ropes become somewhat easier to handle; however, the first rappel on a laid rope usually involves untangling the rope bird's nest.

Goldline mountain laid climbing rope and similar laid ropes will feel much better to the hands once used. The outermost nylon fibers will break down, and the surface takes on a fuzzy feeling. This breakdown does weaken the rope slightly, but the fuzz helps protect the interior rope from further abrasion.

Summary of Caving Rope Characteristics

To summarize some of the preceding points on ropes for caving, it is recommended that a main rope be 7/16-inch (11- to 12-millimeter) nylon. The breaking strength for a main rope should be approximately 6,000 pounds (2,718 kilograms) or greater. On some occasions 3/8-inch (9- to 10-millimeter) ropes can be used where there are long approaches to the site and every ounce of weight must be taken into consideration. However, if used as main ropes, the smaller sizes should be used very carefully, as their breaking strength is greatly reduced to approximately 3,500 pounds (1,586 kilograms), leaving no room for error or accident.

Laid ropes are popular because of their price and favorable abrasion-resistant qualities. However, for longer drops or drops where the rope is hanging free from the wall, the static kernmantle (braided) ropes are far superior.

 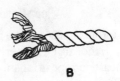

Rope construction.

A. *Kernmantle construction, showing sheath and inner core.*

B. *Laid construction in which multiple strands are twisted about one another.*

The most common rope in use today for caving is Bluewater II. Bluewater II was developed by cavers and features a tightly woven sheath to help prevent mud and water from penetrating the core. Bluewater II, composed of type 66 nylon, variety 707, is rated to approximately 7,000 pounds (3,170 kilograms), and even if the sheath were to wear through, the core would still have approximately 4,900 pounds (2,220 kilograms) of holding strength remaining. Also offered by Bluewater is Bluewater III, composed of type 66 nylon, variety super 707, which claims a bit more abrasion resistance, but is also a bit more dynamic. We have also heard of sheath slipping in Bluewater III; however, Super Bluewater III, which supposedly no longer has that problem, is now available. Another type of static kernmantle caving rope that is now being widely accepted by cavers is being produced by Pigeon Mountain Industries.

Nylon Sling

Another major component of climbing systems is nylon sling. Nylon sling is generally used for harnesses, runners, tie-offs, and similar purposes (see Chapters 11 and 12). Nylon webbing or tape (as the Europeans refer to it) is generally of flat construction and often of flat tubular construction. The widths vary, with 1 or 2 inch being most common, followed in popularity by ½ or ⅝ inch. The breaking strength of the webbing varies directly with the width. Webbing is used almost exclusively for harnesses because it is quite comfortable due to its flat construction.

Rope Care and Maintenance

When purchased, rope should be measured and cut to a length approximately 5 percent longer than needed in order to allow for shrinkage. The first piece of business at hand with a new rope is to fix the ends to prevent unraveling. When working with laid ropes, the best method is to wrap the last 5 inches tightly with vinyl tape, then cut the center of the taped portion with a hot knife. The hot knife will seal the end of the rope.

Another method is to melt the final inch of the rope with a flame, and then, wearing gloves, to twist the 3 to 4 yarns in the normal direction. This will place molten nylon between yarns.

With kernmantle ropes, one should melt the end sheath to the core to become one piece of nylon for a length of approximately ½ inch. Then rotate the rope evenly over a flame for an additional 3 inches; this causes the sheath to contract tightly over the core to prevent sheath slippage near the end. (Note: be sure to wear gloves. Do not let molten nylon drip onto your hands; it is extremely sticky and burns severely.)

Another method of securing rope ends is to use shrinkable irradiated PVC tubing, which is cut into lengths, slipped over the rope ends, and heated until it shrinks tightly. A helpful practice is to print the rope length and the year placed into use in indelible ink underneath this clear plastic rope whip so this important information concerning the rope is readily available (Montgomery, 1977).

Good rope is essential to safe SRT. It must be respected and treated carefully. There are several rules of rope care that experienced cavers follow quite strictly. First and foremost, do not step or walk on the rope. This forces grit, rock fragments, and crystals into the rope, as does unnecessary dragging. Once in the rope, these minute particles act like miniature knives, and each time the rope flexes they cut small rope fibers. For this reason, when transporting rope underground, it is recommended that it be transported in bags or packs, whenever possible, to avoid damage.

Ropes are generally organized by either coiling or chaining. The easiest method is coiling. The rope is generally coiled around the soles of the feet, over the knees, back to the feet, and so forth. When beginning the coils, leave approximately 3 extra feet. After a few coils, place an overhand twist around the coils to stabilize the end and continue to coil the remaining rope until there is approximately 10 feet remaining. Begin wrapping this remainder around the coils, spacing these countercoils 6 to 10 inches apart. When you reach the other end, next to the overhand knot, tie these together to finish securing the coil.

The other common method of managing a rope is called the chaining method. First, double the rope back and forth, making the total length approximately 25 to 30 feet. Take one end and form an overhand loop. Once this is done, you need only bring successive loops through each other to form something that resembles a daisy chain. When complete, the chain will be about 10 feet long and easily handled.

When rope is used over an abrupt edge or over any abrasive surface, the rope should be adequately padded. When rigging a drop it is mandatory, except

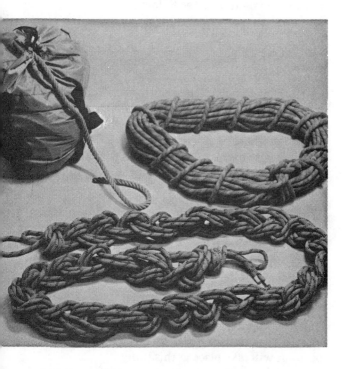

The three most common methods of organizing rope for transport include:

(Left): *Stowing it in a bag by simply starting with one end of the rope and stuffing it into the bag;* (Right): *Forming it into a tight consolidated coil;* (Bottom): *By chaining.*

under very special conditions, to clean the drop of all loose rock. If possible, collect loose rock and place it back away from the edge; if this is impractical, knock it off the ledge while no one is below. Then drop the rope over. Upon the first descent it may be necessary for the person rappelling to pull up the rope and dislodge more unstable rock. Do not release rock and allow it to fall down a drop where a rope is standing, since severe rope damage or severing of the rope may occur. This is a good reason to coil all excess unused rope out of the way at the top and bottom of the rigged pitch.

Ropes should be washed as they become dirty, since washing releases the grit inside the rope. A recommended method is the following:

1. Braid the rope into a chain.
2. Place in washing machine.
3. Use hand-warm water for nylon and Terylene, and cold water for polyethylene and polypropylene.
4. Continuous repeated rinsings do a decent job; however, the addition of detergents keeps the released particles suspended, preventing them from settling down into the rope again.
5. Be sure to rinse well after using detergents.
6. Air drip dry, avoiding direct sunlight. Avoid hot-air dryers.

Whenever possible, pad the washer window of front-loading washing machines with canvas. Concentrated fabric softeners will help to limber up a stiff rope, and will actually form somewhat of a barrier between the rope fibers and the grit. Bleaches should be avoided, especially if they are chlorine-based.

It is a good idea to wash the rope when new, before its first use. This will assist in extracting lubricants used in its manufacture, and if any shrinkage is to occur, it will take place at this time.

It is advisable to keep the rope out of direct sunlight whenever possible, as ultraviolet rays are damaging. Keep the rope away from all hot places, such as car windows and furnaces. Store in a cool, dry place and avoid chemicals and acids. Wash the rope often.

Inspect ropes before each use. With laid ropes, one

can attempt to untwist the rope and inspect the interior. If its interior is powdery, laid rope should be retired. Also, feel the rope for irregularly increased or decreased diameter and soft spots.

It is more difficult to inspect sheathed ropes. However, if the sheath appears in good condition, the core is probably in the same condition. It is recommended that you examine the sheath with a ten-power magnifying glass. With sheathed rope, if approximately 50 percent of the sheath yarns are disrupted, retire the rope. If the worn portion is small, you can cut the rope on either side of the damaged spot and use two shorter lengths.

Ropes should be retired if they have absorbed heavy stresses, such as a fall. In this case the damage may not be visible.

When retired, a rope should be marked as such so that no one attempts to use it. If possible, paint the ends black, or cut it into many short sections.

KNOTS

The rope is of little use unless one can anchor it or hook into it. Therefore, in order to make full use of the rope one must learn some basic knots and understand the theory behind them.

There are hundreds of knots in common use today. However a few versatile, efficient, and effective knots are far safer and more useful when known well than are many specialized knots. A virtue of a good knot is simplicity. Any caver should be able to look at a knot that someone else has tied and know at a glance that the knot is or is not tied correctly.

Most knots have a tendency to work loose when tied in nylon ropes; hence all knots should be cinched down. Unless otherwise noted, all knots should have two overhand safeties tied against the primary knot, using the tail of the knot. Six to twelve inches of free tail should be left after the second safety knot is tied as a safety factor. It is extremely important that the caver tie efficient, neat knots.

All knots weaken the rope to some degree. Generally anywhere from 20 to 60 percent of the rope's unknotted strength is lost. Weakening occurs due to the turns the knot forces the rope to take, causing non-uniform stress. The strands on the outside of the turns are subject to unusually high stresses, as they are stretched when the knot takes a force.

It is very difficult to determine exactly to what degree a knot weakens a rope system. Many testers and rope manufacturers state the efficiency of a knot by determining what weight a rope will hold with the given knot in the system, as compared to the weight the unknotted rope will hold:

$$\text{Knotted Efficiency} = \frac{\text{Weight held knotted}}{\text{Weight held unknotted}}$$

This method does provide a good indication of the effectiveness of a given knot, if the figures are close to reality; however, some agencies and individuals preparing these figures rely on unknotted strength figures as provided by the rope manufacturers, and these figures may be far enough off to cause a significant deviation. Only when the researcher carries out independent tests on unknotted strengths are figures reliable. Also, each researcher invariably uses slightly different testing techniques, which may affect the figures to some degree. Another, and probably the largest, cause of discrepancies in cross comparisons is that the holding strength of a knot differs greatly when different types and sizes of rope are used. A given knot may demonstrate great holding strength in one type of rope and show limited holding strength in another.

Three knot efficiency averages are listed below. Remember that strengths vary drastically depending on the testing procedures and apparatus; so these figures are approximations and may vary.

Knot	Efficiency
Bowline	65%
Overhand loop	49%
Figure 8	70%

From the figures one can see that the bowline weakens the rope by 35 percent, for an efficiency of 65 percent as compared to the strength of the unknotted rope. In other words, if the rope used is rated at 7,000 pounds, its tensile strength is reduced to 4,550 pounds when a bowline is used to anchor it.

The knots described below are reliable for use in caving.

The *bowline* on a bight is one of the most common knots used to tie a loop in the end of a rope. The bowline is exceptionally efficient, easy to check, and easy to untie even after holding a load. The free rope portion should end up on the inside, and should then safety the knot with an overhand around the side of the bowline loop. To be properly safetied, the safety overhand should be in a plane parallel to the bowline. The bowline is generally considered the knot of choice when anchoring one end of the rope. It is easily employed to secure the rope to a rock, carabiner, or similar point.

The bowline can be strengthened by using a double bite in the rope and placing the free end back through the bite, entering through the opposite side once more.

The *figure 8* knot is very easily and quickly tied, easy to check, and quite strong. The figure 8 is most commonly used when a medium to small loop is desired. The figure 8 should also be safetied by tying an overhand snugly against the main knot.

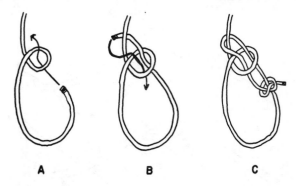

A   **B**   **C**

Bowline on a bight knot. *This basic, multipurpose knot is easy to tie, check, and untie, even after it has absorbed a substantial load. It should be safetied with an additional overhand knot, as shown in C.*

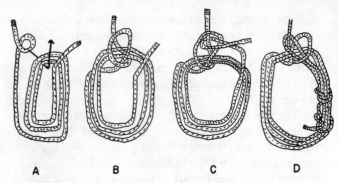

A   B   C   D

Bowline on a coil. *The method for tieing a bowline on a coil is illustrated. This is commonly used for a caver attaching himself to a belay rope. Due to the increased surface area provided by the multiple body-encompassing coils, support would be provided over an increased surface area in the event of a fall.*

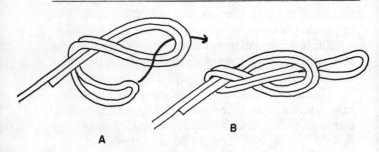

A   B

Figure 8 knot on a bight. *This is a commonly used knot for obtaining a loop for attachment.*

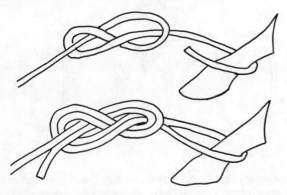

Method for tieing a figure 8 knot around an object.

The *overhand* knot is also very quickly tied, but is not as strong and is much more difficult to untie after loading, thereby making the figure 8 the knot of choice. The figure 8 knot can also be tied in the middle of the rope when a middleman loop is desired. (A middleman loop is a loop tied in the middle of the rope to provide a tie-in point.) It is important to remember that the standing rope should be tied to the outside of the loops.

The *double fisherman's knot* is an exceptionally strong knot. It is one of the very few knots that does not require safety overhands; however, it should have sufficient leftover ends to ensure safety even if some slippage should occur. This knot is composed of symmetrical halves, each tied separately, then pulled and snugged up against each other. It is virtually impossible to untie once it has held a load. The double fisherman's is used to join two ropes of similar diameters together. It is also used to form a loop by joining both ends of a rope together.

The *prusik knot* is a unique knot with specialized applications. It is constructed using a smaller-diameter rope sling around a larger-diameter rope. It has the

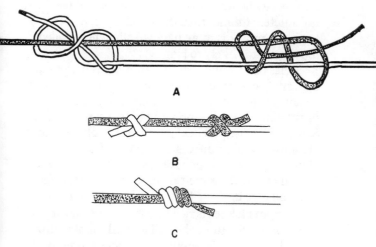

A

B

C

Double fisherman's knot. *This knot is used in tieing together two ropes of similar diameter.*

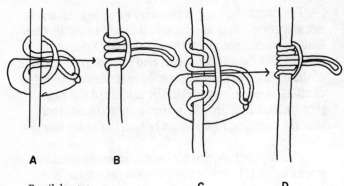

Prusik knots.

A-B. *Tieing the 4-wrap prusik.*

C-D. *Tieing the 6-wrap prusik.*

unique property that it may be moved up and down a standing rope if it is gripped by the knot while holding no load, but resists slipping when weighted from its sling. It is commonly used in pairs to climb up a standing rope. Its use will be discussed in more detail later.

The type of material used for tying the prusik will affect the knot's efficiency and effectiveness. The cord should be of resilient, round construction, which will improve its holding performance, and should be 2 to 3 millimeters thinner than the standing rope. If too large, the prusik is more likely to slip when loaded; if too small, it is likely to jam.

It has been found that this knot holds better when oppositely constructed ropes are used. That is, if the standing rope is of kernmantle construction, the prusik loop generally should be of laid construction. Some cavers use prusik slings made of polypropylene, claiming that they are easier to move after weighting. However, polypropylene has low abrasion resistance as well as a lowered melting temperature, and when used must be inspected thoroughly and often.

The prusik knot is tied by passing one end of a continuous loop through itself around the standing rope, then passing it through itself once more; this is called a four-wrap prusik. The holding power of the prusik knot depends directly on the number of wraps with which the knot passes around the standing rope. The four-wrap prusik is the most common form of the knot for personal use. However, if the rope is muddy, icy, or the knot is holding more than body weight, as in rescue applications, pass the free end through the knot one more time to form a six-wrap prusik.

In rescue operations where high loads may be encountered, the prusik knot is much safer than a mechanical ascender. If the load increases over the holding strength of a mechanical ascender and the ascender fails, either by physical breakdown or cutting through the rope, a catastrophic failure will be experienced. However, if the load exceeds the prusik's strength the knot will generally begin to slip and slide down the rope. By slipping, the knot is transferring the force into friction and movement downward. When the force is dissipated, the knot may well begin to hold again. In other words, when used properly the prusik generally will give the caver warning before it fails completely.

The *ring bend*, *sling knot* or *water knot* is generally the only one used in flat webbing. It is exceptionally strong and is quite easy to check for correct structure. This knot is easily tied by first tying a loose overhand knot in one end, and then following this in the reverse direction using the other end. This knot is very secure and generally does not require any safeties; however, it should have a few inches excess on each end. Once this knot holds a load it becomes quite difficult to untie.

11
RIGGING AND ANCHORS

RIGGING, OR THE COR-
rect preparation and
placement of a
standing rope, is the first link in the chain
of your vertical caving system. It is important that the
person rigging the drop know a multitude of rigging
options and techniques. Certainly he must be familiar
with equipment construction and the real and
potential stress that equipment may encounter.

Even if an individual other than yourself ordinarily
rigs the drops in your caving group, it is important that
you and every vertical caver learn the art and science
of rigging. You may be required to take over the job of
rigging in an emergency. Also, as is the case with all
life support systems, rigging should be checked and
double-checked by all individuals present. Remember
that anyone, including experts, can make errors; do
not feel as though you are intruding by double-
checking the rigging. Your efforts are for everyone's
safety, including your own.

ANCHORS

In 1975 a member of the Laredo Speleological Society
died when he fell approximately 50 feet into the
entrance pit of Pumkin Cave in Texas. As he began
descending into the entrance the iron stake to which
his rope was tied broke. The National Speleological
Society (1977) reported, "Analysis: Although the

information is sketchy, the accident was attributed to carelessness, unnecessary haste, and not using a belay. *If the tie-off point is at all questionable, the rope should be tied to 2 or more independent points"* (our italics).

One must continually strive to rig in the safest, most secure manner available. A rigging system is no stronger than its weakest component. Your anchor is of vital importance in rigging, for it does not matter how well you tie your knots or how strong your rope is if your anchor is not strong and secure.

Natural Anchors

When selecting an anchor, if possible it is far better to find a natural anchor rather than placing an artificial one. Also tieing the rope directly to a natural anchor is often of advantage to the caver, as this aids in economical use of the equipment that must be carried.

Aboveground near the entrance, trees provide exceptionally strong, secure anchors, as long as they do not have shallow root systems. Large rock outcroppings also provide solid anchoring. As we have already stated, any knot tied in the rope weakens that rope due to the sharp turns the knot requires the rope to take. For this reason, tensionless rigging is preferred. This is an arrangement in which the rope itself holds the load and the knot experiences no stress. For example, if a tree is being used for an anchor, take the rope and pass it around the tree a few times, then form a loop in the end by tying a figure 8. Clip a carabiner into the loop and clip back into the main rope. Due to the friction provided by the rope wraps around the tree, the knot should not be subjected to any stress. If the anchor is at all questionable, incorporate another secondary anchor into the system; this secondary anchor should be strong enough to hold the entire load if the primary anchor fails.

Inside a cave there are often natural anchors available. Boulders, ribs, flakes, jughandles, stalagmites, columns, and other similar formations often provide excellent anchors. If these are used for anchors, make every attempt to avoid defacing them. Some individuals may argue that natural cave features should not be used in this manner; yet their use is often less destructive of the cave than is possible permanent defacement caused by placement of artificial anchors.

Montgomery (1977) notes that speleothems should always be treated carefully. Due to their orderly crystalline structure, they have the ability to fracture in two along a crystal cleavage. Any speleothem under 70 millimeters in thickness is a poor prospect for an anchor. In order to avoid any possible leverage, the anchor point on a formation should generally be next to the formation's point of attachment to the floor, wall, roof, and so on.

It is important to inspect the formation to which you are anchoring the rope. Oftentimes the speleothem may have formed on dirt or mud, which provides an insecure base of attachment, and the speleothem itself may pull free. Assure that the speleothem is attached to a solid rock. When considering rock irregularities such as knobs or flakes as potential anchors, cavers often tap the rock gently with a hammer and listen to the sound. If it sounds hollow or weak, do not use it.

With many speleothems, such as columns, it is possible to use tensionless rigging, as was discussed with the use of trees. Wrap the rope three or four times around the speleothem and tie a figure-8 loop or bowline through which the standing rope passes, or use a carabiner as described above.

In caves where there is a breakdown present, oftentimes one can tie off to a large block. When tying off, again tie to a point where there will be no leverage. The block should be large enough, at least 2,000 pounds, so that it will not budge or roll. Make sure that the rope cannot be pulled off or under the block if a strong force must be held.

When attaching to natural anchors, especially limestone, inspect the area with which the rope will be in contact for burrs, ridges, and spikes. These irregularities are often quite small, but are also usually quite sharp. If one must tie directly to a rock with sharp edges, it is wise to take a hammer and pound these sharp protrusions to a fairly smooth surface. If this is undesirable due to conservation principles, the rope must be padded to prevent abrasion, for abrasion will cause severe strength loss to the rope.

In many cases webbing is used to wrap around natural features and then the rope is clipped into the webbing. Generally a couple of 1-inch tubular webbing slings are used to ensure more than adequate strength. Also, on some natural rock protrusions, a rope, due to its round configuration, could possibly roll off. A sling, because of its flat construction and increased surface area, will hold quite securely.

Vertical cavers in Australia are using wire strops (traces), just as slings would be used, for much of their rigging. The wire strop is a short piece of steel cable approximately $\frac{3}{16}$ inch (5 millimeters) in diameter

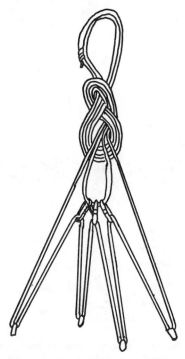

Equalizing anchor. *Used for consolidating multiple anchors, any one of which, used as the sole anchor, could be insecure; however, used in conjunction with one another, they prove safe.*

with swagged loops at either end for carabiner attachment. Because the strops are constructed of cable, they are flexible and certainly much less prone to abrasion than are ropes and slings. They should also be rust-resistant. Strops can be used quite successfully on rock where the use of rope is impractical.

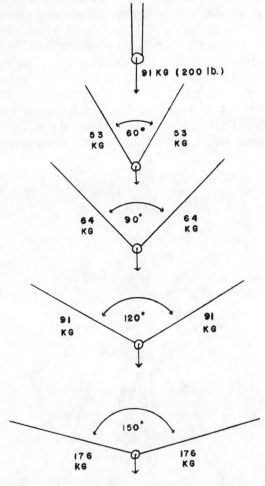

Resultant forces for displaced dual anchors. *As the angle of the rope connecting the two anchors increases, so does the resultant force experienced by each anchor. The angle should not exceed 120°, as resultant forces far exceeding the load applied will then be experienced by both anchors.*

When you are tying off to two or more anchors or are using a loop around a large anchor, it is important to note the angle at which these multiple anchor system slings come together to form the principal attachment point, or the angle from which either side of a loop joins to the other side. If the angle formed is greater than 120°, the anchors will be loaded in excess of the weight applied. Avoid rigging that produces angles greater than 120°. By simple physics it is found that at 150° the force would be double the weight applied, at 165° four times as great, and so on.

Chocks

In the last decade, as a result of the increase in climbing activity aboveground and the awareness of increasing environmental damage caused by use of pitons, there has been a movement toward the use of nondamaging, artificial anchors called chocks. Chocks are aluminum wedges that come in hexcentric (six-sided), tubular, tapered, and many other shapes. They range in size from about the size of a dime to larger than a man's fist. These jam nuts have holes drilled through them to permit attachment of a sling, or for some smaller ones cable is used to provide adequate strength. A carabiner is attached to these slings and connected to the standing rope. Cord is stronger than webbing and is also more abrasion-resistant, but webbing is thinner and more flexible, a good feature for some placements.

A chock stone is placed into a crack and positioned so that it will jam into the crack even tighter when it takes a force. *It is extremely important that the direction of force be determined correctly, as a misdirected force will often pull the chock out of its placement.*

Removal of chocks is generally quite easy. The caver merely has to give a tug in the opposite direction from which the chock was inserted. If jammed in fairly tightly, or if the placement is in a very deep or confined area, a chock tool may be needed. A chock tool is nothing more than a thin piece of metal with a hook at one end. It is used to manipulate the chock around in areas where the hand cannot reach. Some individuals use an adjustable shelf bracket as a simple chock tool.

Although smaller chocks with wire slings ⅛ inch (3 millimeters) or smaller should be avoided, any medium-sized chock that is placed correctly will have excellent strength. Tests by Magnussen have demonstrated that well-placed chocks consistently held loads of 1,000 kilograms (about 2,200 pounds).

As a matter of interest, it was found that when placed behind flakes, tapered wedges created forces well in excess of loading by virtue of their design and tended to pry the flake away from its attachment. A #2 Chouinard stopper that has an angle of 8° theoretically will exert a wedging force seven times that of the load applied (Montgomery, 1977).

In general, chocks are quite secure anchors, but a single chock should never be used as the sole anchor; rather, it should be used in conjunction with other anchors. As with any new technique or piece of equipment, the use of chocks should be practiced thoroughly on the surface before employing them underground.

Pitons

As we noted, the trend is toward chocks as artificial anchors, rather than use of the more destructive piton. Although the piton is almost completely phased out on the surface, where its use once flourished, it is still used by some cavers for anchoring purposes where wall climbing to obtain a high lead is necessary and no natural anchors are available, where chock placement is not possible, or where bolt placement is not practical.

A wide variety of piton types and sizes is available. The types used most often by cavers are the medium-sized angles, horizontal blade pitons, and leepers. Large angles and vertical blade pitons are generally useless to the caver. Today the majority of pitons are made of some type of chromium and molybdenum (chrome-moly). These pitons are exceptionally strong and durable. In the past, pitons were made of a malleable iron that conformed to the crack. This type had a short life, and many also displayed decreased strength; these types should be avoided. Pitons with welded rings should also be avoided.

To place a piton, one must study the crack very closely, looking for tapers, nubbing, irregularities, and depth. Select a piton and that portion of the crack that best fit together. The piton should be able to be inserted one-half to three-fourths of its length before requiring pounding. Pound the piton part way, then test it by giving it a slight blow perpendicular to the crack to determine its resistance to shifting. If results are favorable, finish driving the piton. Although a high ring pitch does not necessarily indicate solid placement, as was once commonly believed, it is a good indication. If a high ring suddenly drops down to a dull and hollow sound, the caver should assume a poor placement.

A single piton should not be used as the only anchor, but is reliable if used in combination with others. Pitons that cannot be driven all the way must be tied off with a hero loop. A hero loop is a small piece of webbing tied into a continuous loop, which is tied around a piton close to the rock, to avoid any bending caused by leverage. Piton placement is an art and should be mastered aboveground before going underground.

Inspection of the rigged anchor or anchors should be thorough. If in doubt about an anchor, back it up with another one or two. Sometimes you can clip a sling to the anchor. Place your foot in it and jump up and down. This may give you a clue as to whether the anchor is or is not solid. If it moves, it most likely is not a satisfactory anchor.

Bolts

Bolts are exactly what the name implies. They consist of various types of boltlike pieces of metal that are driven into the rock after a hole has been drilled to accept them. When placed correctly bolts are extremely strong and secure. There is much controversy over the use of bolts because they permanently scar the rock; however, when there are no natural anchors available, the bolt is generally the first choice for an artificial anchor by modern day American cavers. Bolt anchors are generally far more secure than pitons or chocks. Another advantage of bolt anchors is that they can be placed almost anywhere in any solid rock. This makes it possible to rig pitches so the rope hangs free rather than against a lip, or to rig the rope so that it hangs out away from a waterfall rather than underneath it.

There are several types of bolts available on the market today. The two most popular styles in the United States are the self-drilling shield type and the Rawl type.

The self-drilling shield type is probably the more popular among cavers. These types are available in many sizes, with the most popular size being ⅜ inch (9 millimeters). The shield has teeth at one end that drill through the rock. The other end of the shield has a threaded center into which the bolt driver is screwed firmly. The driver is held with the toothed end of the shield against the rock. The driver is then hit with the hammer, pounding the shield's teeth into the rock. The shield must be slightly rotated after each blow by rotating the driver.

To set a bolt, first you must investigate the rock into which you plan to place the bolt. Take your hammer and tap this area of the rock. Listen to the sound, which is often indicative of the condition of the rock. By tapping you can clean up and make a uniform flat surface on the rock. When cleaning the rock, do not deface any rock area larger than is absolutely necessary. Avoid setting bolts into weathered, crumbly, flaky rock, since the bolt may pull loose, taking with it the rock immediately around it.

It is best to install the bolt so that the force will be at right angles to it; this is called shear loading. Although bolts will hold to some extent even when placed in ceilings, it is recommended that they be placed in walls or floors where the force will be 90° to their attachment. Montgomery (1977) noted that when placing a bolt in a wall, a 5° angle downward will help prevent the bolt from pulling out if it loosens. Once the area for bolt installation has been determined, begin drilling the hole, monitoring the shield to make sure it is continually held in the same position and rotated after each blow with the hammer. If the shield is held at varying angles you stand a chance of fracturing the rock or enlarging the hole to the point that strength is severely reduced. Several times during the drilling process, the shield must be removed and tapped against the rock to dislodge compacted rock powder that accumulates in its center. When the shield is removed, the caver should blow out any rock powder that remains in the hole, using a small section of hose. The hole should be drilled until the top of the shield is flush or just slightly below the rock. Sometimes in very hard rock, such as marble, it is necessary to use a second shield to finish drilling the hole. If the first shield has no teeth left, the new shield provides a fresh cutting edge.

When drilling is completed, remove the shield, clean out the rock powder, and insert the conical plug in the toothed end. Insert the shield into the drilled hole and pound the shield down to the bottom of the hole until the top is parallel with the rock. When the shield is pounded down on the conical plug, the shield is split and wedged against the walls of the hole as the plug moves upward in the center of the shield. Thus the holding power in the placement is near its base, where solid rock is generally present.

Finally, unscrew the driver. The shield should be solid. The caver now takes a hanger and a high-tensile bolt and bolts the hange down securely into place. The hanger is simply an angled piece of metal with a round hole through which it is bolted into the anchor and another hole facilitating carabiner attachment. Again, be sure when attaching the carabiner that the carabiner's gate will not receive any force against the rock if the rope shifts. The gate should face up.

A note on hanger attachment: if the hanger is to be left in place, use Locktite or epoxy on the threads to prevent others from removing it. If you plan to take it when you leave, you should leave the cap bolt in, coated with a bit of grease. This prevents the shield from filling up with rock, dirt, and grit.

Any strange bolt and hanger encountered in caving should be considered unreliable until investigated thoroughly. As mentioned, one good way to check strength and security is to connect a runner to the hanger via a carabiner and jump up and down. If it moves, be quite suspicious of its strength.

When bolting, a caver should carry the components of a bolt kit in a small pouch or container. These should include hangers, driver, wrench, and hose to blow out powder. If the self-drilling type is used, the kit should also include shields, plugs, and cap bolts. Or, if you are using the Rawl type, include Rawl drives and Rawl studs, extra drill bits, and a sharpening stone. Both the hammer and the driver should be tied to you in order to prevent their loss if dropped.

The time required to set a bolt will depend on many variables, such as type of rock, type of drill, and so on, but will usually take approximately fifteen to twenty-five minutes.

Rawl drives and Rawl studs are the other popular types of bolt used today. These come in various diameters, the most popular being the 6 millimeter (¼ inch thick) and the 10 millimeter (⅜ inch). The stud type has a threaded head to accept a nut that can be removed to retrieve the hanger; this type is available in 37-millimeter (1½-inch) and 50-millimeter (2-inch) lengths. The drive type has a permanent head and comes in 30 millimeter (1¼-inch) lengths. These cylindrical bolts are compressed in the middle, making their center portions a larger diameter than the remainder of the bolt.

A hole is drilled with a high-impact, high-tensile-strength drill bit, which is held with a driver. The driver is hit with the hammer and rotated, as was the other style of holder. In the case of the Rawl it is important that the hole be deep enough so that the bolt does not bottom out, for a very significant portion of the bolt's holding strength is lost if bottoming out occurs. Again, be very careful to drill the hole straight. Do not allow the hole to be enlarged; this often happens when the hole is being drilled in places that are hard to reach. If the drill bit is allowed to move around sloppily, the hole's diameter will be too large and severe loss of holding strength may occur. It has also been found that the split in the middle of the bolt is prone to aging and fatigue, which at times aids in loosening the bolt. Although the Rawl type of bolt is common, it does have some drawbacks. For example, the drill bit must be sharpened or replaced as it becomes dull, whereas the self-drilling shields provide a new cutting surface with each placement, since the teeth are an integral part of the shield.

In summary, when selecting the anchor, the ultimate goal is to select a bombproof anchor and rig it correctly. Natural bombproof anchors are not always available. When this occurs, it then becomes necessary to provide an artificial anchor that will ensure strength and security. *When using artificial anchors it is best to use them in groups of two or more.* Some cavers are lazy and will take the easy way out by placing bolts or pins when, if a little time and effort were expended, they would find natural anchors that meet the criteria for safety. The caver who takes time to work with the natural environment, instead of against it, in selecting natural anchors, becomes closer to the cave and can appreciate it more for what it is. This is not to say that a caver should sacrifice safety for conservation, but rather that a rational, responsible, middle-of-the-road approach should be taken, and indiscriminate bolting should be avoided.

RIGGING

Rigging includes the anchoring of a rope to safe solid anchors and arranging the rope down the drop to provide a safe descent and ascent; it is a many-faceted technique that must be mastered by vertical cavers. As we have been discussing, the first step is for the rigger to locate a satisfactory anchor or anchors to which the main rope can be attached. Tensionless rigging around a bombproof anchor is ideal; however, this is not always possible. When anchors must be used in groups to ensure a secure attachment, they must be rigged in the best possible arrangement.

In a situation where a main anchor is used and a

backup anchor is connected to it, it is important that there be no slack in the rope between the primary and backup anchors. In the case of primary anchor failure, any slack present will allow the load on the rope to drop an unspecified distance, causing the second anchor to absorb a shock load. However, with no rope slack present, the second anchor will begin to take up the force immediately upon primary anchor failure. If an artificial anchor is placed because no natural ones can be found, the backup anchor should be directly in line with it, but separated from the primary anchor by a short distance, especially if the anchors are bolts. If one anchor fails, in many situations the rock may be damaged or unstable, and if the second anchor is close, it may fail also.

When one anchor is doubtful, sometimes using three or more of these anchors with an equalizing harness will be quite safe. In this situation the load is spread over all of the anchors, and if one fails, the others will absorb the force equally.

Once the primary anchor system has been determined and the rope has been anchored, the rope must be positioned on the drop. The ideal rigging would allow the rope rigged directly from its primary anchors to drop free all the way to the bottom, avoiding all obstructions. The rope would also be rigged so that it would be easy to get on and off at the top. This type of arrangement is not generally feasible; so the rigger strives to do the best he can with the circumstances presented.

Length of Drop

It is important that the rigger determine the length of the drop as closely as possible in order that the correct length of rope can be chosen. If it is not possible to look over the edge and determine the depth, an estimate must be made. This is commonly done by dropping a rock over the edge and noting the time it takes for the rock to reach the bottom. There are a number of formulas used today to determine approximate distance. Although none of them are exact, they give a good estimation under certain circumstances.

Montgomery (1977) uses the formula

$$D = 5t^2$$

In this formula D is depth in meters and t is time in seconds. This formula works well for drops when the time is 5 seconds or less.

Another formula used by some cavers to determine depth is

$$D = 89.7t - 156$$

In this formula D is depth in feet and t is time in seconds. This formula appears to give fairly close results.

There are many problems with using any type of rock-dropping, depth-time estimates. First, the shape and density of the rock used varies. Thus air resistance and gravitational forces acting upon the rock will also vary slightly. Humidity, altitude, and temperature will also cause deviations. As the distance to the bottom of the drop increases, so also does the time taken for the sound to travel back up the drop. These effects may be small, but they do bear on the results.

Another common problem is that the rock does not necessarily experience an unhindered free fall. The rock may come in contact with the wall or ledge, sending a premature sound to the top that may be mistaken for the sound of the rock hitting bottom, which will give a shorter reading. At the other extreme, the dropped rock may come to rest on a ledge and dislodge another rock, which continues on down. The drop is then often estimated to be deeper than it actually is because of the delay.

When dropping rocks, be extremely careful to make sure that there definitely is no one below and that no rope is hanging where a rock could hit it. It is also recommended that you be tied in before venturing close to the edge—that is, connected through a safety loop to an anchor, thereby preventing the possibility of a fall.

Many factors affect estimates, so, unless you can see your rope on the bottom, always be prepared to ascend the rope in the event that it does not reach. Never assume your rope reaches the bottom if you cannot see it, and as discussed in Chapter 13, always tie a knot in the end of the rope just in case it does not.

When lowering the rope down the drop be careful not to get a bird's nest of rope hung up part way down. On long drops, it is unwise to throw the rope down because the weight of the rope can exert exceptionally strong forces on the anchors as the force of the falling rope is absorbed.

Gardening

It is necessary to clear away all loose rock, dirt, and possibly bushes near the top of the drop before the rope is lowered over the side. The rock and debris should be set back away from the edge so that there is no possibility of it falling on anyone below at a later point in time.

As the first caver descends, he should be constantly on the lookout for any loose rock or debris that could be dislodged by successive cavers or the rope. If he finds any, he should move this material back away from the edge. This is not always possible, and the next best thing is for the caver to pull the rope up and dislodge the debris. If the rope is below when the debris is dislodged, you can be almost certain of rope damage or severing.

Abrasion and Rope Protection

The most dangerous situation in SRT is the possibility of main rope breakage due to abrasion. It is extremely important that all ropes rigged be carefully inspected for any contact points with the rock that could abrade the rope. Any point of contact with the rope is a potential rub point that could lead to abrasion. A skilled rappeller can generally descend the rope smoothly and avoid abrasion; however, no matter how skilled, the caver will set up a bouncing cycle on the rope as he shifts weight during ascent. This bouncing causes sharp edges to saw their way through the rope. Rub points vary in their effectiveness at abrading the rope, depending on their position in relationship to the rigging. The bounce distance and the amount of prusiking or rappelling to which that section of the rope will be subjected will determine total abrasion sustained by the rope at that point. Obviously the bounce distance will be the greatest at the bottom of the rope; however, little prusiking and rappelling will be done here. In actuality it appears that the greatest danger of abrasion experienced by the rope is located approximately halfway up the drop, with the most intense area just above the halfway point.

When rigging a wet pitch where you are dealing with moving water, such as in a waterfall, the rigger must investigate the pitch very carefully, otherwise rub points may be obscured by water and overlooked. *Do not leave a rope rigged in moving water unless absolutely necessary,* as the water has the ability to move the rope and abrade it. This is especially true with nylon rope, as its abrasion resistance is reduced when wet. Oftentimes, after the caver has descended, he will be able to pull the rope to the side, out of the water's path, and tie it off until it is needed for the trip out.

It is often the case that on a pitch where no bomb-proof natural anchors are available to create a free drop, the naturally anchored rope may be redirected through an artificial anchor placed out on the wall above the drop to create a free fall. In this case, the redirecting anchor need not necessarily be bombproof. Do make sure, however, that the ascent will still be possible if it gives way.

Another method of avoiding rock-rope contact on longer drops is to set an anchor below the point of potentially serious abrasion. In this fashion abrasive rock will be at the very bottom of that section of rope. Even though it is one continuous rope, it is rigged as two drops. This anchor may be artificial or natural, and it is naturally backed up because the rope is continuous.

When it is not possible to rig the rope to avoid abrasive rock contact, the rope must be protected by padding, so that the padding receives the abrasion rather than the rope. The more rope protectors used, the longer it takes a party to descend a drop. Because skilled rappellers do not present a great danger of abrading the rope, in rappelling it is often the last caver down who sets up rope protection if it needs to be extensive. This is not to say that the rope should not be protected for rappelling, but often areas of contact will present potential problems only upon ascent. Be sure the rope reaches bottom, or the first caver may have to ascend an unpadded rope.

Sometimes it is quite difficult to determine where the rope will rub upon ascent due to rope stretch. Many a caver has padded the rope on his descent and upon ascending has found that due to rope stretch the pad has shifted, and the rope has been abraded nearly completely through. If this happens the caver must then knot together the rope above and below the abraded section, thereby bypassing the damaged section, reprotecting the rope.

Study the pitch very carefully when you are selecting points of protection. Remember, the more rope protection devices attached to the rope, the more time it takes to get up or down. Also, every time the protective pads are removed and replaced, the more chance there is that they will be replaced slightly differently, increasing the possibility of misplacement and hence abrasion. Generally the majority of padding is needed near the top where the rope goes over the edge or lip. In these cases it is sometimes more efficient to allow the tail of the rigged rope to lay parallel to the standing end, ending just below the padding with a figure 8 tied in the end. When ascending, upon reaching the pads, the caver simply transfers over to the tail, which needs no padding because it is short and is not subjected to stretch-bounce abrasion.

There are essentially two types of protective devices commonly used today as rope protection devices. The best type for serious cave exploration is called a protector. We are extremely happy with the type developed in Australia, which Montgomery (1977) describes as a piece of heavy material about 5 inches wide and about 2 feet long, held together by a Velcro strip that runs the entire length of the material. It has a cord attached to it, which is tied off to place it. You can tie the cord to the rock or to the main rope. The protector wraps around the rope and is closed with

Velcro. To pass the protector, you separate the Velcro, unfold the protector, and continue closing it after passing. If the protector is tied to the rope, you can ascend over it. However, if rappelling, you will have to untie the cord and replace it once you have passed it. With this type of protector, the rope cannot roll out of or underneath the protector, as it can with a mat type.

The other commonly used type of protective device is called a mat or pad. This is generally 1 foot wide by about 3 feet long and is made of canvas, bluejeans, leather, old rug remnants, and so on. It is laid against the rock and is tied off with a cord attached to the top. As with the protector, it can be tied to rock or to the rope. If rug remnants are used, be sure they are not composed of nylon, as nylon rubbing on nylon tends to melt.

Another style of rope protection device that is occasionally used is made from a flexible hose, slit to allow placement on the rope. The hose diameter is selected so that it will fit snugly around the rope. This type also has a cord attached to one end for securement. Because the rope sometimes tends to work its way out of the hose through a straight slit opening, the slit should instead be arranged so that it forms a spiral pattern around the hose.

12

HARNESSES AND CARABINERS

THIS CHAPTER DESCRIBES harnesses, carabiners, and other equipment that is used in all types of vertical caving. Descenders are described in Chapter 13, ascenders in Chapter 14; equipment used for rigging is described in Chapter 11.

HARNESSES

The caver's basic component for any rappelling or ascending system is some type of seat harness. It is to this harness that one of the descending or one of the ascending devices will be attached. The seat harness should be fail-safe, easy to tie, comfortable, and versatile. When we say fail-safe, we mean that if one portion of the harness fails, another part will immediately take up the weight. It should be easy to get into and out of when the need arises, and hence easy to check for correct donning. Buckles and knots should be easily checked for correct positioning and security. The seat harness should be comfortable, for a caver may be suspended in it for long periods of time. Sitting in a harness that cuts off the circulation in your legs is extremely painful. Versatility is a beneficial feature to possess in your harness, for if problems arise, it is good to know that you can modify your system and that your seat harness will adapt.

Most harnesses are constructed from flat or tubular

nylon webbing (or tape, in Europe). Webbing is much more comfortable than rope or cord by virtue of its increased surface area. Webbing is jointed by sewing, knotting, or buckles. The water knot is the most common knot used in webbing (see Chapter 10). It is strong, fairly flat, and comfortable. Webbing and thread are available in nylon or Terylene. If acid or alkaline batteries are being carried, it is wise to choose material that will not be damaged by the type of electrolyte used. Terylene is destroyed by strong alkalis such as the caustic soda type electrolyte found in nickel-iron lamps. Nylon is destroyed by phenol, cresol, and the acids such as the electrolyte found in lead-acid cell battery lights.

Though there are buckles on many types of harnesses on the market today, the trend is away from them and toward softer, more comfortable joints using knots or sewing. Sewing is the strongest method of joining webbing. There are several stitching patterns used for sewing the webbing together, including boxes, criss-crossing, and others; however, it has been found after some research that the best joint is that using eight stitches per inch on the sewing machine, overlapping the webbing ends about 3 inches, and sewing a series of longitudinal rows of stitches (Magnussen, 1972). A 1-inch piece of webbing should have a minimum of ten rows of stitching. Magnussen recommends #24 Star Ultra Dee polyester for Terylene and CONSO #16 nylon for nylon webbing. McClurg (1980) recommends that half of the rows be sewed 2 inches and the other half of the rows extend the full 3 inches; the rows extending to the end will indicate failure before the entire joint fails.

Harnesses and any other items constructed from webbing must be treated with care, just like your ropes. They should be washed when dirty, and you should avoid dragging them through mud and dirt whenever possible, as they will suffer abrasion. Because of the greatly enlarged surface area, webbing is quite vulnerable to ultraviolet deterioration. Although this situation may not affect cavers as much as some other individuals, the condition of the webbing should be constantly monitored. If wear appears on the side of the webbing, retire it, as it will have a tendency to rip. On harnesses it is also a good idea to look for weld abrasion—that is, where a rope has run across a portion of the harness and the heat from friction has begun to melt it. Remember that nylon on nylon melts quite quickly with the addition of friction. *Do not risk your life on a damaged harness; repair or replace it.*

Seat Harnesses

Not long ago cavers constructed and sewed the majority of their harnesses themselves. Today there is an overwhelming variety of commercially prepared harnesses available on the market. Many still require minor modifications, but work well. However, any serious caver should be familiar with a variety of descending, ascending, and harness systems, for one never knows when one will need, in an emergency, to construct a safe, workable system out of materials at hand. Therefore, we will discuss the simplest systems first.

Most cavers, and for that matter climbers also, will always have at least one sling constructed of 1-inch tubular webbing and approximately 10 to 12 feet in length tied end to end forming a continuous loop. From this single loop a caver can construct a simple seat harness, chest harness, safety loop, belay tie-in, and many other items. Let us first describe the seat sling.

The simple seat sling is called a Swiss seat or diaper sling. You will need only approximately 8 feet of webbing to form this, so shorten your webbing as necessary. To don the diaper sling, the caver passes the doubled loop behind him, holding one end in each hand in front, allowing one strap to hang down behind. Now the caver has both sides of the sling behind him, with the ends held in front. He then reaches between his legs with his free hand, his other hand holding both ends in front, and grabs the loose, hanging strap and pulls it through his legs to the front, leaving the remaining nylon strap at about waist level, and with a carabiner clips all three pieces together. If correctly prepared, the caver can now sit down fairly comfortably, suspending his weight from the carabiner. This type of harness will work, but too many novices disregard the fact that it is not fail-safe. This sling need only break at one point and the harness will unravel off the caver. It is for this reason that an independent waist loop should be added. With this addition the caver will have a backup system.

A much more comfortable and safer seat harness is called the swami belt. It is generally constructed out of a 25- to 30-foot piece of 1-inch webbing, although some cavers use 2-inch webbing. There are a number of ways to tie a swami belt. One way is to find the center of the webbing and, using figure 8 knots, tie a leg loop on either side of center by taking a loop and tieing the knot approximately 7 to 9 inches from the center mark. The leg loops should be fit snugly but not tightly. The two ends are then wrapped in opposite

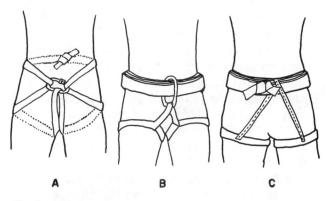

A   **B**   **C**

Simple seat harnesses.

A. *Simple diaper seat harness which is considered somewhat unsafe, as a failure at any point in the system would prove catastrophic. Safety can be increased through the use of an independent waist strap.*

B. *Leg loops and waist strap (front view). This simple, safe, seat harness is composed of two independent components.*

C. *Leg loops and waist strap (rear view). Note the strap used to hold up the leg loops.*

directions around the waist (it is a wise idea to wrap the ends once through each of the leg loops and also through the connecting portion between the legs) and are secured to each other with a snug water or square knot with trailing free ends a few inches long.

Another method preferred by some individuals is to mark the center as before, measure approximately 3 feet on either side of center, then run one end parallel to this 6-foot length above, and the other end parallel below. Now you have a single strand of webbing extending on each end of a three-strand section in the middle measuring about 7 feet in length. Now again tie your leg loops using the figure 8. Each tie is about 7 to 9 inches from center using all three strands. Again, the leg loops should be snug. Each individual will have to experiment to get the correct fit. You finish tieing this in the same way described above for the first method, only this time you will have triple straps between leg loops.

To hook into this seat harness you take a large locking carabiner and clip it through all of the waist loops and the piece bridging the leg loops, whether it be one or three strips.

We will now discuss a couple of the more popular commercial harnesses. Forrest Mountaineering manufactures a two-piece climbing harness that some cavers find works quite well. The bottom half is simply a figure 8 design, a continuous loop, sewed in the middle. The legs go through the loops, which are available in 3-inch flat webbing, making it a bit more comfortable to sit in by virtue of its increased surface area. The upper half is simply a 3-inch piece of webbing with tapered loops sewed in the ends. A carabiner can then be passed through both ends of the upper belt and the leg loop bridging section. This company also recently began producing a one-piece seat harness.

A few years ago a British climber named Whillans developed a seat harness now named after him. This harness, produced by Troll Products, is exceptionally strong and does not inhibit freedom of movement. Normally the harness has a rope passed through three points of attachment to achieve a fail-safe mode. Cavers may want to substitute a large locking carabiner for this attachment. The Whillans does tend to support the caver at a backward angle, which some cavers have found unsatisfactory for various ascending systems. This harness is also available in Terylene webbing for those cavers using electric lights with acidic electrolyte batteries. This reduces the risk of any spilled electrolyte weakening the harness.

There are a number of other seat harnesses on the market today, and many of them are good. Regardless of which harness the caver chooses, he should use his harness and work out any problems with it before venturing underground. At the bottom—or worse, in the middle—of a 1,000-foot pit is no place to discover that your harness doesn't work correctly.

Full Body Harness

Troll also manufactures a full body harness that connects a chest harness with the seat harness. This harness, although a bit bulkier, is an excellent piece of engineering, especially for difficult technical exploration.

Chest Harnesses

Chest harnesses are gaining in popularity as more and more ascending systems incorporate the chest harness to secure an ascender, ascender box (see Chapter 14), carabiner, or pulley (see below). The chest harness should be placed as high as possible on the chest, and should be as snug as possible without inhibiting breathing. Like the seat sling, the chest harness must be designed with strength in mind, as you may find yourself supported entirely by your chest harness.

Again, the simplest chest harness can be formed from a piece of 1-inch webbing tied into a continuous loop. To attach an ascender, pull it through until it is positioned in the middle of the sling. Now take one loop, put your left arm through, and pass the loop over your head. The ascender should be about center chest. To finish take the remaining loop, pass your right arm through it, and pass the loop over your head. You are now securely attached to the ascender.

To attach a carabiner to the chest for various clip-ins instead of the ascender, we use a slightly different configuration. Take your sling, again a continuous loop, and cross it. Now position the cross in the center of your back and put your right arm through the loop coming around from the right, and the left arm through the loop coming around from the left. Now take the two loops on your chest and attach a carabiner through them. You now have a point of attachment for a safety line, tie-in, prusik knot, and so forth.

The most comfortable chest harnesses are the sewed 2-inch webbing type. They work quite well and may be constructed with a little effort.

It is a very good idea to fashion some type of safety

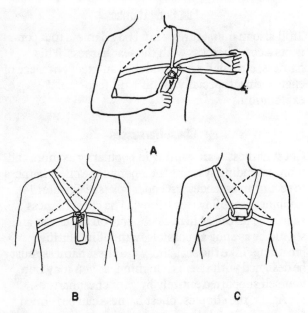

Simple chest harnesses *(front view)*.

A-B. *Method for attaching an ascender to a simple chest harness, constructed of a single, nylon web sling.*

C. *Simple chest harness providing a point of attachment for a carabiner.*

Sewn chest harness. *This chest harness is constructed of nylon webbing, sewn rather than knotted, and buckles.*

loop to attach the chest harness to the seat harness. This provides another backup system.

Foot Harnesses

Foot harnesses, more commonly known as stirrups, are used to attach the majority of ascending systems to the feet, except in some rope-walking systems in which an ascender may be attached directly to the foot through strapping. In general, a loop is fashioned by tieing a figure 8. The loop should be large enough to pass over the boot but should remain snug enough that it will not shift sloppily. To prevent the stirrup from coming off the foot in the event of a harness failure and a fall backward with these stirrups as the only source of attachment, cavers construct "chicken loops." These are simply binding straps that go around the ankles to prevent the stirrups from coming off. Generally the chicken loop is donned before the caver's boot, as it is designed small enough so that it will not fit over the boot. When the caver puts the stirrup on, he passes it through the chicken loop, then around his foot. These stirrups should be constructed out of 7- or 8-millimeter cord, rather than webbing, if possible, as its abrasion resistance is far better. If webbing is used, knotting is better than sewing for the same reason.

In Australia and New Zealand, some cavers are using quick release foot stirrups using C clasps. These are obtainable at sailboat shops. The foot attachment is simply a loop made of ⅝-inch webbing threaded through a C clasp with half of the loop also threaded through a piece of 1-inch tubular webbing, which is positioned under the instep to protect the inner foot loop, with the C clasp positioned on top. On these foot loops there are two straps sewed on opposite sides, one side possessing a buckle. The two straps are buckled securely together forming a chicken loop. Another C clasp is tied to the line descending from the ascender. The foot harness is worn throughout the cave, and the ascender can be attached quickly and efficiently when needed. We have found this system quite efficient for multi-drop cave systems.

SAFETY LOOPS

It is exceptionally handy when engaging in vertical work to carry an assortment of slings and loops made from webbing and 7- or 8-millimeter Perlon cord. These can be used for many different purposes. Rigging systems, backup systems, safety tie ins, prusik knots, and dangling your pack below when ascending or descending are all possible uses. (On long drops the pack is much more comfortably carried when suspended below on a sling attached to the descending system, rather than carried on the back.) Slings and loops can also be combined to form a hand line, haul line, or anchor line.

CARABINERS

Carabiners, often called biners, are oval, metal links that have a hinged gate and opening side that snaps back into the closed position once pressure is reduced. Although some carabiners are still made of steel, most are of an aluminum alloy yielding reduced weight and better antioxidation properties. Carabiners are commonly available in oval, D, and modified D shapes, with or without locking gates. The D carabiners were introduced for a stronger construction. The D design is such that, upon loading, the long side will receive more weighting and stress than will the shorter side. This is important if one wants to open the gate when the carabiner is loaded. On an oval, because it is

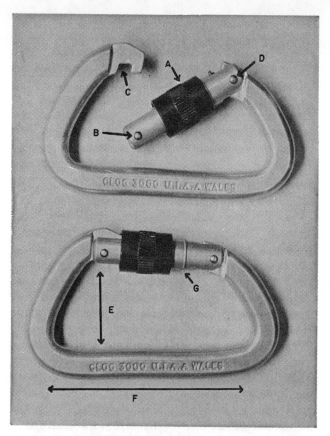

Offset locking D carabiner displaying features common to many carabiners. A. Locking slure; B. Locking pin; C. Locking notch; D. Hinge pin; E. Short axis; F. Long axis.

---

symmetrical, loading is equal and often it will be difficult to open the gate even under the standardized body weight used in testing (176 pounds). However, many quality carabiners of symmetrical design will open when slightly loaded. When carabiners fail, however, they usually unbend, beginning at the gate, obviously the weak point. One can see why the D design would experience a greater load before failure. Offset-D or pear-shaped carabiners facilitate the clipping of more items into them than most other carabiners.

Carabiners are available in locking models, on

A   B   C

Carabiners.

A. Standard oval carabiner with gate open; B. Standard locking D carabiner with gate open; C. Offset D locking carabiner, gate open; All locking carabiners must be locked for safe operation.

---

which a locking sleeve screws up and down to lock the gate shut and provide increased security. When selecting locking carabiners, you should inspect the gate-lock mechanism. Some have pins, others use threads. If threads are sharp they may damage ropes or slings. Look for flat-topped threads. Most quality carabiners have an average breaking strength of 3,000 to 5,500 pounds (1,350 to 2,500 kilograms, with some up to 5,000 kilograms), when loaded properly along the long axis. It is extremely important when placing a carabiner into position to ensure that the load cannot shift to the short axis, thereby loading the gate, which is the weakest point on the carabiner. Gates fail with loads as small as 300 pounds. Contrary to popular belief, the locking sleeve only improves security; it does *not* strengthen the gate. Generally it is the hinge pin at the opposite end that fails (Blackshaw, 1977).

Carabiner Maintenance

A misconception held by far too many cavers is that carabiners are indestructible. While carabiners are extremely strong and rugged, nevertheless they need regular inspection and care. They should be cleaned of dirt, mud, bat guano, and similar materials regularly, and the gates should be lubricated with some type of penetrating lubricant, such as WD-40. They should be checked for free gate action. If the gate does not snap immediately back into proper position, retire the carabiner. If a carabiner has experienced a fall of more than 10 to 15 feet, it may possess hairline fractures invisible to the eye that will show up only under X-ray.

Checking them in this manner would be prohibitively expensive; therefore, if in doubt about a carabiner, retire it.

Most cavers and climbers prefer to mark their carabiners for identification, for due to their similarity they are easily mixed up with fellow cavers' carabiners. Many individuals use strips of brightly colored tape or spray paint. Because these sometimes wear off, a few cavers stamp their carabiners with their initials. If you use this method, be careful to stamp only the gate, since stamping the body will weaken it.

LOCK LINKS

Lock links or rapid links are steel oval links with a screw opening and no hinged gate. They are extremely strong when the opening is screwed closed. The opening screw must be closed or the strength is severely reduced. The French Maillon Rapide Link #9 tests to 10,000 pounds (3,730 kilograms) when closed, but less than 1,100 pounds (410 kilograms) when the sleeve is open. When closed the #9 is quite strong considering it is only about two-thirds the size of a standard oval carabiner. Although it is harder to put a group of clip-ins inside the Rapide link, as the opening is only half the size of a carabiner, it has no gate, which on a standard carabiner often lodges against ropes or carabiners already inside.

These lock links are useful for rigging rescue pulleys for harnesses and other varied applications where high strength and low bulk is desirable. *Remember that the screw gate must be closed for any application.*

DAISY CHAINS

Daisy chains are manufactured by Forrest Mountaineering. These handy items are nothing more than a sling of ⅝-inch webbing about 4 feet long. The two sides of the sling have been sewed together approximately every 6 inches to form multiple positions for carabiner attachment. These can be used for position-

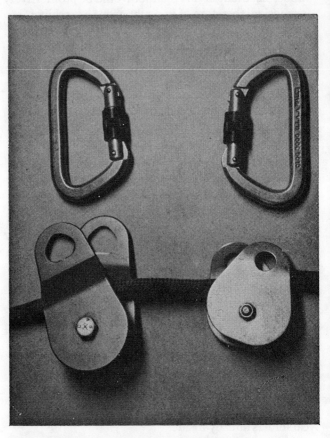

(Left): *Heavy duty rescue pulley;* (Right): *Lightweight personal pulley.*

Carabiner sides are shifted to allow attachment to rope at any point. Upon attachment by carabiner to pulley, the pulley is locked onto the rope.

---

ing a belay stance, tie-ins, ascending systems, spacing, and so on.

PULLEYS

Every vertical caving group should have in their possession a minimum of two pulleys. Pulleys are extremely efficient when large amounts of gear need to be hauled, or if a rescue situation should ever arise. They are an integral part of mechanical advantage systems for moving and lifting. The pulleys available today are generally available in two sizes. There is a smaller one, which is generally aluminum color, intended for personal use. These are manufactured by a number of climbing hardware companies. For heavy loads and high stresses, as would be encountered in rescue or moving large loads, the larger types are definitely called for. Recently, Search and Rescue Associates (SARA), working with H. R. Anderson, has produced some exceptionally high-quality pulleys.

Both of their styles of pulleys are of similar construction. They use aluminum sides that may be rotated around the center pin, which holds the nylon or aluminum wheel in place. This side rotation allows them to be attached to the rope at any point, thereby eliminating the need to thread the rope end through.

The stronger SARA rescue pulleys come in two styles. The red-sided ones have a bushing, while the blue-sided ones use sealed bearings. Where extremely high loads or extended periods of time in use are expected, the sealed bearings will provide better performance. Be sure the wheel runs freely. If not, there is a possibility of overheating.

13

VERTICAL CAVING TECHNIQUE: DESCENDING

IN VERTICAL CAVE EX-
ploration today, the
fixed rope is used for
lowering oneself down
basically two purposes:
from the tie-off point to the bottom, and the reverse,
returning to the top from the bottom. This chapter is
concerned with the former: the equipment, theory,
and technique of descending a rope safely.

Descending, commonly known as rappelling or
abseiling (European), is today generally accomplished
with some type of mechanical friction device. Simple
physics tells us that an object (the caver) at a higher
elevation possesses more potential energy than does
an object at a lower elevation, and that energy is
neither lost nor created, but simply changes form.
When a caver descends a drop he begins with more
potential energy than he ends up with after allowing
gravity to work on his weight. This energy is not lost,
but is translated through friction into heat and stored
mechanical energy. It is the careful, controlled conver-
sion of this energy with which we are concerned.

All types of rappelling require an instrument,
whether it be the caver's body or some manufactured
device, which converts potential energy through
friction into heat. Anyone who has used the body as a

friction device knows about heat production, and possibly about rope burns.

CLASSIC BODY RAPPEL

Although the body rappel is extremely uncomfortable, it still has its emergency uses, and may at times be used in conjunction with mechanical rappelling devices. To achieve the correct rope configuration, the caver faces the rope's anchor with his back to the drop. The rope passes through his legs, around the right hip, and then goes across his chest from the lower right to the left shoulder. From here the rope passes diagonally to the right hand, which is held at approximately waist level. The caver's left hand is placed on the rope in front of him for balance. By allowing rope to slide through the right hand, the caver thereby regulates his speed of descent. (The pressure will tend to make you assume a fetal position. Do not allow yourself to get in this position, as it is nearly impossible to straighten back up.) The caver needs nothing more than a rope to accomplish this descent, which makes it attractive for emergency use. However, this type of rappel is quite uncomfortable, and it is therefore normally used only for very, very short drops or in emergencies.

RAPPEL DEVICES

Today there are many kinds of rappel devices (also referred to as descenders) available. We will go over the simpler ones first, moving to the more complicated ones later. All of the rappel devices described here are attached to the caver's seat sling or harness by means of a locking carabiner.

Carabiner Wrap

This type of friction device is quite simple, using only one carabiner. The rope is wrapped two or three times around the side of the carabiner opposite the gate. The carabiner should be of the locking type. Be sure the rope does not rub against the sling, as the nylon rope will melt through the sling very quickly. Again, one

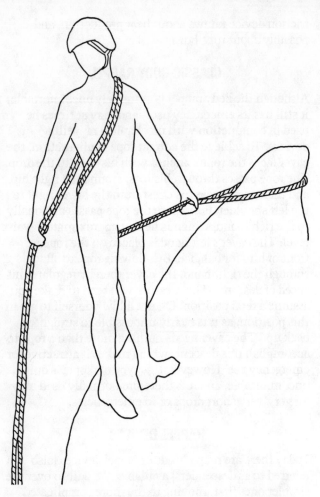

Basic body rappel. *This rappel method uses the body as a friction device. However, due to friction and heat buildup, this means of rappelling is extremely difficult and dangerous. Normally it is used only in emergencies or in short drops of five to ten feet.*

hand is held in front for balance, and the other, held low, regulates the amount and speed of the rope to be passed through the carabiner. If speed increases, making it too difficult to keep a slow pace, increase friction by moving your braking hand to position the rope across some portion of your body. This method can be employed with any mechanical rappelling device.

Although the carabiner wrap method is used by many military personnel, it is not recommended as a standard means of rappelling. Not only is it not as safe as other methods, but it weakens that particular carabiner through heat and abrasion, and it weakens the rope.

Brake Bars

Brake bars are simply round aluminum rods approximately 4 inches long with a hole drilled through one side to fit a carabiner. The other end of the brake bar has a slot machined across it to allow it to lock into the other side of the carabiner. The rope is placed through the carabiner, up over the brake bar, and back through the carabiner. Because of the machined slot in the brake bar, it can hinge up so you can simply put the bight in the rope, push it through the carabiner, and snap the brake bar back in place. This is much simpler than threading the rope through, starting at one end. *Be sure the brake bar is situated correctly.* If the rope is inserted backward, the brake bar will snap open as soon as any force is put on it. The carabiner brake bar setup is clipped into the caver's harness via a locking carabiner. If locking carabiners are not available, as a second choice use two nonlocking carabiners with gates reversed.

A caver may use, as needed, any number of these carabiner brake bar setups. They should be connected with continuous links or locking carabiners. Generally one brake bar is used with double ropes. Double brake bar setups should usually be used with a single rope.

Figure 8

The figure 8 rappelling device is becoming quite popular for short to intermediate drops. To rig the figure 8, a bight is taken in the rope and passed through the large ring on the 8; the smaller ring is then stuck through the bight. The small ring is clipped into the harness again, and the caver uses one hand for balance and one for control. The figure 8 is exceptionally safe, as it is nearly impossible to hook up incorrectly.

Longhorn 8

The longhorn 8, manufactured by Mountain Safety Research, is essentially an extension of the idea of the figure 8. It has curved catches on it so that the rappeller can wrap the rope around these hooked catches to slow or stop the descent completely. (Again, remember that nylon on nylon melts.) The main advantage of the longhorn 8 is that it does not have to be unsnapped from your seat sling to hook in.

All of the foregoing rappel devices are static; that is, they produce essentially uniform friction, and do

Figure 8 descender. *This very popular descending device is used for short to intermediate drops. It is extremely safe, as it cannot be hooked up incorrectly.*

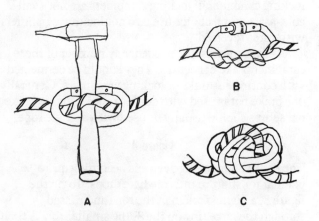

Improvised rappelling devices.

A. Use of a hammer handle and carabiner; B. Carabiner wrap where the carabiner is used as the sole source of friction; C. Use of four carabiners to create friction. Note that care must be taken to position the gates properly so that the force of the rope will not open them.

not allow the device itself to change in such a way as to produce more or less friction. Some increased friction can be obtained by using the controlling hand to pull harder on the rope to make the rope turns tighter, but this does not involve a mechanical change in the rappelling device.

For serious vertical cave exploration where substantially long drops are encountered, such as those of 150 feet or more, it is important that the caver use some sort of variable friction rappel device. In use on a long drop, the rope arrangement through the device at the top of the pitch is arranged to create less internal friction because the mere weight of the standing rope hanging below the friction device may be quite significant, causing increased friction. Indeed, this weight may be sufficient to lock up a rappel device completely and prevent any rappel, unless the rope is forcefully fed through the device, a very tiring and inefficient method. As the caver rappels down, the amount of rope hanging below is continuously reduced, hence the weight becomes less. Because of lessened weight and hence lessened friction, speed will increase unless the mechanical descending device is adjusted to create more internal friction. For these reasons, as well as the fact that they dissipate the heat more effectively as a result of their larger sizes, most serious vertical cavers use one of the rappel devices described below.

The Rack

This is more properly known as the rappel rack and was designed by John Cole in 1966. It is essentially a U-shaped piece of round steel bar upon which a series of brake bars is added. Cavers usually use a series of six bars. These bars are positioned so that they swing open in opposite directions alternately, and the rope goes over one and under the next. The bars are also able to slide up or down. Holding the lower brake bars in his hand, the caver is able to push them up. As the bars move upward the rope is forced to take tighter turns, thus creating more friction and slowing the descent.

By spreading the bars farther apart, the friction is reduced and speed is increased. Another method of regulating friction, hence speed, is by beginning the descent with four or five bars when the rope below weighs enough to create increased friction. As the caver descends and the friction produced by the rope decreases, he may flip in additional brake bars to produce additional friction. By pulling the free end of the rope up and over the end of the rack, the caver can lock the rack up, arrest his descent, and free both hands.

The first three bars of the rack should be slightly filed in the center to produce small grooves in which

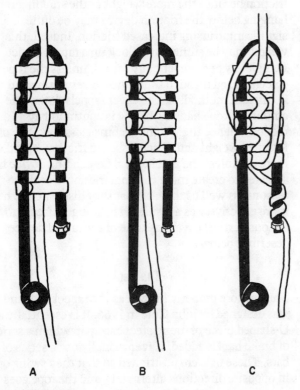

A   B   C

Rack (descender).

A. *Uncompressed brake bars allow rope to run through the rack;* B. *Compressed brake bars increase friction, slowing the rate of descent;* C.*When the bars are compressed and the rope tied off around the rack, any movement is prohibited.*

the rope should track. Never allow the rope to track off center, as this not only produces nonuniform stresses, but also may damage the rack itself through abrasion and heat. It has been reported that if the rope tracks off center, it may become very difficult to shift the bars to adjust friction. The first three bars will wear more than the others, and once worn should be switched with the bottom three at some point so as to get uniform wear. When the bars have worn down to the point where they do not cause the rope to take tight enough turns, they should be replaced.

Occasionally on long drops the weight of the hanging rope will cause the first two bars to pinch, creating much friction and heat, which is not dissipated efficiently. Not only is heat damaging to the ropes, but handling the brake bars in this situation is next to impossible, even with gloves. Many cavers are modifying their racks to suit long drops better by replacing the top two 18-millimeter bars with 25-millimeter machined square aluminum bars, or by replacing the top two independent bars with two pairs. This provides much more efficient heat dissipation because of increased mass. To avoid the pinching effect of the top two bars, one can place 20-millimeter-long brass tubing spacers between them (Montgomery, 1977).

The standard rack is U-shaped at one end and open at the other with an eye for carabiner attachment. The opening allows the rope to be moved in or out to add or subtract brake bars. Be sure when selecting a rack that the eye is of secure construction. Even if the rack itself is strong enough, some tend to begin bending with loads of 250 kilograms and fail with 500 to 1,000 kilograms by unwrapping at the eye (Stiles, 1971).

The rope should never run over the rack end, as this will weaken it. The rope should always run over a bar on the end.

Super Rack

A modification of the rack to form a super rack began to gain popularity in 1973. The super rack is again a U design; however, the point of attachment is at the bottom of the U, and the two free ends are threaded and nuts are screwed in place to prevent the bars from coming off. Generally there are five 25-millimeter square aluminum brake bars present, and all are always used. The bars are notched to position the rope and avoid the square corners. Spacers are generally positioned between the first two bars to prevent pinching. Because of the increased mass of aluminum in the bars, heat dissipation is much improved.

The super rack works well on long drops where hanging rope weight is encountered; however, near the bottom or on short drops when rope weight is slight, some cavers report that because of the decreased friction, speed is often much harder to regulate, and the caver may descend too rapidly.

Whaletail

The whaletail was originally invented in the United States, but was modified to its present form in Aus-

Super rack (descender). *This rappel rack has large bars for increased heat dissipation. For this reason, it is generally used on long drops.*

tralia. The whaletail is a piece of aluminum with a series of slots machined into it so friction can be varied according to the number of slots through which the rope is wound.

RAPPELLING TECHNIQUES

Rappelling is one of the easiest, most exciting areas in vertical cave exploration. It is also a very safe aspect of vertical caving if the caver uses good judgment. Although a substantial percentage of caving accidents happens during rappelling, most of such accidents can be divided into two general categories. The first involves novices who do not have the proper equipment and have had no instruction in the proper techniques. The second involves experienced individuals who through overconfidence fail to follow safety procedures.

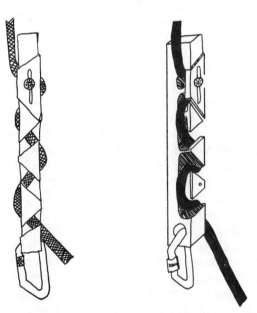

Whaletail descender. *This descending device is commonly used in Australia. Note that the gate at the top must be locked for security.*

When the bottom of a pit cannot be seen or there is any possibility that the rope will not reach the bottom of the drop, it is a very wise procedure to tie a figure 8 knot in the end of the rope, forming a small loop. Many a caver has rappelled off the end of the rope without such a precaution.

To initiate a rappel the caver first faces the properly anchored rope with his back to the drop, which should be well back from the preparing caver. He then takes the rope and properly positions it through the descender he is using. The descender should be attached to his seat sling by means of a locking carabiner. *Once the rope is threaded through the descending device, make sure the locking carabiner is locked.* At this point the caver should take up all slack in the rope between the anchor and himself by feeding the rope through the descending device.

Now the caver needs to arrange the standing rope through his braking hand into the desired configuration about the body. (The braking hand is generally the individual's favored hand.) Many cavers favor having the rope leave the descender to travel around their side through the braking hand in such a way that substantial friction can be induced by pulling the rope around the hip toward the back. The body thereby provides increased friction. Normally simply increasing or decreasing the hand pressure on the rope will be sufficient to regulate speed. Some cavers prefer to run the rope through the legs with the braking hand directly behind the buttocks. Still others prefer the rope to pass through the legs and around the hip and thigh to the braking hand in front. Some prefer to run it around the back to the opposite hip. The body-rope configuration decided upon will stem from personal preference, the type of equipment used, and the type and length of the drop. The nonbraking hand is generally positioned on the rope above the descender for balance. This hand is not used for speed regulation or control, but simply for balancing.

Those individuals using racks will find that they

often prefer to leave their braking hand in front, below the rack. The left hand is used to cradle the brake bars, moving them up or down. Because of the rack's length, balance is not sacrificed. Make sure the descending rope does not rub against the seat sling, as it will melt through it.

The caver now begins to back toward the edge, double- and triple-checking his descender for proper rope positioning and to be sure the descender is securely attached to his seat sling via a locked carabiner. It is a good idea to check occasionally, on the way down as well.

With a brake bar setup, if the rope gets slack in it, as it sometimes does, bars have been known to slip open. Also, with brake bars, be absolutely positive about position. Many individuals have died because the rope was threaded backward in relation to the brake bars (suicide rigs); a minute force was put on the system, the bars popped, and the rope fell free.

The Edge

The caver plants his feet at least shoulder width apart, and placing his weight against the anchor, backs to the edge. Slowly, one foot at a time, he walks over the edge, allowing the rope to feed slowly through his braking hand. Oftentimes there will be so much friction the caver will have to feed the rope through the descender until he is on his way. However, never let go of the rope with your braking hand.

It is the first few steps over the edge that are by far the hardest. In reality it is quite simple—you simply walk down backwards, regulating speed with your braking hand. The initial phases of walking over the edge become a bit more intense when the edge is an overhanging lip. In the case of an overhang, simply lower your buttocks down to below the level of your feet, *gently* push off springing your knees, unplant your feet, and you will swing in and under to where you will be hanging free. When free, you simply sit in your seat sling as if in a chair and lower yourself down.

Be careful when going over a very abrupt edge with

a rack. When you come down you do not want your rack to end up halfway over the edge and become deformed and bent.

Descending

You want your rappel to be a slow and controlled one. Descent speed should not exceed about 20 yards per minute, and less is recommended. Do not try to impress your friends by bouncing out in long leaps and bounds as demonstrated on television. This and abrupt stops put great stresses on the system—anywhere from 94 to 169 percent (McClurg, 1980).

While enroute, if you find you need additional braking that exceeds what you can accomplish with your braking hand, a very quick and effective way to increase friction and hence braking is to use your leg and/or foot. Swing your leg back, hooking your foot around the rope, thereby wrapping it around the leg. If this is still not sufficient, hook the rope again with the other foot.

It is important to use proper call signals throughout the descent.

When rappelling, the caver must secure all loose clothing, hair, and electric wires out of the descender's area. Anything loose tends to be pulled into the descender where it then jams. If this should occur, the first and most important step is to stop and evaluate the situation.

In the case of caught hair, action must be taken immediately. The only feasible solution is to cut, carefully break, or pull the hair out. If the situation is allowed to continue, your scalp will be pulled into the descender, producing a painful bald spot. If an ascender is at hand, you may be able to attach it and move upward far enough to untangle yourself by releasing weight on the descender. Using hair ties or tucking the hair up under the helmet are highly recommended precautions.

Many experienced cavers recommend gloves to avoid rope burns and abrasion. There is some basis for the wearing of gloves on the braking hand; however, especially on shorter drops, if you need gloves to avoid rope burns from abrasion, you are probably exceeding a safe descent rate. Personal preferences will decide this issue; however, simply wearing gloves does not mean you are able to travel any faster.

Heat is produced through friction during a caver's descent. It is important to monitor the heating of descending devices, as they have the ability to become hot enough to melt through a rope. If the descender is exceptionally hot, it is also important not to stop and remain in one exact spot, as this permits the hot bar or area on the descending device to affect a very small section of the rope. This may appreciably weaken or damage the rope.

Just in Case

It is a very wise idea to carry your vertical ascending gear with you on any substantial drop of 50 feet or more. If you find that your rope does not reach bottom, you merely switch over to ascending gear and ascend back to the top. When switching over to ascending from descending, you must suspend your weight from the main rope above the descender (through the use of an ascender attached to the main rope) in order to unweight the descender and disengage it.

Crossing a Knot

It is not uncommon in deep pits and technically rigged caves that the need arises to cross over a knot in the rope while on a rappel. The principle is the same as switching from descending to ascending. In order to descend past a knot, the caver must stop above the knot by about a body length, and attach his ascenders. (If you are going to pass over a knot, you should already know this, and it would be prudent to have already donned your ascending system.) At least one ascender must be attached to the main rope above the descender to allow disengagement of the descender after unweighting. Once you have attached your ascenders and detached your descender, you simply prusik downward, passing the knot by detaching and

reattaching each ascender below the knot, one by one.
Once below the knot you reengage your descender,
place your weight on the locked up descender, remove
your ascenders, and continue on down.

Belaying

In learning to rappel, it is psychologically reinforcing
to have the rappeller belayed through the use of a separate rope. However, it has been found that the belay
rope often causes problems with entanglement and
dislodging rocks; these are often considered to present
greater danger to the rappeller than does lack of belay
with a separate rope. Therefore, in the modern use of
SRT the belay systems using an additional rope are generally not used, except in special circumstances. Obviously this means that any failure in the primary system
will possibly result in catastrophic results. Therefore,
the primary system must be of fail-safe design.

While a separate belay system is not generally
used, the descending caver should be belayed from
below whenever possible. This bottom belay is quite
effective (provided, of course, that there is no equipment malfunction). The belayer holds the bottom of
the rappeller's rope and monitors the caver's descent. If
the caver yells, "Falling," or the belayer sees the caver
out of control, he needs merely to add tension to the rope.
The belayer is essentially doing the same job that the
caver's braking hand does; however, the belayer can increase tension to a greater degree than can the rappeller.

Increased tension on the rope creates increased
friction, hence the descending caver comes to a stop.
The belayer can actually control the descent of an
unconscious caver all the way to the cave floor quite
effectively. Remember that on longer drops the belayer
must take up rope stretch before tension can be
achieved. *It is extremely important that the belayer be
clear of the rockfall area below the descending caver.*

Self-Belay

It is generally a more accepted procedure for the
descending caver to use a self-belay. To do this, the

caver attaches some type of ascender or prusik knot above his rappel device, holding it in the disengaged mode; if control is lost, he merely needs to engage it by letting go, and the ascender will bring the caver to a halt.

In recent years the effectiveness of this system has been questioned. It is often a natural instinct to hold on even tighter to this self-belay device, since it is your balance hand. When gripped, it will not engage. The most effective self-belay device is a modified Gibbs ascender called a spelean shunt. A quick release Gibbs is used with a locking carabiner passed through the eye and around the housing. A piece of webbing is tied from the eye to the chest harness. If control is lost the caver merely leans back, engaging the Gibbs. The carabiner provides a handle to release the activated Gibbs. The chest harness should be attached to the seat harness for safety.

Reaching the Bottom

When descending into a pit and reaching the bottom, be careful that as you get off the rope it does not spring upward out of reach. If the rope is not sufficiently long, it may spring out of the caver's reach when body weight is removed, due to the stretching characteristics of nylon ropes (especially dynamic types such as Goldline). This is embarrassing at best, and could present a serious problem.

INSTRUCTION AND PRACTICE

It is important that the novice caver seek instruction in the equipment and techniques of caving. Every caver should know his equipment implicitly. He should be able to work with his equipment blindfolded, as at some point the caver may well find himself in the situation where he has no light and must finish a descent or ascent in the dark. Underground is no place to learn to use a new piece of equipment. *Practice with your equipment outside on open rock and drops. Do not go underground until you are thoroughly familiar with any new equipment and new caving techniques you intend to use there.*

14
VERTICAL CAVING TECHNIQUE: ASCENDING

I N MOUNTAINEERING or rock climbing, the climber generally climbs up first and then climbs down. If the ascent is too difficult, the climber remains safely on the bottom. In caving, once the caver rappels down, he must regain the top to end his trip. We once heard of a group of so-called cavers who managed to rappel into a 500-foot sótano in South America. They were at the bottom when they realized they had neither sufficient knowledge nor equipment to return to the top. Details are sketchy, but apparently after a number of days a helicopter entered the large pit to rescue the victims. Quite embarrassing.

While descending is quite simple, ascending (prusiking) is another matter entirely. The majority of this chapter will be devoted to the equipment and techniques commonly used to get the caver up a fixed standing rope.

The vertical caver generally uses three separate ascending devices consisting of knots or ascenders of mechanical construction. The knots are simple, safe and economical. While they lose points in efficiency when they need to be removed and reattached, they are still important to know, understand, and respect as a tool to be used, especially valuable in emergency situations and rescues. Any caver who will be involved with any type of vertical caving should be familiar with ascending knots and should be able to use them any time. We will then consider the systems used in conjunction with the ascenders to achieve upward progress on a rope.

KNOTS

The Prusik and Related Knots

The prusik knot was developed by Karl Prusik in Austria. He reported on a simple ascending system using the prusik knot in the *Austrian Alpine Journal* in 1931. Although this original system was important in his time as a way for a climber to achieve a self-rescue ascent out of a crevasse, the ultimate purpose is the same today as it was then—to go up. As described in Chapter 9, the knot is tied using a continuous sling of a smaller diameter rope tied around the standing rope. The knot allows itself to be moved up or down when unweighted, but will lock up when weight is applied.

It should be noted that most of the laid rope in the United States is right-handed, upon which right-handed prusik knots hold better. The bottom half of the knot should spiral around in the same direction as does the laid rope.

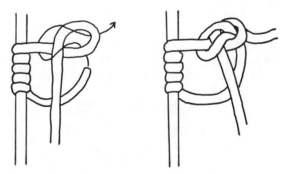

Helical knot. *This ascending knot serves essentially the same purpose as a prusik knot.*

The other popular ascending knot composed entirely of rope is the helical knot. When tied correctly the helical knot's holding power is far greater than that of the prusik. It is considered by some individuals to be easier to loosen and move. This knot uses a piece of cord sling material and is usually initiated by wrapping the free end downward; it is then secured. It is important that the proper amount of slack be incorporated in the knot, for if it is constructed loosely it will tend to slip, and if tied too tightly it will be difficult to move and will jam. There are differences of opinion as to how well the knot works; however, many cavers use it and are happy with it.

Bachmann Knot

The Bachmann knot is a semimechanical knot using a carabiner as well as the sling. The carabiner is clipped into the sling and then the sling is wrapped downward around both the standing rope and the carabiner. As the sling is wrapped around, it is clipped through the gate of the carabiner on each sucessive wrap. The side of the carabiner opposite the gate is the side wrapped with the rope. The carabiner is not used as a handle, as the knot will slip when weight is applied to the carabiner. To move the knot, the caver grabs the sling closely below the carabiner and pushes the bottom of the carabiner upward. By incorporating the carabiner, the chances of the sling rope locking completely up, as the prusik and helical knot sometimes do, are reduced. Use of the carabiner aids in loosening the knot much more efficiently. Thrun (1973) mentions that through rearrangement of coils the knot may reverse itself without requiring untying, and because of the

Bachmann ascending knot. *This semimechanical ascending knot employs the use of a carabiner to loosen the knot.*

carabiner's weight, the knot may slip down the rope unless it is attended.

Sling Rope Selection

The selection of ascending sling material for the purpose of tying ascending knots is a controversial subject at best. Generally the diameter of slings will be ¼, 5/16, or 3/8 inch (6, 7, or 8 millimeters) with 5/16 inch (7 millimeters) probably the best all-around size.

Nylon slings are perhaps the most durable of the synthetics, but nylon has more stretch than the other types, has a tendency to jam at times, and its efficiency in ascending systems may be reduced because of its stretch.

The basic chemical makeup of polypropylene and polyethylene ropes is similar. They are unaffected by water and possess limited stretch, but both are soft and hence suffer from abrasion more than some other types of sling material. They tend to grip extremely well, but they will melt through quite easily if they ever slide down the standing rope. Tenstron, which is in the polypropylene family, is quite popular as ascending sling material and is available through many caving suppliers. When using any poly-type rope and cord, be constantly vigilant and always monitor its condition for possible damage.

Manila, sisal, cotton, dacron, and Mylar cords generally are not used or recommended today, although some cavers still use high-quality manila for prusiking. There are other fibers on the market, but investigate them thoroughly before employing them in your system.

MECHANICAL ASCENDERS

There are several brands of mechanical ascenders on the market today, as well as some homemade ones. Most of the mechanical ascenders currently used work on the same basic principle. They use a camming device to pinch the rope, which creates enough friction to obtain a static hold. Mechancial ascenders are preferred over knots by the majority of cavers because they can be loosened and moved up and down with relative ease. Many can be quickly detached and reattached to the rope using only one hand. Their life is longer than that of knots; however, when worn they cost much more to repair or replace, and they are bulkier and heavier than knots.

Jumar Ascenders

The most popular and one of the oldest mechanical ascenders is the Jumar ascender. It has been made in Switzerland since the end of the 1950s. This ascender consists of a cast aluminum body incorporating a cast steel, spring-loaded cam with a plastic spring safety clip, which when closed prevents the cam from being accidentally retracted fully and hence prevents the ascender from becoming detached from the rope. There is a hole at the top of the body of the Jumar for attachment in hauling applications. There is also a hole at the bottom of the Jumar body, under the handle section. The Jumar should be rigged so that body weight is suspended on a cord or webbing, which is threaded up through the slot around the handle and back through. The caver should avoid any rigging where the loading is on the thinner piece of casting along the bottom. Direct carabiner attachment to the Jumar should be avoided, as metal on metal can weaken the ascender through abrasion. Balance is better accomplished by holding onto the upper portion of the Jumar body, although the handle does prevent you from smashing your hands when ascending against the rock. Jumars come in pairs that consist of a left-handed and a right-handed model. When each is used with the corresponding hand, one-handed operation is easily accomplished. The Jumar is exceptionally easy to take on and off the rope. The safety catch is retracted, thereby allowing the cam to be pulled down, at which point the Jumar can be detached or put back on.

The 1979 Jumar models have a slightly revised safety catch. They can be adjusted to hold the cam disengaged without the need of holding it with your hand. To move the Jumar up on the rope one simply pushes; to avoid any friction one can finger down the cam slightly, retracting it away from the rope. Be careful not to move the safety catch. The cam must be fingered down to move the Jumar down the rope, then released to reengage. Although the Jumar brochure states that Jumar ascenders can be used on rope diameters varying from 7 to 14 millimeters (¼ to ⁹⁄₁₆ inch), they tend to jam more readily on 13- to 14-millimeter (½- to ⁹⁄₁₆- inch) rope.

Anytime a Jumar is being attached to a rope, check to assure that the safety catch is engaged. The Jumar's strength is much reduced when used on nonvertically rigged ropes, as it twists and cuts the ropes (Ullin, 1973). It should be noted that there is a recall for the yellow 1979 model of Jumar. These should be returned for a checkup, as some have a faulty closure spring on the safety lever.

The cam on the Jumar is cast with short teeth that grip the rope. It has been found that these teeth wear the rope a bit more than the Gibbs ascender, but generally the wear is minute. The Jumar is also known to be brittle, and when dropped or when shock loading has occurred, creating severe impact, it should be retired or carefully inspected using X-ray evaluation techniques, as it may develop cracks in the body not visible to the naked eye.

One other drawback to the use of the Jumar is that it performs poorly on muddy and icy ropes. The ice and mud impregnate the teeth, prevent secure gripping, and the ascender slips. By pushing the cam tighter into the rope with the thumb, engagement can sometimes be achieved. A toothbrush is a convenient tool to have along to clean the mud or ice out of the teeth. After years of use, the teeth on the cam will become worn, which will eventually lead to slipping. Replacement cams are available from REI.

Roloff Ascenders

The Roloff ascender, manufactured by members of the Mother Lode Grotto, California, resembles the Jumar

Modified Gibbs rope shell with inserted roller. *Efficiency in many rope-walking systems can be increased by inserting a roller in the top of the Gibbs rope shell, thus reducing drag.*

with slight variations, one being the hole at the bottom to the body designed for carabiner attachment. This ascender is no longer commercially available; however, one may run across a used pair.

Gibbs Ascenders

The Gibbs ascender manufactured by Gibbs and Doll, was introduced in 1969. The Gibbs has gained great popularity worldwide, and is now almost as popular as the Jumar in the United States. It is designed to be used on rope of a diameter ranging from $\frac{3}{16}$ to $\frac{9}{16}$ inch (5 to 14 millimeters). The Gibbs ascender consists of a rounded aluminum, U-shaped rope shell open to one side, into which a cast aluminum cam is positioned and held firmly in place through the use of a stainless steel pin. Two types of pins are available. One is inserted through the shell and cam and is locked in place by inserting a spring through a hole in the pin end. The other type of pin, called a quick release pin,

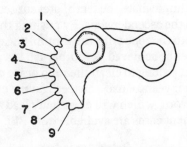

Gibbs cam. *When wear becomes noticeable on the seventh tooth, which is generally the first one to receive wear on the Gibbs cam, the cam should be replaced.*

utilizes two small, retractable ball bearings that extend out of the pin end, thereby locking the pin in place. All three pieces are attached together.

The Gibbs has several advantages over the Jumar. The first is strength. Each Gibbs is tested to 454 kilograms (1,000 pounds), whereas the Jumar is tested only to 300 kilograms (660 pounds). The Jumar is found to cut rope at a much lower load, and if the rope is cut, the Jumar has a much greater tendency to slip down the rope on the sheath.

The Gibbs cam is closed (locking the rope) by application of body weight; on a Jumar a spring locks the cam. The direct weighting of the Gibbs cam tends

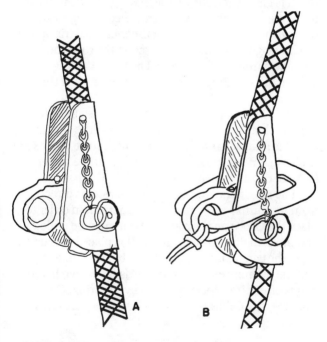

Gibbs ascender.

A. *The basic Gibbs ascender consists of an inner cam and outer rope shell. It is a very popular ascender in rope-walking ascending systems.*

B. *Gibbs ascender modified to construct a spelean shunt which is a safety rappel device permitting an out-of-control rappelling caver to stop.*

to give a much more positive closure and inhibits sheath slippage as well as giving good performance on wet, muddy, or icy rope.

Because the standard Gibbs cam is not spring loaded, it produces no drag on the rope, thereby requiring less effort to raise it. (A spring-loaded cam has just recently been introduced by Gibbs, which some cavers like for use on ascending systems where the rope is not tensioned.) The cam is designed with wide, blunt teeth, rather than the needlelike teeth found on the Jumar. These teeth are not affected by abrasion to the same extent that those on the Jumar cam are, but should be replaced when the seventh tooth is glazed and shows the first sign of wear. It has been found that the newly introduced spring-loaded cam wears faster as a result of the increased friction on the unweighted cam. As you ascend the rope the ascender simply follows you. The rope-walking system of ascending was developed because of this feature.

The Gibbs does not seem to be affected by shock loading that leads to brittle fracture, as does the Jumar, and this is an advantage. Due to this feature, Gibbs are used by some climbers as a self-belay where leader falls are commonplace.

The major drawback of the Gibbs stems directly from its clumsy three-piece construction. In order to place the Gibbs on the rope, the pin must be pulled and the cam disengaged. The shell is placed around the rope, the cam placed in the shell, the holes lined up, and the pin reinserted. This process takes two hands and is often time-consuming and very tiring. Once on the rope, the Gibbs is generally faster, requiring less

Clog ascender. *This is a relatively simple mechanical ascending device.*

effort; however, it it extremely slow and inefficient when one must pass a knot. Gibbs ascenders are stronger and much less expensive than Jumars and are quite efficient for single long drops and where extra strength is a factor. Jumars, however, are extremely versatile and their on-off time is very short, which makes it easy to pass knots quickly and to switch ropes.

CMI 5000 Ascenders

Recently Colorado Mountain Industries (CMI) introduced an ascender that resembles the Jumar, but with greatly increased strength. It is tested to 5,000 pounds (2,273 kilograms) and possesses two strong attachment holes on the bottom and one on top. When this ascender first appeared on the market, some users reported having trouble disengaging the safety catch and cam with one hand. The CMI 5000 seems to be quite good, although only the test of time will reveal its full capabilities and wear features.

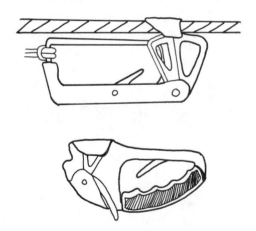

Jumar and Clog Expedition Ascenders.

Top: *The Jumar ascender is the most popular ascending device among cavers. It's versatile and easy to handle.*

Bottom: *The Clog Expedition Ascender is a popular ascending device, similar to the Jumar. However, in the Clog the body consists of plate aluminum rather than a casting as in the Jumar.*

Clog and Clog Expedition Ascenders

Clog Climbing Gear, located in Wales, manufactures two types of ascenders. The Clog Ascender is produced from a piece of plate aluminum that is rounded on both sides. The rope is positioned in one side, the cam's pivot in the other. Near the bottom is a hole designed for a carabiner; this also serves as a safety device, for the carabiner must be removed before the cam can be disengaged sufficiently to permit extraction of the rope.

The Expedition Ascender is similar with a safety catch added, the carabiner hole eliminated from the bottom, and with a handle. The authors have found the Expedition Ascender quite efficient and easy to use with one hand. To attach, simply tie cord or sling through the base of the handle.

Petzl Ascenders

Petzl ascenders are manufactured by F. Petzl in France. They are similar in construction to the Clog, except that the smaller one has two carabiner attachment holes, one in the top and one in the bottom. The safety

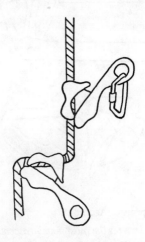

Hiebler ascender. *This ascender, which was developed in Europe, is considered by many cavers to be dangerous due to its tendency to pop off the rope. However, because of its exaggerated camming action, it is the only simple ascender that works on a steel cable.*

catch can be locked into an open position. The version with a handle is much the same as the Clog Expedition Ascender; however, there is a carabiner attachment hole at the bottom.

Hiebler Ascenders

The Hiebler rope clamp is manufactured in Germany. It possesses no cam; rather, the entire ascender tends to act as a cam. Because of the direct attachment and their emphasized camming action on the rope, Hiebler ascenders hold well under the poorest of conditions. They have even been used on a rope core after sheath failure. They reportedly also work on wire cable. This all sounds good, especially since they are inexpensive and lightweight; however, they do have severe drawbacks. You lose efficiency with every cycle up the rope, as they cam downward, and they have a reputation for popping off the rope when weighted incorrectly and when moving upward. One of the authors had a pair pop off while suspended 100 feet off a cave floor; fortunately, a safety prusik was being used. Safety pays.

Maintenance of Mechanical Ascenders

It is extremely important to inspect, clean, and maintain your ascending equipment. You should wash your ascenders in lukewarm water with a bit of detergent. This will aid in cleaning the mud and dirt away. Rinse, dry, and then lubricate them with silicone. Inspect all cord, webbing, and knots. If significant abrasion or damage is found, repair or retire before next use.

The Motorized Ascending Device (MAD)

The Motorized Ascending Device (MAD) was the first motorized device of its kind and was developed by Nevin W. Davis. This device uses a 1-horsepower, two-cycle gasoline engine to drive a V-drive pulley. The device is attached to the caver with a carabiner. The rope is threaded through its wheels and a safety Jumar cam, which will engage if motor failure is experienced. The MAD climbs at a rate of approximately 40 feet per minute, gets about 2 miles to the gallon, and weighs about 22 pounds. Although MAD has been used on several drops, it has the drawbacks of noise, weight, and pollution from its exhaust, especially when confined in small areas.

Ascender Boxes

The ascender box is used by many cavers. It is worn on the chest to keep them into the rope, thereby improving their vertical stance, which in turn improves their efficiency and total energy output. The box is made of aluminum and has two parallel pulleys. The standing rope goes through one side, and the other side is for a sling if your system incorporates this.

There are two ascender boxes currently on the market: the Gosset and the Bluewater chest boxes. Although the Gosset is about twice as expensive as the Bluewater, it is worth the price if you are serious about vertical work. The Bluewater ascender box is much more difficult from the standpoint of placing rope and slings into it. Also, it must be disassembled into four separate pieces, each of which could be dropped or lost. The Gosset is very rugged and all pieces are at-

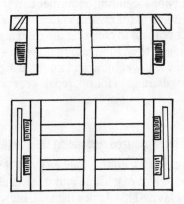

Gosset ascender box. *Attached to the chest, this aids in maintaining a more vertical position in some ascending systems.*

tached together. Another good feature of the Gosset is that either side can be opened independently of the other.

ASCENDING SYSTEMS

The ideal ascending system would be lightweight and very compact. The system would be easy to use and versatile, allowing easy crossing of knots and overhangs and providing good progress against walls. The system would be safe and fail-safe—in other words, even if one ascender failed, the system would back it up. The system would also be efficient and would give you the most vertical height per unit of energy expended.

Any system requires at least two ascenders and probably three. The caver attaches himself to these ascenders through cord or webbing, or attaches the ascender directly to a seat, chest, or foot harness. Most systems use webbing or cord running from one ascender to the feet, generally with a safety loop to the seat to prevent a back flip if one of the other ascenders fails. We will describe the exact arrangement and construction of these systems later. The sling material used for constructing your system should be static cord for efficiency; to gain the most distance for your energy you want to avoid stretch, for you give up height each time the cord stretches under your weight, inhibiting upward progress. Be aware that using static cord will transfer a shock load to an ascender if a fall is experienced. When a short fall is possible, such as climbing over the lip at the end of an ascent where the ascender may be clipped ahead as a safety, be sure to incorporate a dynamic safety loop into the system of the safety ascender.

The system used and personal preference will dictate which type of ascender is most applicable; however, ascenders that possess two points for sling attachment, one above and another below, are most versatile.

As with descending, it has been found that using a separate belay line is often more dangerous than the supposed increased safety it lends. For this reason, separate belay lines are rarely used. If your system uses only two points of attachment you should carry an extra ascender to provide a third point of attachment. We said the system should be fail-safe, meaning that even in the event of an ascender failure the system would still hold solid and would not allow the caver to fall with no support to either the chest or seat harness. In other words, both primary ascenders or at least two ascenders are attached to the chest, or more commonly the seat sling, either directly or through the use of a safety loop.

Energy, efficiency, and comfort are all related in the ascending system. The amount of energy necessary to get a caver from the bottom to the top varies directly with the system's efficiency. Although style and experience are also important, the system should make use of every bit of energy expended. Increased comfort also helps energy efficiency to a certain extent. Many things aid in making the system more efficient. The snugger the harness, the less inefficiency due to sloppiness. The lengths of cord used should be measured precisely. The more vertical the caver can maintain his body position, the more efficient the energy output per unit of vertical distance gained. Also, efficiency is generally increased by pushing the feet back and behind rather than in front of the body.

It is extremely important that vertical cavers know how to construct a number of safe, workable ascending systems. Knowledge, experience, and resourcefulness are keys to safe, enjoyable vertical caving. A wide variety of ascending systems have been developed over the past decade. There are a number of basic systems and a multitude of modified systems that work well for a variety of caving applications. We will describe a limited number of basic, solid, proven systems. If you become serious about vertical work you will undoubtedly develop your own modified system that works for you and your caving applications. We will simply try to describe a basis to build upon.

We can break down the various types of ascending systems into the alternately sitting and standing systems and the so-called rope-walking systems. The former systems are simpler and will be considered first.

The Texas System

The Texas ascending system was the original sit-stand ascending system. One ascender is attached to the seat sling, and the other ascender is attached to one or both feet. The original Texas method used only one foot. This was good for ascending against the rock, as the free foot could push away. The feet could be switched when one became tired. Today many cavers attach both feet to one ascender via an inverted Y cord. In this arrangement, one foot can be extracted, if needed, to push away from the rock face. In addition to the inverted Y cord, the lower ascender should also possess a safety cord running to the seat sling. That safety cord should remain slack unless the top ascender malfunctions. In the event of a malfunction this safety cord will support the caver from his seat, eliminating the possibility of flipping over backwards.

To use this system the caver sits down suspended by one ascender. He moves the other ascender upward by kicking his feet upward and pushing the ascender up by hand. He then stands in his foot loop, and as weight is transferred he moves his seat ascender upward and retransfers weight. This cycle is repeated over and over. Because the caver is sitting and resting for half of the cycle, the Texas system is not as tiring as one might think, although without some simple modifications this system would not be applicable for extremely long ascents due to the tiring of the arms, which must hold the caver into the rope.

Because of the simplicity of this system, it is excellent for emergency use. The foot slings can be constructed from a piece of webbing approximately 12 feet in length. Tie a figure 8 in the middle to create the loop that is attached to one ascending device, then tie two more loops, one in each end, just big enough to squeeze your boots into. Don't forget chicken loops. Attach a sling from the seat harness to the upper ascender and a safety loop from the seat harness to the

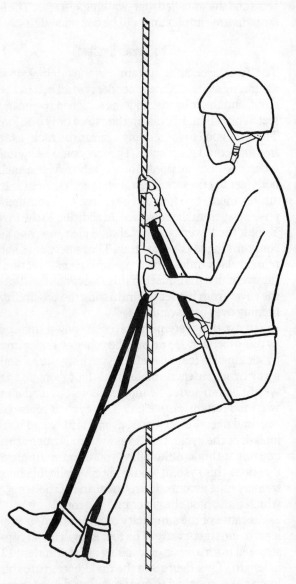

Two-footed Texas ascending system. *This is a basic two-ascender system in which both feet are attached to the same ascender. Due to its simplicity this system is very versatile. A third ascender should be carried for added safety. Chicken loops should be worn around the ankles, as illustrated.*

lower ascender. Because your hands are essentially free, this system is very much safer when a third attachment is added.

The Frog System

The frog system uses two ascenders, generally Jumarn type. The upper ascender is attached to both feet, with a safety loop connected to the seat sling. The lower ascender, connected to the seat harness, is suspended just above it and connected on top to a chest harness or neck loop. This neck loop or chest harness should hold it quite tightly, so that the caver should not be able to stand up straight when not on the rope. To avoid possible strangulation in the event of the chest Jumar's seat attachment breaking, the neck loop should be rigged with a buckle or some other device so that it will break at a little less than body weight. This system is constructed well for getting on and off the rope quickly, even in squeezes, because both ascenders are positioned above the waist. For crossing obstacles, knots, overhangs, and so on, this system is excellent. When preparing to stand, concentrate on standing up, pushing legs down and back rather than out in front. It is also advisable to carry a third safety ascender attached to the seat sling. This can be used in the event of an ascender failure.

When ascending, the caver must have at least two points of attachment to the rope at all times. Upon crossing a knot, ledge, or other obstacle, he needs to detach one ascender from below and reattach it above. When he does this, he has committed himself to only one point of attachment during transfer. This is definitely not recommended. Instead, he must attach his safety ascender to the rope and then transfer his primary ascender. When transfer is complete, the safety ascender can again be disconnected. It is recommended that you have this safety ascender rigged with a dynamic safety loop. It can then be used as a safety tie-in, as mentioned earlier, and in case of a fall the dynamic loop will help absorb the force and not shock load the ascender.

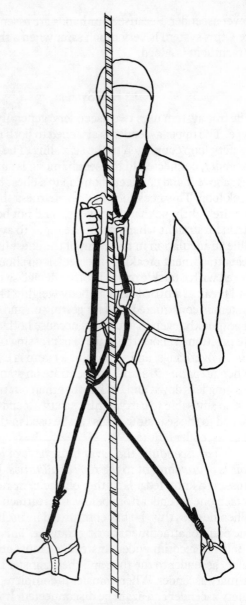

Frog ascending system. *Developed in Australia, this two-ascender system is quite versatile. The top ascender is connected to both feet with a safety loop to the seat harness. The chest ascender is attached to the seat harness; it is held taut through the use of a neck strap. Note the chicken loops on the foot harnesses.*

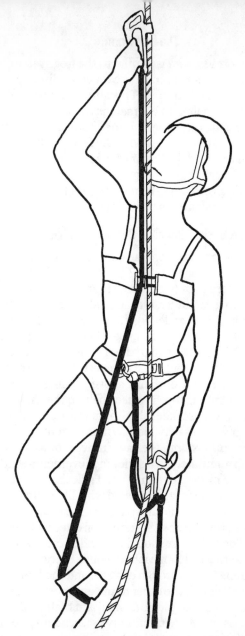

Basic Mitchell ascending system. *This is a very popular two-ascender system in which each foot is attached to a separate ascender. Note safety line from ascender to seat harness for increased safety. The chest box helps maintain an upright position.*

The Inchworm

The inchworm system is similar to the frog system, except that the foot ascender is connected directly to a bar, and is worn on the feet. This aluminum bar, called the Mar-bar, is bolted to a Jumar via a U bolt at the bottom; passing through the Jumar from either end of the bar is a cord that rides above the feet. As the feet are moved up, so is the Jumar Mar-bar.

We now begin our description of the rope-walking system, which employs the movement of each foot and leg independently of the other.

The Basic Mitchell or Cuddington Phase I

The basic Mitchell system, also called the Cuddington Phase I, was described in 1967 by Dick Mitchell. The original system uses two ascenders and a chest harness with a locking carabiner. One ascender is attached to the left foot, the ascender positioned down as low as is comfortable, just above the knee when standing. The other ascender is attached to the right foot, the foot sling running up through the chest carabiner with the upper ascender positioned just above the chest carabiner. The standing rope is placed behind the carabiner. The lower ascender should also be attached to the seat sling via a safety loop. With a system constructed in this fashion, the caver moves the ascenders and feet up alternately in a series of movements that resemble the motion of climbing a ladder.

Because of the friction created with lines running behind and through the chest carabiner, cavers added a chest box to the Mitchell system soon after its introduction. The chest box should be divided into two sections, with a roller in each to reduce friction. The standing rope is run through one side and the long foot sling is run through the other to the upper ascender. The ascender box should be as snug and high on the chest as possible. As with other two-ascender systems, a third, safety ascender connected to the seat sling with a safety loop should be carried.

The Cuddington Phase III System

It has been found that when ascending pitches that are not vertical, or when crossing knots, overhangs, and so forth, the chest box or chest carabiner of the Mitchell system do not work efficiently. When ascending such pitches the caver can convert to the more efficient Cuddington Phase III system by simply removing the standing rope and the foot stirrup sling from the chest box and attaching his third Jumar—which is often referred to as a safety Jumar, and is connected to his seat harness—to the long foot stirrup sling. The length of the safety loop should be such that this third Jumar is positioned on the sling slightly below the upper Jumar. The third Jumar provides a safety backup and allows better balancing and an easy resting position. It is adjusted on the long foot stirrup to position the body in a comfortable upright position. This ascender can be detached and used as a primary ascending Jumar. These three Jumars provide great versatility, since you may interchange between Texas, Mitchell, Cuddington Phase III, and other modified systems.

The Floating Gibbs Rope-Walker System

The original rope-walking system introduced by Gibbs and Doll used one Gibbs attached directly to one foot and the other Gibbs strapped to the opposite knee with a weight-bearing stirrup running down to the foot. The knee band was used for nothing more than to aid in the raising of the ascender. It was not intended to take any weight. It was this ascender, which did not work effectively for many cavers, that led to the development of the floating cam. Today this knee Gibbs is still positioned at knee level, attached to the foot via a sling and stirrup of 1-inch webbing safetied by a chicken loop. But this knee Gibbs has an elastic cord attached to it at one end, with the other end of the elastic attached to the seat sling or chest harness. There is no attachment to the knee.

There should be a safety loop from this Gibbs to the seat sling for safety. The elastic cord, commonly called shock cord, should be at least 5 to 7 millimeters

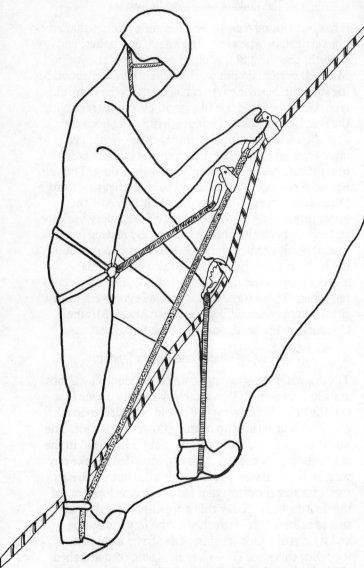

Cuddington Phase III ascending system. *Through the use of a third safety ascender, the basic Mitchell ascending system can be converted to the Cuddington Phase III ascending system which is much more efficient on high-angled slopes. To do this, the caver removes his ascending sling and rope from the chest box used in the basic Mitchell ascending system and attaches his third safety ascender to the long ascender sling removed from the chest box.*

(approximately ¼ inch) in diameter. Through the use of this shock cord, the Gibbs is automatically pulled up, eliminating the need to use your hands. The best method of attaching the shock cord to the Gibbs is through the use of a small metal plate, which is drilled so that the Gibbs pin fits through it and is held securely under its head. You should not tie directly to the top of the eye in the Gibbs cam, as this will tend to lever the cam off the rope. This could possibly result in the Gibbs slipping. Some cavers attach the elastic cord to the pin-retaining chain.

The original system also lacked a third point of attachment, which is an important safety feature. Now a third Gibbs is attached most commonly to a shoulder strap, which is secured to the chest harness and is oftentimes an integral part of the harness. The cam of this upper Gibbs is sewn into the shoulder strap by means of sewn tapered webbing. When in operation, this upper Gibbs floats as the caver ascends. This ascender not only adds safety but also aids in maintaining the caver's vertical body position.

Today the Gibbs attached directly to the foot generally has the cam sewn into a continuous band of 2-inch-wide webbing. This band should be sewn to fit snugly around the boot and should have an integral buckling chicken loop.

As previously mentioned, the elastic from the floating knee Gibbs may be anchored to the seat harness or the chest harness. If attached to the seat harness, it is neat, very simple, and out of the way. If tied to the chest harness, the elastic shock cord is longer and has more pull, which makes it a bit more efficient; however, some cavers prefer not to use the longer version because it is more cumbersome.

The upper Gibbs oftentimes produces considerable friction, as the rope drags against the top edge of the housing when ascending. Isenhard (1974) suggests cutting a notch in the top of the shoulder Gibbs and inserting a small pulley wheel. This pulley wheel will be the portion of the Gibbs to come in contact with the rope and will greatly reduce friction and drag.

The strap to which the shoulder Gibbs is attached

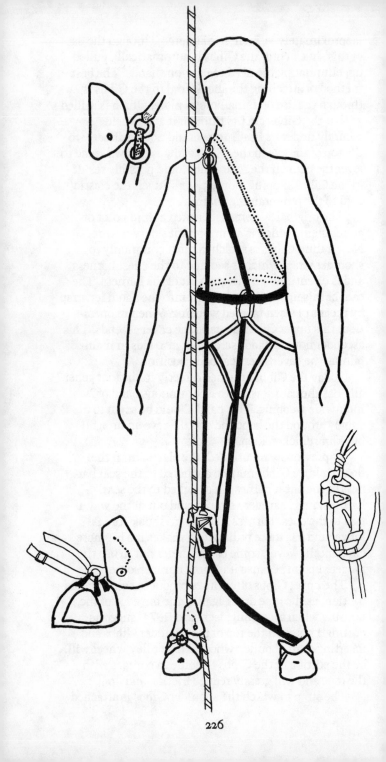

should be anchored directly into the seat harness cara-biner, go over the shoulder, and buckle into an adjust-able buckle attached to a strap sewn into the rear seat harness. Rigged in this fashion, the caver can unbuckle the shoulder strap and move the shoulder Gibbs in front of him. This phase is necessary to overcome overhangs and knots and when ascending against walls.

To make upward progress, the caver, once at-tached, stands up as tall as possible, thereby moving the shoulder cam up as far as possible. He then moves the left leg up as far as possible, moving the floating Gibbs up, and lifts his right foot up with the Gibbs on it until the foot Gibbs touches or nearly touches the floating Gibbs. The caver's arms are positioned above the top Gibbs and used for balance. To rest, the caver merely sits down, his weight held by his seat harness suspended by the shoulder Gibbs.

If the caver has trouble moving the lower Gibbs up the rope near the bottom of the pitch and there is no one to help by placing downward tension, as would be the case with the last man, he can tie a pack on the end. Be sure the pack can be pulled up easily later. It is better if the caver takes the rope and makes a loop in it, placing his left foot in the loop to create tension, allowing the right foot to move up easily.

The Gibbs floating cam rope-walking system is an exceptionally fast ascending system, winning the NSS prusiking races year after year with speeds for the 100-foot race of under 30 seconds. It is extremely efficient for long drops, free drops, or vertical drops without obstacles such as knots, rope protectors, redirected anchors, and so forth.

The rope-walking ascending system. *A method for ascending a fixed rope which is considered very efficient. However, this system is more difficult to use when crossing knots and other obstacles than are some of the other systems. It is quite efficient for single drops. Shoulder ascender helps maintain an upright stance. Middle ascender, attached to the left foot, and with safety cord to the seat harness, is floating. Bottom ascender is attached to the right foot.*

The Three-Knot System

As previously mentioned, it is extremely important that all vertical cavers know how to rig ascending systems with minimal equipment. The three-knot system is one of these systems. The caver needs only a piece of webbing to form a simple chest harness, and three pieces of cord for tying prusik knots. The caver ties a prusik knot and attaches the loop to the chest carabiner. He should be able to push this knot easily all the way up so that there is no slack in the prusik loop. He then ties another prusik, and in the other end of the prusik loop he ties a figure 8, into which his foot fits snugly. He follows the same procedure for the remaining foot. The lengths of these slings must be arranged so that they are able to move up and obtain as full a bite as permitted by the body, and not be stopped short by another knot.

The foot sling knots should, when pushed up on their cycle, fall a few inches below the chest prusik knot. The lower foot sling should be slightly shorter than the upper foot sling, so that when both feet are level with each other the foot sling knots fall an inch or two apart on the rope, just under the chest prusik.

The caver begins the system of ascending by standing up and moving the chest knot up as high as possible, then moves one foot knot up, then the next. Both feet should be together now. The caver then stands up, pushing the chest knot up, and begins the cycle over again.

If lengths are correct and the caver practices this system, it will actually work quite well. The three-knot system has been used to ascend 1,000,-foot pits with no problems.

Emergency Ascending Systems

A caver should never find himself without the equipment necessary to get up a drop, but sometimes these situations occur in very unusual circumstances. Montgomery (1977) describes an emergency ascending system that may work as a last resort. If a caver finds himself confronted with a situation in which, if he remains at the bottom, he will have no chance of surviving, then a poor, semidangerous ascending system would be the natural choice. With one mechanical ascender or knot attached to a seat sling and chest sling if possible, the caver gains foot purchase by wrapping the rope around the foot with the knee bent, then stands up and moves the ascender upward. Another method to gain foot purchase is to pull a loop of the standing rope up above the head, construct a hitch above the head, and step into the lower loop standing up. By moving the hitch upward the caver may obtain two or three steps before he must retie the hitch.

If a length of standing rope is on the ground at the drop's base, a section can be cut and tied to form a simple seat harness or chest harness. Depending on the type of rope, it may be possible to use it to tie a six- or eight-wrap prusik knot, which should hold to some extent. Resourcefulness may well be the other key to the problem.

OTHER ASCENDING TECHNIQUES
Rappel to Prusik and Prusik to Rappel

For any number of reasons it may become necessary for the caver to reverse directions on the rope. The process is actually quite simple once mastered. The caver should practice these techniques in daylight and close to the ground until he has them mastered and can do them blindfolded. One rule must be strictly adhered to: *the caver must always have two points of attachment to the rope except when on rappel, and then a self-belay such as a spelean shunt should be used.*

When the caver finds he must switch from descending to ascending, he stops and attaches an ascender above the descending device and continues to descend until the weight is taken off the descending device. He then must attach another ascender or safety knot to the rope, then remove the descender, finish attaching his ascending system, and proceed upward.

To switch from ascending to descending, the caver suspends his weight from the upper ascender and attaches his descending device to the slack rope below, locking it up. He then uses his ascenders to back down the rope until his weight is suspended from his descending device. He then disconnects his ascenders and rappels down.

Crossing a Knot

Crossing a knot while ascending is extremely easy, as the ascenders are simply detached and reattached on

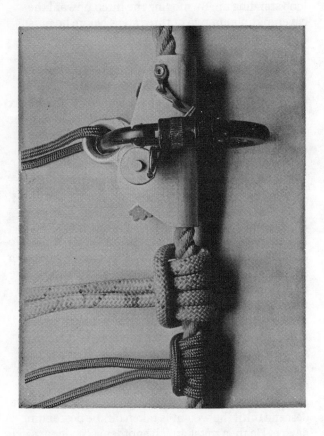

Top: *Spelean shunt used as a safety device for rappels in which a belay rope is not being employed;* Center: *Four-wrap prusik knot tied with 8-mm power cord;* Bottom: *Six-wrap prusik knot tied with 6-mm power cord.*

the other side of the knot, one at a time. For some ascending systems, such as the Gibbs floating cam system, the lower ascender may be quite difficult to maneuver past knots, and the techniques should be practiced until it is a straightforward operation.

Overhangs

Negotiating overhangs and lips is never any fun. In general, when approaching an overhang, the caver can push against the rock with his feet or one hand. This will pull the rope away from the rock, and the upper ascender can then be pushed up, since the weight is no longer pushing the rope into the rock. The other ascenders should follow easily. If the overhang is squared off and no rock from which to push off is available, the first choice is to reach above the overhang and attach an ascender, accomplishing the same outcome as was just described. If this is not possible, one may have to resort to gymnastics to surmount the obstacle. If possible, leave a second rope rigged parallel to the main one, such as a tail of the main rope near the lip. The caver can then transfer an ascender to this secondary rope, and by transferring his weight to this he will be able to move his other ascenders up the primary rope. At this point he may use either rope to finish his ascent.

Speed and Efficiency

Underground is no place to set a speed record. The ascending caver should set up a smooth, rhythmical progression that eliminates rope bounce. Every time the caver's weight is transferred, the rope will tend to stretch and retract, which initiates rope bounce. If the caver tries to move at an extremely fast speed, he not only becomes exhausted but becomes uncoordinated in his ascent cycles, which adds dramatically to rope bounce. As discussed in Chapter 11, rope bounce abrasion is the vertical caver's most dangerous enemy. The caver should concentrate on eliminating rope bounce as much as possible and should never use the springing action to help in upward progress. The caver should develop a smooth, coordinated cycle that is not so fast as to exhaust, but on the other hand is not too slow, since prolonged periods on the rope are extremely tiring as well. Twenty feet per minute is a good even speed. On shorter drops of under 200 feet, a slightly faster speed will be preferred by some, and on longer drops of 1,000 feet or more, a slower speed may be preferred.

Style and coordination aid in efficiency, but so does the system used and its bite. A good bite with each cycle is 18 to 24 inches. Once initiated, this bite distance should not be difficult to maintain. Some cavers can gain bites of almost 3 feet, but this is not common.

Two on the Rope

It is quite commonplace when exploring extensive cave systems with fairly substantial drops to employ tandem prusiking as a method of decreasing total on-rope time. A good example is Sótano de las Golondrinas, with its 1,000-foot-plus free entrance drop. It generally takes a fit caver with a decent ascending system a little over an hour to make the ascent. With six cavers, it would take seven to eight hours for the party to exit if only solitary prusiking were used. The time can be cut almost in half with tandem prusiking. On occasion, even three on a rope may be safe, but we will consider two as the optimum number.

The cavers should climb the rope maintaining close contact to avoid the risk of rockfall and to keep communication easy. The system works best for free or vertical drops rather than slopes, for in the latter case the lower climber's weight on the rope may make it impossible for the lead climber to make progress, as his ascenders will be held against the rock by the weighted rope.

It is very common to run a tail or second rope parallel near the lip, where the first caver simply transfers over to the secondary rope, allowing him to reach the top much more easily.

Practice

As with nearly all techniques used in vertical caving, ascending techniques should be thoroughly practiced in the daylight before going underground. The easiest way to practice prusiking is to rig a pulley 15 to 25 feet up to a solid anchor such as a tree or roof rafter. Run one end of a rope through the pulley until the end touches the ground. The remaining portion of the rope is placed through a descender, which is also attached to a solid anchor at about 3 to 4 feet off the ground. The climber rigs himself to the rope end coming down from the pulley. He begins to prusik up the rope toward the pulley. As he does, his partner begins to let the rope through the descender at about the same rate. The climber may prusik hundreds of feet and never reach over 5 to 10 feet off the ground, and he expends as much energy as if he were actually going up from a deep pit. The caver should also practice crossing knots and switching from ascending to descending and vice versa. There is no substitute for experience.

Scaling Poles

Scaling poles are sometimes used to reach high leads. The scaling pole is usually composed of five to six sections of aluminum tubing that either screw or bolt together. A rope or cable ladder is attached to one end and is hoisted upward. The base is securely placed and the top is generally secured by guy lines. The caver climbs up and enters the passage. If others are to follow, the first caver will need to set up proper rigging and anchors. Although scaling poles have their place in serious cave exploration, they are dangerous because they are prone to metal fatigue. If they are not made from aluminum, internal rusting can be a problem. Check each section carefully before each use.

WATERFALLS

A great many caves have active water moving through them. If a caver is to explore the cave system he must learn how to work with waterfalls as safely and efficiently as possible.

When a caver is confronted by a waterfall on a drop that must be rigged and descended, his first choice would be to rig the rope in such a way that it does not come in contact with the water. This can sometimes be accomplished by the placement of primary anchors or redirecting anchors. Redirecting anchors can oftentimes be placed out on a side wall in front of the waterfall. Be sure a safety traverse line is used if the climb out to the main rope is exposed.

If all else fails and the rope must be rigged through the waterfall, the following points must be considered.

Increased Water Flow

When rigging any drop in active cave systems (those with flowing water), one should consider the consequences of the possibility of increased water flow. Many almost inactive stream cave systems will become quite active during heavy rainfall. Whether the drop has running water at the time of rigging or not, the possibility of flooding should be considered.

Force

The force of a waterfall varies with its height as well as the amount of water it contains. The caver should keep in mind that at the top of the waterfall the force is often not as great as at the bottom. If the caver is barely able to overcome the water's force on rappel at the top of the waterfall, upon beginning his ascent he may well find that the waterfall displays increased force at the bottom as compared to that at the top. If he cannot climb against this increased force, he may be in a critical situation.

Hypothermia

Hypothermia is the primary killer of cavers. Still water conducts heat twenty-five times more efficiently than air, and moving water increases this conduction rate.

Waterfall avoidance. *Descending or ascending through waterfalls should be avoided. In this illustration a caver uses a traverse line for safety to reach the rigged rope on an outlying wall.*

Consider all factors very carefully before undertaking cave exploration that incorporates vertical caving in conjunction with waterfalls. A caver who has begun his ascent or descent in a substantial waterfall may have made a commitment that could kill him, as it is often very difficult or impossible to reverse one's direction on the rope under a waterfall. Even a caver in good condition before beginning his ascent in the area of a waterfall can become numb in a very short distance and incapable of performing such simple movements as moving ascenders upward. If something is not done quickly, a caver in this situation will die from hypothermia or drowning.

Protection

Any caver who is serious about exploration in caves possessing active water should invest in a wet suit to protect against the possibility of hypothermia. The danger of chilling does not end with the bottom or top of the drop. Unless a wet suit is worn or dry clothes are available, the wet caver can become chilled very quickly.

When ascending or descending a drop where the caver will be in moving water, he may want to turn his backpack upside down. Upright backpacks that do not possess a very tight top closure will fill with water and become unmanageable.

The caver obviously cannot depend on a carbide lamp for light in waterfalls. The most common method is to use a Wheat or MSA electric lamp; these are fairly resistant to water. Experienced cavers often position a second mounting bracket to the side of the main mount on the helmet. When a waterfall pitch is encountered, the carbide is extinguished and the electric turned on.

Although waterfalls are sporting, they can also be deadly to the unprepared and inexperienced caver.

15

CAVE DIVING

CAUTION: IT WOULD BE difficult to find a mode of exploration more dangerous than cave diving. Despite the development of sophisticated new equipment and the proliferation of articles on safe diving technique, the incidence of injury and death among cave divers remains alarmingly high. We urge novice and expert alike *not* to attempt this hazardous adventure before taking courses—from a professional—in the craft. Contact the National Speleological Society, Cave Diving Section, 2832 Concord Drive, Dacatur, Georgia 30031, or the National Association for Cave Diving, P.O. Box 1813, High Springs, Florida 32643, for further information.

Cave diving using scuba equipment started in Florida in the mid-1950s. Unfortunately, as it increased in popularity, so also did the number of accidents and deaths. Interest in the sport increased dramatically in the 1960s and '70s, and it gradually became safer because of the work done by cave divers in developing techniques and more reliable equipment. Still, the risks of cave diving are not to be underestimated. Certified scuba divers continue to enter submerged caves feeling that they are qualified for this type of diving. This is just not the case. Diving in a cave is an entirely different experience to diving in open water. In a cave it may not be possible simply to ascend to the surface, and visibility may at times go from 200 or more feet to zero in a matter of seconds. Light failure can have serious repercussions, and cave systems often exist in the form of a maze, which makes retracing one's path difficult, even with fixed lines. Generally accepted emergency procedures for buddy breathing (sharing air) often are impossible to employ in restricted cave passages.

We do not intend to teach an individual to become a cave diver—entire books have been written on the subject, and a course or courses in cave diving should be attended before one decides to give it a try. Instead, we will briefly outline some of the major aspects of the sport.

The overwhelming majority of cave dives are performed in solution cave systems (see Chapter 2). The action of water on limestone in submarine cave sections is the same; however, to understand submarine caves, we must expand on a few areas and definitions.

SPRINGS

Caves associated with springs are very popular with cave divers. Generally, water from rain and other sources percolates down through the ground and begins to collect and flow under the force of gravity.

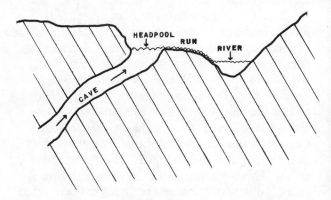

Spring. *This is a type of water-filled cave that may at times be entered by cave divers. Water exits the cave entrance where the headpool exists; the water then flows down the run to its drainage, usually a stream or river.*

This water will flow downward until it finds a weak point in the overhead rock, at which point it will emerge with the energy equal to its hydrostatic head pressure. Hydrostatic head pressure is caused by the gravitational force of the water located upstream.

The water will generally form a pool, called the head pool, where it emerges from its underground passage. From here, if it is a true spring, the water will flow downhill to a stream or river. This portion is called the run. If the head pool is covered with sufficient water during a flood, the hydrostatic pressure could be affected to the extent that the spring flow could run in the reverse direction. In other words, the pressure of the water above the old head pool will exceed the former hydrostatic head pressure. Fresh water will exert approximately .432 psi for each foot of elevation. If the hydrostatic head were 3 psi and during flood the head pool were covered by an additional 10 feet of water exerting approximately 4.32 psi on it, the flow would cease and possibly reverse.

SPRING SIPHON

A spring siphon is generally found where a river runs underground near the surface. As it flows, the water continues to eat and dissolve away the rock through physical and chemical processes, and at some weak point the overlying structure may give way to create a depression exposing the subterranean river. The result is a spring cave from which water enters the depression. From the depression water continues on into the siphon cave. The siphon and head pool are often combined in this situation.

SINK

A sink is also a depression exposing a body of water. Its formation may have been similar to that of a spring siphon; however, when the overhead collapse took place, or at some other time, the siphon became plugged and the outflow ceased, producing a calm body of water with no detectable flow. Another

possible method of formation is that a spring has lost
sufficient hydrostatic head to continue flowing.

UNDERGROUND LAKE-SUMP

Oftentimes cavers will be exploring a cave whose roof
dips, lifts, and curves along a passage and will round a
corner to find that the roof slopes down and meets the
water, stopping all further dry exploration. This point
is called a sump. Large numbers of cave systems end in
this manner. In many cases the roof will lift again
ahead, but no one knows for certain until it is
investigated. Many a caver has tried to dive sumps by
holding his breath. In some cases siphons are negotiated as a matter of course on a standard trip. While it is
often relatively easy to hold one's breath and dive
through into the next air pocket or room, these types
of sumps are still capable of killing people. Special
training is required for serious exploration of sumps.

SPECIAL CONSIDERATIONS FOR CAVE DIVING
Visibility

Reduced visibility can cause major problems and must
be monitored at all times. By far the most common

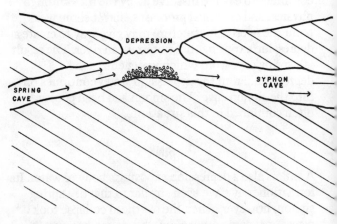

Spring-siphon. *A water-filled depression joins a spring cave, from
which water comes to a siphon cave where the water exits.*

reason for reduced visibility is turbidity caused by suspended silt. Most water in caves is extremely clear. However, one poorly placed fin kick stirring up silt will reduce exceptional visibility to zero in seconds. We will discuss methods to avoid this below, as well as emergency procedures to survive the situation.

Some caves will have reduced visibility from the start, stemming from algae content, chemical concentrations, and so forth (Mount, 1973). These types are not very common, and exploration of such systems should be avoided.

Visibility should never be reduced due to lack of a light source.

Currents

In any siphon-spring and at times in other types of aquatic caves, a current will be detected. Currents must be accounted for. A swift current could prevent entry into a cave system, being too strong for the diver to overcome. Generally this presents no major problem, as the dive is simply called (aborted); however, if a cave diver ventures into a system with the current in his favor, he may be unable to return to the entrance,

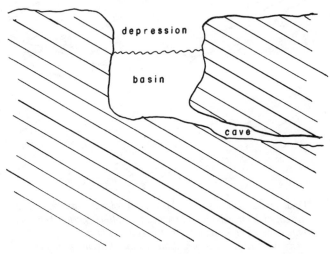

Water-filled sink. *This is a commonly dived type of water-filled cave.*

as he requires increased air when fighting the current. If the current is not monitored very carefully, the diver could run out of air and drown.

On occasion even a slight current can increase to an exceptionally strong force if it must move through a restriction.

Some cave systems have ever-changing flows. This is especially true of some caves connected to the sea. If hydrostatic pressures fluctuate, currents and direction of flow will also change. This is common where radical tide changes occur. In caves connected to the sea this can be extremely dangerous, as the current can reverse during the dive. Such systems must be investigated thoroughly before any attempt to dive them.

Physical Construction

The physical construction of the submerged cave system must be studied and potential problems understood. Large passages often lead to disorientation when walls, floors, or ceilings cannot be seen. Deep passages lead to a host of potential problems such as nitrogen narcosis, decompression sickness, oxygen toxicity, and

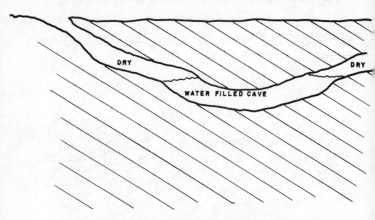

Underground lake or siphon. *Such a body of water may occur in a dry cave which ends abruptly with a water-filled section, beyond which there may or may not be dry sections. These water-filled sections constitute a cave section that may be explored by cave divers.*

many others. Divers should limit their depth to 130 feet or less. (The study of human physiology under increased pressure while scuba diving is a very complex subject; the bibliography lists some texts covering this area.)

Mazelike passages can make it easier to get lost, which is one of the most common causes of death. One should always use a continuous line while diving. Line and reel techniques are discussed below.

Physical restrictions in the cave can range from minor ones that the diver can scrape his way through to the major ones that require the diver to remove his tanks and push them ahead. Restrictions must be approached and penetrated with care.

Air

Air is the most definite limiting parameter in cave diving. Without an air supply the diver obviously will die, as he cannot simply ascend to the surface and free air. The NSS has found that the loss of air is the second most common cause of cave diving fatalities. *Air supply must be monitored continuously.* In the past there were no submersible pressure gauges (SPGs) available on the market, and cave divers used regulators without this device. They carried out extensive air consumption preplanning, which worked to some extent; however, the diver could never be absolutely sure about the amount of air he actually had. Today there is no reason why anyone should cave dive without an SPG.

In 1968 Sheck Exley, one of the world's foremost cave diving experts, proposed this rule: one-third of the starting pressure is to be used for penetration and one-third for returning, leaving one-third as a reserve for emergencies. The diver divides his beginning air pressure by three, subtracts this from his initial pressure, and thus determines his turnaround pressure. When this rule is applied to a three-man cave diving team, for example, the team must turn around when the first member reaches his turnaround pressure, thus adding some additional safety margin. It is of the utmost importance that each member have essentially the same volume of air. If one member with an efficient breathing rate enters with a single tank, and his teammate with an increased breathing rate enters with double tanks, uses one-third of his volume, and experiences a malfunction at the point of maximum penetration, the teammate with the single may not have enough reserve air to allow his buddy to buddy breathe back to the entrance. Exley's rule, allowing two-thirds for the trip out and reserve, should be considered as a bare minimum, and oftentimes the diver should allow additional reserve air depending on current restrictions and other factors.

It should also be mentioned that fatigue increases a diver's air consumption and hence decreases efficiency. Thus a fresh diver may manage penetration using one-third of his air, but he may require more than one-third to exit. If silting has occurred, the time to exit will be greatly increased, compounding the problem.

Lights

Every diver must have three separate light sources. Each light source must have the capability of lasting the entire dive. If any of the three lights will not last the entire dive, more than three lights must be carried. All lights must be waterproof diving lights. The primary light should be exceptionally rugged, reliable, and as small as possible while not sacrificing candle-power. All dive lights fail sooner or later. Out of 100 cave dives, the chance of the primary light failing is 86.7 percent. With three lights per person, the chance that all of them will fail drops to .08 percent (Exley, 1979). We recommend taking a primary light with a 30 watt beam, a strong secondary light, and two small backup lights.

Line and Reel

The lack of a line and reel has been found to be the largest single factor leading to cave diving fatalities. *Cave divers must always use a continuous single guideline.* This is your guide back to the surface and allows you to retrace your route even under such potentially dangerous situations as light failure or complete silting out. The first man in the team is the reel man. He should carry a nonjamming reel capable of carrying 500 feet (150 meters) of ⅛-inch (3-millimeter) white nylon line. Do not use natural fibers, as they will rot. Polyethylene and some other synthetic lines should be avoided, as they float and increase the chance of entanglement.

The reel man, who is also the captain, enters first, tieing off the line on a submerged rock or object, and then ties it off again just inside the cave entrance. It is important to arrange these tie-offs so that if a swimmer or other person dislodges or unties your guideline, one of your secondary tie-offs will hold it. As mentioned, the reel man is first in and should also be last out, thereby keeping everyone else between himself and the entrance, providing everyone with a continuous guideline. As the party penetrates farther, the line should be tied out of the way around small projections using as few tie-off points as possible, but as many as necessary, generally one every 50 feet. In cases of lost visibility, when a party must follow the line out, it has been found that each tie-off consumes time and hence air; therefore try to set up the minimum number of tie-offs necessary to do the proper job and reduce the chance of entanglement; make these wraps as simple as possible.

Entanglement must be carefully avoided. When you cross a line, swim over it so that you will be able to see the problem if entanglement does occur. If you become entangled, attempt to reverse the movement that initiated the entanglement. A buddy can often be of great aid in helping to free an entangled diver.

Use tape to tuck in protruding portions of equipment. Reverse your fin straps and tape them. Wear your knife on your forearm, not on your leg where it can easily be snagged. Sometimes in severe entanglements the diver may have to remove his tanks in order to untangle them. Cutting the line should be considered a last resort. If it is necessary to cut it, make sure the nylon line does not go shooting down the passageway out of sight. If the line is cut for any reason, be sure to have a grip on the portion that leads out. Make sure that all divers are between the cut and the entrance before you cut the line, whether you are cutting it to replace a frayed section or simply attempting to disentangle yourself or your buddy.

It is not always necessary to follow the line by placing it in the circle formed by touching your forefinger to your thumb. When clear water is present and silting is not expected, visual contact is sufficient. However, upon silting or light failure it is of utmost importance to get everyone on the line.

Altitude

It should be noted that some cave diving is not done at or near sea level. This necessitates a consideration that is often overlooked and rarely stressed sufficiently in the basic scuba classes. When a dive is done at altitude, the ambient pressure is reduced as compared to that at sea level. This directly affects partial pressures of the breathing gases, which directly affects tissue absorption of these gases. Special dive tables must be used and depth gauge corrections employed when diving at any level other than sea level.

SCUBA GEAR

Rapid advancements have been made over the last few years in scuba gear, especially for cave diving. Redundancy is the key to safe cave diving equipment. Backup systems should exist for every piece of equipment. Today it is recommended that every cave diver carry two independent regulators, allowing either to be shut off in case of malfunction, with the remaining one having access to the entire air supply.

Valves and Tanks

On a single tank it is important that the diver use a slingshot valve providing two separate air outlets. It should be noted that single tanks rarely provide sufficient air for any serious exploration.

On double tanks it is necessary to use a dual valve

manifold. This provides two air outlets independent of each other; however, each has access to the entire air supply.

J valves are not recommended, as they are of no use to the cave diver and provide another piece of equipment to fail or possibly become entangled with guidelines.

Most serious cave divers are currently using twin 72-, 80-, or 100-cubic-foot tanks.

Regulators

The regulators used in cave diving today are of single hose construction. Any top-of-the-line single hose regulator will do. The primary regulator used for cave diving must have an SPG, accessory inflator hose for filling your buoyancy compensator.

The primary regulator should have the second stage equipped with a 5-foot-long intermediate hose to aid in sharing air using the Rimbach method (see below). The second stage with the long hose is generally used as the primary by the cave diver. If he gets the out-of-air signal from his buddy, he already knows where the long second stage is. He simply hands it to the out-of-air victim, recovers his other second stage, and they exit the cave.

In order to avoid snagging, the diver brings the long second stage regulator under his right arm and around the neck to the mouth for normal use. It is mandatory to place a secondary regulator on the other air outlet on the manifold, so that if one regulator fails the diver simply needs to turn off the air source to the faulty regulator. Using the other regulator, he should then surface.

Both air sources should be turned on at the beginning of each dive so that air does not need to be turned on in an emergency, thereby wasting time. Also, make sure you can reach your on-off valves, so that in case of free flow you can shut off the valve leading to the faulty regulator.

As with all diving, you should know your buddy's equipment inside and out, as you do your own. Your life may depend on your buddy's equipment.

Buoyancy Compensators

Buoyancy compensators (BCs) are of three types—front units, back units, and jackets—all of which may be used for cave diving. The buoyancy compensator should have a power inflator. You should previously have used this piece of equipment extensively in open water in order to know its buoyancy and how it supports your body in relation to a feet-up position. Experiment with your BC so that you can get the desired body position before attempting any cave diving.

COMMUNICATION

Communication is one of the most valuable ways to avert problems underwater. You must be able to communicate effectively underwater in order to relay a message concerning a potential problem to your dive team. There are a number of hand signals used for cave diving communication. These are too numerous to be covered here; therefore only some of the more common ones are shown. Individuals who will be involved in cave diving should refer to *Hand Signals for Diving*, which is the current authoritative text on hand signals. You should become familiar with these and practice them with your dive buddies often. An underwater slate is practical for writing messages.

When cave diving, wave your light back and forth with a deliberate side to side sweeping action to get your buddy's attention. Do not delay in signaling to get his attention if you have a problem, for it may take a while before he realizes you are in trouble.

EMERGENCIES

Cave diving, besides having a potential for specific emergencies, such as those described below, also has the potential for any emergency related directly to open water scuba diving, such as nitrogen narcosis, decompression sickness, oxygen toxicity, carbon dioxide poisoning, embolism, vertigo, squeezes, reverse block, and others. An authoritative text should be studied for information on these potential problems.

Silting

Silt and clay are composed of minute particles derived from organic and inorganic matter. These particles are so light in weight that once suspended in water it takes a very long time, sometimes days, for them to settle back out. A careless movement with one's fin can disturb silt, causing it to cloud the water and thereby decrease visibility to zero in a few seconds. For this reason, special techniques for moving through passages have been developed. These are too numerous to describe here, but some involve different body positions, pulling along with fingers on projections, or sometimes swimming upside down. Some cave diving techniques you may run across in this regard are called finger walking, fly walking, and shoveling. The idea is to limit unnecessary movement as much as possible.

Some caves will have silt and mud even on ceilings. In this case a caver's exhaust bubbles will disturb the roof as he moves through the passage and may cause percolation and thus silting. Even with complete silting up, the diver should be able to follow his guideline back to the surface.

It is important to monitor behind you continuously for silting. It is quite easy for silting to go unnoticed until a diver turns around to return and finds he has kicked up silt and reduced visibility to zero. Immediately upon discovering silting, the entire team should get on the guideline and exit, using the Rimbach system to stay together. In this system, all team members should be on the same side of the line, one hand encircling the guideline, the other hand holding onto the diver ahead by his upper arm, or sometimes in constricted passages by his thigh. By pressing forward on your buddy, you are telling him, "Go ahead; everything is OK." By squeezing, you are saying, "Stop," and by pulling back you are communicating, "Come back, I need assistance." If you are in the lead and contact is lost with the diver behind, stop and wait until contact is made again.

If has been found that for each additional diver in a group, the time to move through a given passage increases greatly, and it increases even more extremely under conditions of limited visibility. Therefore, cave diving teams should be limited to a maximum of three or four individuals.

Loss of Air Supply

Loss of air supply should almost never occur if the dive is planned properly, air is monitored carefully, and proper equipment is used, but the possibility of this emergency does exist. Upon loss of air, signal your buddy with standard hand signals; he should then hand you his long-hosed second stage. The team should then form a single file, with the out-of-air diver in front of the donor, and should proceed directly out using the Rimbach system, if applicable. Obviously, here it becomes quite important that divers have a 5-foot intermediate hose to the second stage. Without this length it may become quite difficult or impossible to use the Rimbach system in constricted areas.

Entanglement

The chances of entanglement are greatly reduced through proper use of reels and lines; however, if you do much cave diving, entanglement may occur. When entanglement does occur, reverse the action that induced it. If this does not free you, run your hand down the line to the point of entanglement, and slowly untangle it. Rapid, erratic movements will only make the entanglement more severe. Never swim under the line, since this is a good way to begin entanglement.

If you become entangled at some point out of your range of sight and reach, such as on your back, your buddy should be there to assist. If you have to go it

Rimbach System. *This is used for exiting a water-filled cave in emergency situations where cave divers encounter loss of air or zero visibility. The diver behind holds the leading diver's arm or thigh. Slight forward hand pressure means continue. A squeeze means stop. A slight reverse pressure means reverse. The air-sharing recipient leads, the donor follows.*

alone, remove your tanks carefully and untangle the line. Donning and doffing of tanks as taught in all basic scuba classes should be practiced in open water until the exercise is mastered completely.

Cutting the line should be considered a last resort. Before cutting it, be sure that all divers are between you and the entrance, and be sure to have a grip on at least the end leading toward the entrance so that you do not lose the line. Also, if the line is allowed to shoot past your fellow divers, the possibility of it entangling with them is increased. If you must cut the line, cut it next to a tie-off point if at all possible so that the line to the entrance will remain taut.

Getting Lost

If divers are trained properly and the dive is planned correctly, you should never find yourself lost or any of your diving buddies missing. However, in case of accident or misjudgment, you must be ready to deal with the emergency that arises in this regard.

You should constantly be checking to be sure all of your party is together during a cave dive. The second you become aware that the team is missing a member, stop. Look for the missing diver's light and listen for his exhaust. If you are running a reel, tie it off. Assuming the diver does not appear shortly, and if your team has sufficient air, begin a systematic search at the point of farthest penetration where separation could have occurred. Work your way back to the entrance. If you find it necessary to search away from the line, be sure to use an emergency reel or splice spool. Use a continuous line, and never break any of the above rules. Good indications of the location of a lost diver are silting and bubbles from his exhaust caught in the ceiling.

If you find yourself separated from the group, stop and wait. Your buddies will probably appear soon. Be sure that you are in physical contact with the line. Wait until your air pressure reaches the turnaround point, then head out. If you are using a reel, tie it off and leave it; do not take it back out until you are sure everyone is out. If you are unsure of the correct direction to the entrance, there are a number of ways to determine it. Look for markers on the line. Line markers should always point to the closest entrance. If no markers are present, look for a trail of trapped air bubbles on the roof left from the penetration dive. Silting is a good indication that there was a diver present at the location in the recent past. If the current can be felt, downstream should lead to a spring and upstream to a siphon. By disturbing a small bit of silt and watching it, you may be able to detect the current when its velocity is so slight that it is not physically felt. Look for scallops on the walls; they will point downstream. Always look for your team's lights and listen for the sound of their exhaust. One method for finding the line, if you are not on it, is by using your reel or splice line. Tie off one end of it securely and begin a systematic search, utilizing a circular search pattern with the tie-off point as its center.

Getting Stuck

A diver who becomes stuck in place should first reverse the movement that resulted in his getting stuck. Buddies should avoid pulling on a stuck diver, except as a last resort, as this may increase the extent of jamming. Before proceeding through cave restrictions, study them carefully in order to avoid this problem. Sometimes it is preferable to enter restrictions feet first, since if you become stuck it will be easier to free yourself by exiting headfirst.

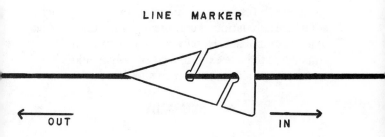

LINE MARKER

← OUT   IN →

Line marker. *This plastic marker is placed on a cave diver's line, indicating the direction in and out of the cave being dived.*

STRESS AND THE PANICKED DIVER

Increased stresses are inherent in cave diving. A panic situation is much more probable where stress is high. Panic is a direct reaction to high stress. No light, no possible direct ascent, confinement, and restriction are all sources of stress. Loss of control related to current and buoyancy control are also very serious sources of stress. For these reasons, it is probable that the percentage of divers who panic increases in the cave diving environment.

If you find yourself on the verge of a panic situation characterized by rapid, shallow breathing and increased heartbeat, stop and force yourself to take deep, controlled inhalations. Concentrate on the job at hand and slowly work toward your goal.

If you find yourself confronted by a panicked diver, his state stemming from panic, nitrogen narcosis, or some other reason, first stop and think. The only thing worse than a drowning death is a double drowning death. If you believe the panicked diver may be more than you can handle, do not attempt it. In open water situations, students are taught that if the crazed diver is too much to handle, you should monitor him until he passes out, then get him to the surface, stabilize him, and begin mouth to mouth and CPR, if necessary. This method may or may not apply in cave diving, depending on the specific situation.

To tow a diver out of the cave, the rescuer should grab the victim's tank valve with one hand and tank base with the other. The rescuer should attempt to compress the chest of an unconscious diver in order to aid in the exhalation of compressed air from his lungs to avoid embolism. However, the victim should be considered to have experienced embolism and standard first aid for embolism should be initiated.

SUMMARY

1. Attend a certified diving course for training.
2. Use proper cave diving scuba equipment.

3. Have emergency gear, know how to use it, and practice emergency procedures often.
4. Always use a single continuous guideline.
5. Use the one-third rule for air planning as a minimum.
6. Have at least three lights per person.
7. Do not dive too deep; the recommended limit is 130 feet.
8. Do not kick up silt and be aware of silting.
9. Keep a rational head.

16
POTENTIAL HAZARDS AND CAVE SAFETY

CONTRARY TO POPULAR belief, cave exploration is quite safe if simple rules are followed and good judgment is employed. However, a number of potential hazards are involved in cave exploration, including obvious ones such as falling or getting lost as well as less obvious hazards. It is primarily the less obvious ones with which we will be concerned in this chapter.

LOST

Getting lost in one of the major concerns of novice cavers. Fortunately it is a rare occurrence, although almost every caver who has been caving for any length of time has, at one time or another, been briefly disoriented. In the past, and even today, cavers occasionally encounter masses of entangled string weaving back and forth through a cave's passages. This is a sure sign that a party whose members have had no introduction to cave exploration has passed that point at some time. If the cave is small enough that balls of string will reach its extremities, it is undoubtedly too small to get lost in anyway.

When cavers retrace their route in order to exit a cave, the return route looks very different than it did while they were entering. The best method to follow in order to learn the return route is to turn around often while traveling inward in order to see what the passage looks like when headed in the opposite direction. If the party is still concerned about becoming disoriented, it is best to leave temporary, ecologically sound route markers, which should be removed in the course of the party's exit. Many cavers who find themselves disoriented will have become confused concerning the route in large rooms or at junctions. Hence it is a wise idea to mark such places, either physically or mentally. Pay attention to distinctive formations and passage configurations. The use of a compass and a note pad for jotting down information regarding the route is a great help in extremely complicated or large cave systems.

If your group finds itself disoriented, the best course of action is to sit down where you are. Once rested, and having discussed the situation and each person's ideas as to where the desired passage is located, the party can then send out small scout teams in the surrounding area to search for the correct but elusive passage. This search should be organized with the teams reporting back to the central location according to plan. The correct route is often not the most obvious one. The disoriented party is ordinarily quickly reoriented after a systematic search.

If you find yourself separated from the remainder of your caving party, you should sit down and think about your previous route. Turn your primary light down in order not to waste it, or if you have a candle, light it instead. Call out every few minutes and listen for sounds of the other members of your caving party. Undoubtedly you will be found quickly. At times you may want to use a systematic search pattern to find the main route, similar to the method used by the group. One should never cave alone, however, so if there is no danger of hypothermia, you should remain where you are and let the larger caving party do the searching.

In frequently visited caves the main route is often easy to recognize because the rock is mud-colored and at times worn smooth from caver traffic. The floor will often exhibit paths and at times these may be deeply indented. Formations may be discolored at about shoulder level, having been used as handholds by careless, muddy-handed cavers. In the past it was common practice for cavers to smoke or paint arrows on the cave walls to mark their route. This is no longer an acceptable practice, but these older markings may still be encountered. The rule is that these arrows when placed should always point toward the nearest entrance. You should never trust these implicitly, however, as uninformed so-called cavers may have pointed them in the opposite direction.

CONTAMINATED AIR

It is commonly believed that many caves possess air contaminated with one substance or another. In actuality less than 1 percent of known caves possess bad air. In this section, in addition to contaminated air, we will be discussing cave air with abnormally high or low levels of some commonly occurring component. This is done for the sake of simplicity and with the understanding that in the strict sense of the word this air is not contaminated.

Hypoxia and Elevated Carbon Dioxide Levels

Low levels of oxygen have been reported in some caves or cave portions—usually small slots or holes set down low. Carbon dioxide is heavier than oxygen; therefore, a caver breathing in oxygen and giving off carbon dioxide who is located in a depression with poor air circulation could conceivably reduce the supply or even deplete the air of oxygen. This situation is rare, as most caves possess good circulation (unlike many abandoned mines).

The human body that does not receive adequate oxygen suffers from *hypoxia*, which is defined as a deficiency of oxygen in body tissues.

Many individuals believe that a candle or carbide lamp will be extinguished due to lack of oxygen before the caver experiences any trouble in low-oxygen-level areas. This is not a good rule to follow, for as Halliday (1974) states, normal air possesses approximately 20 percent oxygen. Candles will be extinguished when the level reaches about 16 percent. Dangerous hypoxia begins when the level reaches about 15 percent, but carbide lamps have been known to burn in atmospheres possessing only 8 to 10 percent oxygen. Human death will occur at appoximately the 7 to 8 percent oxygen levels.

Halliday also states that 5 percent carbon dioxide in the atmosphere is a high enough concentration to cause serious discomfort and prevent strenuous activity, although the human body can endure concentrations as high as 30 percent carbon dioxide when enough oxygen is present.

Ammonia

Caves that possess large concentrations of bat guano sometimes exhibit high levels of ammonia, a by-product of decomposing guano. Due to its strong smell and the irritation it causes to the eyes, nose, and respiratory system, a caver generally is repelled by excessive levels of ammonia before he would ever be exposed to dangerous levels of the gas. Cavers active in guano- and ammonia-laden caves should use a proper type of gas mask to filter the ammonia out of the air.

Hydrogen Sulfide and Other Sulfur Gases

Hydrogen sulfide, which smells like rotten eggs, contaminates the air of some caves. Such caves are most often located near geothermal activity.

In areas associated with active or semiactive volcanic activity, the release of sulfur gases such as sulfur trioxide or dioxide has been reported. These gases are extremely dangerous, for when mixed with moisture, such as that of the eyes, throat, and nose, sulphuric acid is formed. If a caver detects the smell of sulfur, he should consider the cave off limits.

Methane

Occasionally a cave is found that has bubbles of gas, usually methane, trapped in the stream-bottom mud. These bubble up through the water to its surface and sometimes ignite in bursts of flame when carbide lamps are held near the water surface. Forest litter or other plant material, washed into the cave and lodged there, produces this flammable gas in the process of decomposition.

FIRES

More contaminated-air-related cave deaths have resulted from carbon monoxide poisoning than all other types of bad air combined. Carbon monoxide is lethal in extremely small concentrations, for it binds with the body's hemoglobin, the oxygen-carrying molecule in the blood. Due to the fact that carbon monoxide binds with an affinity 230 times greater than does oxygen, the carbon monoxide effectively displaces the oxygen, causing death.

In the absence of strong air movements in caves, carbon monoxide is produced and accumulates in the cave atmosphere when fires are built inside caves; hence the repeated admonition: *do not build fires in caves.* For cooking and heating of liquids, use a small backpack stove.

An accumulation of carbon monoxide can also result if the exhaust of internal combustion engines becomes directed into caves.

Guano has been known to ignite, and some reports of it exploding have been recorded. *Never light guano on fire.* In Arizona's Grand Canyon, one particular cave possessing unique giant prehistoric ground sloth remains had its guano ignited by some careless cavers. The fire burned for months despite rigorous and expensive attempts to extinguish it. Large quantities of the scientifically priceless paleontological remains were destroyed.

Acetylene

Carbide cavers must carry their carbide in waterproof containers. Occasionally one hears of a careless caver who in the process of wading through or climbing in water manages to soak his improperly packed carbide, thereby producing a large amount of acetylene gas. The acetylene catches fire, flashes, or blows up spontaneously; this can be very dangerous. *Be sure you transport carbide properly.*

ROCKFALL

Although caves are generally extremely stable, the area around the entrance sometimes has loose debris and rock. It is important that cavers pay proper attention to unstable rock and debris when entering caves, especially virgin caves.

Accidents reported due to falling rock have often taken place in pits while a caver is ascending or descending. Cavers rigging the drop must be careful to rig in such a way that the rope will not dislodge rocks, and cavers at the top of the drop must be extremely careful not to knock off any rocks; even a small rock falling any distance and striking a caver can cause severe injury or death.

MINES

Caves are not mines and mines are not caves. Caves have been formed naturally over thousands or millions of years. They are generally physically stable and possess good air circulation. Mines, on the other hand, are artificial, man-made, and are constructed over a relatively short period of time. Mines are often extremely unstable and air circulation within them is often poor, with concentrations of poisonous gases not at all unusual. Few accidents occur in caves, but the same cannot be said for mines. *Old, abandoned mines are dangerous* and should be avoided.

FLOODING

Flooding is a serious hazard in many caves, and cavers should take all possible precautions to avoid dangerous or potentially dangerous situations involving this hazard.

Do not enter a cave with active, or potentially active, underground streams if a storm is theatening, if rain is forecast, if it has rained very recently, or if there is rapid melting of the snow pack occurring in the area. We include potentially active streams because in some cases cave entrances without active streams receive heavy runoff from the surrounding area following rainfall. Check the lay of the land surrounding any cave entrance where you will be exploring to determine if such an occurrence is possible in that particular location.

Piles of flood debris at a cave entrance are, of course, an obvious warning that the cave is subject to flooding. Inside the cave, leaves and debris trapped high up in a cave passage or room are good indications that that particular portion of the cave is subject to flooding. While visiting a cave you should be continually aware of any indication that flooding may be occurring. Watch for increased foam at the base of waterfalls.

If you do find yourself in a cave that is flooding, remain calm, quickly determine your alternatives, and choose the most favorable. If possible, exit the cave immediately. If exit is impossible, proceed to the highest level of the cave. Prepare to wait and guard against hypothermia.

ACCIDENT STATUS

In discussing potential hazards to the caver, it is of value to look at some of the statistics compiled by NSS and others regarding caving accidents and fatalities. The NSS prepared a report in 1977 that presented information on caving accidents from 1967 through 1975. During that period, looking at immediate accident causes, falls accounted for 74 accidents; drownings for 24; falling rock or object, 22; failure of rappel or prusik, 18; stumble, 14; exposure and/or exhaustion, 11; burns, 6; illness, 6; asphyxiation, 3; and animal attacks, 1.

Contributory causes included inexperience, 81; inadequate equipment, 43; poor judgment, 34; climbing unroped, 32; losing way, 28; getting stuck, 20; light failure, 17; exposure and exhaustion, 16; bad weather and flooding, 13; worn equipment and party separated, each 7; caving alone, 4.

In this particular study, two-thirds of all cave accident victims were between the ages of 15 and 25, and 88 percent of the victims were male. As noted, inexperience was the major contributory cause.

The same report cited statistics regarding fatal caving accidents for the year 1975 only, not including cave diving accidents. Of the latter, five were reported, but it was considered that this was only a small fraction of the actual number, most not having been reported to the NSS. There were nine nondiving caving deaths reported that year. These included three novices who drowned under flood conditions; two men crushed at cave entrances in separate accidents; and three who were involved in vertical caving accidents.

Richard L. Breisch (1977) compiled statistics on 68 fatal North American caving accidents between 1940 and 1976, not including an estimated 100 fatal cave diving accidents. He cited 48 general accident fatalities. Of these, 23 drowned, 5 died of hypothermia, 3 were asphyxiated, and 3 died from injuries due to falling objects. Twenty fatalities were caused by vertical caving accidents.

These statistics are related here not to make the caver apprehensive but to point out that inexperience is a major contributory factor in caving accidents. Obviously cave scuba diving is in a class by itself, and carries a higher potential risk than other types of cave exploration. In all types of cave exploration, the way to become an experienced caver is to follow the rules, learn from experienced cavers, practice the techniques, and display common sense in the undertaking.

17

FIRST AID AND HEALTH CONSIDERATIONS IN CAVES

ACCIDENTS IN CAVES may result in a variety of medical problems that initially are little different underground than they would be aboveground. However, underground they normally are more difficult to treat; arrival at a medical facility often will be delayed; and rescue operations, if needed, will cause increased stress for the patient. Medical problems may include bleeding, sprains, fractures, head and spinal injuries, chest injuries, unconsciousness, hypothermia and others. Therefore, all cavers should be familiar with both the theory and practice of first-aid procedures, including artificial respiration and cardiopulmonary resuscitation; should be capable of making level-headed, intelligent decisions regarding the most satisfactory and feasible methods of handling a medical emergency in any caving situation; and should be efficient in implementing such decisions.

It is beyond the scope of this book to cover all first-aid and medical measures that might conceivably be needed in a caving situation. Therefore, we will be discussing primarily those closely related to caves and the caving environment, or those that have special implications in a cave situation.

MOUTH-TO-MOUTH RESUSCITATION

Mouth-to-mouth resuscitation is one very basic, general type of first-aid direction that should be well known to all cavers. If you find yourself with another person who has stopped breathing, immediately prepare for and administer mouth-to-mouth resuscitation as follows:

1. It is important to establish air exchange as rapidly as possible. Irreversible damage occurs within four to six minutes after the brain cells are deprived of their oxygen supply.

2. With the victim on his back, place your face close to his. Look, listen, and feel for air exchange.

3. If no air exchange is apparent, immediately roll the head on its side; using your finger, quickly sweep the patient's mouth clear of foreign objects or material.

4. Roll the head back to its original face-up position.

5. Tilt the patient's head backwards as far as possible so that the front of the neck is stretched tightly.

6. Hold the nostrils closed by pinching them with your thumb and finger. Seal your mouth on the victim's mouth and blow a breath into the victim's lungs, watching to see that the victim's chest rises—a confirmation that air exchange is taking place.

7. Place your head close to the victim's to determine whether you can hear air escaping from the victim's nose and mouth.

8. If no exchange is taking place, you may need to accentuate the stretch of the neck to get the tongue out of the way. In order to pull the tongue as far forward as possible, insert your thumb between the patient's teeth and, with your fingers under his chin, pull the jaw forward.

9. Apply mouth-to-mouth resuscitation as follows:

a. Maintain maximum extension of head as just described.

b. Pinch patient's nose shut with your thumb and forefinger.

c. Take a deep breath, open your mouth wide, and place it over the mouth of the patient, making a tight seal.

d. Blow your full breath into the patient's mouth until you can feel the resistance offered by his expanded lungs and see his chest rise. (Each breath should provide about two pints of air, or approximately twice the amount of air in a normal breath.)

e. Remove your mouth to allow patient to exhale.

f. The process of blowing into the mouth, followed by exhalation of air from the patient's lungs, should be repeated twelve to fifteen times a minute for an adult.

g. As the size of the victim decreases, so does the amount of air delivered. (An infant receives only puffs of air from your cheeks.)

h. Mouth-to-mouth resuscitation should be continued until the victim revives or until trained personnel are available to assume care of the patient.

10. Once initiated, mouth-to-mouth resuscitation should not be terminated prematurely, for patients have been known to revive after hours of mouth-to-mouth resuscitation.

SHOCK

Shock is the disruption of the blood circulation, which in turn can upset many vital body functions; these are depressed due to the loss of blood volume, reduced rate of blood flow, or lack of oxygen. Shock can be caused as a result of severe injuries; it may also occur with injuries that in themselves would not ordinarily be fatal, but in conjunction with shock may well prove to be so.

When in shock the body constricts many of its blood vessels, causing shunting of the blood to vital organs. Symptoms of shock include pale, bluish, cold skin, which may be moist and clammy; weakness; rapid, often faint pulse; increased rate of breathing; and in advanced stages, apathy, dilated pupils, and mottled skin.

First-aid measures should seek to improve the victim's blood circulation and supply of oxygen and to maintain the body's normal temperature level. Keep the victim lying down—the position dependent upon injuries he may have incurred—keep him warm, and seek help immediately. First-aid treatment of shock, as is true with other medical emergencies, is something that should be known by cavers before the situation arises, and a comprehensive outline of the treatment of shock is beyond the scope of this book. It is specifically mentioned here, however, because it is an extremely serious condition, which is worsened by hypothermia, and this relationship should be noted.

HYPOTHERMIA

Hypothermia is a state of low body temperature. It is sometimes referred to by cavers and others simply as exposure. Hypothermia can be and has been a killer in caves. We have noted earlier the wind chill factor, the intensification of loss of body heat when the body is wet, and the need for proper clothing, including a wet or dry suit in some situations. However, accidents can occur, cave conditions may be unanticipated, or other emergencies may develop that cause temperature stress for a caver. Therefore every caver should understand what occurs, recognize the symptoms, be prepared to aid victims of hypothermia, and be knowledgeable regarding its prevention.

The human body is homothermic—that is, its inner body temperature is maintained at a constant level. Although the body extremities may often be many degrees below normal body temperature when exposed to cold, it is vital that the inner body core temperature be maintained, for major deviations from this level —either upward or downward—prove fatal.

The body produces its own heat metabolically. Heat can also be gained by the body or lost from it, depending on the temperature of the body and its surroundings, through the following means:

1. Radiation, in which heat is radiated from the body to its surroundings, or, conversely, heat is

radiated from the surroundings to the body.

2. Conduction, in which heat is lost or gained by contact with other objects, such as water when the caver is immersed.

3. Convection, which is the gain or loss of heat caused by moving air. The effect of convection can be intensified by:

a. Evaporation of moisture on the body (from sweating or due to the presence of wet clothing), which can cause the body to lose great amounts of heat.

b. Respiration if there is heat loss or gain due to the differential between body and air temperatures.

Hypothermia occurs when the body loses heat to its surroundings faster than it can replace it. With reduction of the body's core temperature to approximately 96°F, the victim begins intense shivering, which is a means of heat generation. This in itself is a possible hazard to the caver, because it causes coordination to be severely reduced and the possibility of a fall is greatly increased. At this point the body has already reduced blood flow to the extremities, and vascular constriction, which aids the body in keeping warm blood in the body core around the vital organs, has occurred. When the temperature drops to between 95°F and 91°F, the caver will display reduced ability to think, difficulty in speaking, poor coordination, and often disorientation. He will continue to shiver, but his heat production will be inhibited, and his central nervous system will begin to fail. With a drop to between 90°F and 86°F, muscular rigidity occurs with erratic movement, and amnesia may occur. The victim may become unconscious at approximately 86°F or 87°F, and/or display a glassy stare, slow pulse, and slow respiration. Death will ordinarily occur when the core temperature reaches the range between 85°F and 77°F. Few victims survive if their core temperature drops below 80°F.

At the first sign of hypothermia in a caver, every effort should be made to warm and aid the victim quickly. If possible, remove him from the cave immediately. If the victim is wet, immediately give him dry clothing in whatever quantity available. The victim should be protected from air movement, and if stationary in the cave should be elevated above the cold cave floor by means of packs, clothing, rope, or other articles. Heat from carbide lamps or a backpack stove under a protective insulating cover, such as a space blanket or plastic sheet, should be provided. Hot foods and drinks are excellent if the victim is able to take them. Direct body contact with another individual, as in a prewarmed sleeping bag or similar arrangement, will be advantageous in providing heat. It is important that those aiding the victim realize that sources of heat must be supplied to the victim. Merely placing him in a sleeping bag or similar methods will not suffice, for once his body undergoes decreased ability to produce heat—and this occurs fairly early in hypothermia—he cannot raise his body temperature by himself, even with the aid of insulating material about him.

It seems incongruous, but in advanced hypothermia a further drop in the body core temperature occurs when heat is applied to the body surface. The blood vessels near the body's surface, which have been constricted, will dilate when heat is applied. This causes increased circulation and increased heat transfer from the body core to the periphery, resulting in an "afterdrop" in the core temperature of as much as 4 to 7 Fahrenheit degrees. There is some debate regarding the rewarming of a victim—at what rate of heat addition does one risk the danger of initiating severe shock, leading to ventricular fibrillation by drawing the blood out of the core to the dilated peripheral vessels? It seems to be generally agreed, however, as Kreider (1967) states, that "this rewarming should be accomplished as rapidly as possible to reduce the period of time of the 'afterdrop.'"

In advanced hypothermia, resuscitative techniques may be necessary. Do not give up such efforts prematurely. Walraven et al. (1978) advise that "if the patient arrests profound hypothermia, the time of biological death may be extended up to 10 minutes due to the slower metabolic rate." Kreider (1967), describing the death of a hypothermia victim in a cave situation, makes the following observation: "After the rescue team arrived no further emergency treatment was tried because she appeared to be dead. This may have been a mistake, because many people have been revived from this state by rewarming. . . . Wet clothing should have been removed and she should have been wrapped in warm blankets and removed carefully and quickly by litter to a place where she could be rapidly rewarmed." Inquiries by the authors to emergency medical personnel reveal that they ordinarily do not pronounce a hypothermia victim dead until the body temperature has been raised to normal, since some victims who appear to be dead can recover if rapid warming takes place and resuscitative methods are employed.

Several precautions should be employed in order to prevent the possibility of hypothermia. One of these is sufficient amounts of the proper type of clothing, including a wet or dry suit if necessary. Remember also that wool is recommended, since it is much more efficient in conserving body heat, even when wet, than cotton or other materials.

A disproportionate amount of body heat is lost from the head and neck as compared to the rest of the body. Make special efforts to cover and protect these areas in cold temperatures or cold water.

Good physical condition is very important. The fit caver does not become fatigued as rapidly as the caver who is less fit. Fatigue can be dangerous because it reduces the body's ability to produce heat through physical exercise and shivering. Also, the fit caver is far better able to negotiate his way out of a cave when under duress or faced with the potential onset of hypothermia.

Avoid becoming wet whenever possible.

If intervals of inactivity in cold temperatures become necessary, periodic periods of exercise, such as running in place, may be valuable as a means of increasing the body's heat production, but do not do this to the point of fatigue, which will intensify the effects of hypothermia, should you contract it.

Gauge your energy levels and those of your companions and do not allow any of the party to become dangerously fatigued.

Body types vary in their susceptibility to heat loss. For example, all other factors remaining equal, a thin caver may be expected to lose body heat more readily than a caver with an insulating layer of subcutaneous fat.

Caving requires energy, as does heat production by the body. Fuel the machine by eating a nutritious meal before entering the cave, and eat high-energy, quick-energy foods, such as carbohydrates, while caving. If possible, arrange for hot food and/or drinks while in the cave.

HYPERTHERMIA

Hyperthermia is greatly increased body temperature. It is less frequently seen in temperate climate caves than is hypothermia, although it may occasionally occur, and certainly cavers in warm areas of the world, including the southern and desert areas of the United States, should beware of the possibility of hyperthermia.

Causes of hyperthermia in cavers may include high cave temperatures, but in temperate caves are more often tied to metabolic heat production and clothing. Thus a caver wearing a heavy coat or layers of wool clothing who felt quite comfortable while visiting the bottom of the cave or while waiting there for his turn to ascend the rope out of the cave may seriously overheat while undertaking the ascent. During this strenuous activity his body is called upon to exert a great deal of energy, thereby increasing his heat production ten to fifteen times over that while resting or inactive. With excessive clothing blocking loss of excess body heat to the atmosphere, the caver's body temperature increases. This is a primary reason cavers are advised to wear layers of clothing, allowing removal of the desired number of layers, and/or clothing that allows venting as a means of controlling the dissipation of body heat.

Under heat stress, the body's heat gain must be reduced before it reaches a certain level, or fever ensues, which can lead to death if it is not controlled. The primary means whereby the body relieves itself of excess heat is through evaporative cooling of the skin and underlying areas by evaporation of sweat from the skin. The inner core of the body is cooled when its heat is transferred to the blood, which is then directed to the cooler peripheral body areas adjacent to the skin.

Ordinarily evaporative cooling is efficient. Evaporation may be retarded, however, by high humidity or by heavy clothing, as in the example above, and hyperthermia may result. Evaporative cooling is also expensive in terms of water use; large amounts of it are expended in critical situations. Thus it is important that cavers in situations that may contribute to hyperthermia drink sufficient amounts of water.

As blood is shunted away from the viscera to peripheral body areas for cooling, cardiac activity is increased. If the cooling mechanisms are insufficient, the body temperature begins to rise. Dehydration of the body due to profuse sweating often occurs in this situation. When this happens the blood becomes increasingly concentrated, blood flow becomes inadequate, and the core temperature continues to escalate. Cardiac output doubles as the body temperature rises from 98.6°F to 107.6°F, and the heart's oxygen consumption increases 40 percent or more. At approximately 42°C, cardiac output drops and the heart's oxygen consumption decreases rapidly. The central nervous system then fails to function properly and the tissues of the heart, lung, and other body parts suffer damage and their function is impaired, with further deterioration of the victim. Henry (1980) states that "the essence of heatstroke pathology is the accumulation of excess heat in the body until direct thermal injury or dysfunction occurs in some or perhaps all of the body's tissues."

Three general types of heat-related illnesses can be pinpointed. The first is known as heat cramps. These may affect individuals engaged in strenuous activities in hot environments. Loss of large quantities of sweat creates an imbalance in the electrolyte ratio. If salt intake is insufficient to remedy this imbalance, heat cramps may occur. Sufficient ingestion of salt when heavy work is to be carried out in heat is an important preventive measure. Symptoms include muscle cramps and pain in extremities and abdomen, faintness, and profuse perspiration. First-aid measures include removing the patient to a cool place, giving him salted drinking water (one teaspoon of salt per glass, half a glass every fifteen minutes for an hour), and massaging of the cramps.

The second type of illness is heat exhaustion, which may also occur in individuals undertaking strenuous activities in hot environments. With quantities of blood directed away from the body core to the body surface, pooling of blood in the peripheral vessels combined with the pooling in the lower extremities when a person is standing sometimes provides an insufficient blood return to the heart and brain, thus leading to physical collapse. Symptoms include weak pulse, rapid and shallow breathing, generalized weakness, pale and clammy skin, profuse perspiration, dizziness, and sometimes unconsciousness. First-aid measures include removing the patient to a cool place, keeping him in a prone position with his feet elevated 8 to 12 inches, giving him water with salt, removing as much of his clothing as possible, and removing body heat by convection. Evacuate the caver as soon as feasible and seek medical help.

Heat stroke, the third and most serious type of illness, should be recognized as a true emergency; if prompt action is not taken, the patient may die. Heat stroke is a catastrophic disturbance of the heat-regulating mechanism of the brain. It is associated with high fever and collapse, and may result in convulsions and unconsciousness. Symptoms of heat stroke are very different from the two conditions described above, for in heat stroke the sweating mechanism no longer functions and the skin is hot and dry. Symptoms include sudden onset of the condition: hot, flushed, dry skin; dilated pupils; full and fast pulse; breathing that is fast at first, then changes to shallow and faint; early loss of consciousness; muscle twitching, possibly leading to convulsions; and a body temperature elevated to between 105°F and 106°F or higher. First-aid measures include removing the patient to a cool place; removing as much clothing as possible; assuring an open airway; attempting to reduce body temperature immediately by dousing body with water; wrapping victim in wet clothing; and, if convulsions occur, protecting the victim from injuries such as tongue biting. When possible, it is recommended that ice packs be placed under the arms, around the neck, at the ankles, or at other locations where blood vessels lie close to the skin. Transport the victim to a medical facility immediately, or if this is impossible, seek rescue immediately.

BURNS

Burns of two different types may occasionally be sustained in a caving situation. One is thermal. In a cave, burns of this type are often associated with carbide lamps or accidental inflammation of carbide that is improperly vented, with flames from backpack stoves, or with hot or boiling liquids being heated for drinks or food. (An incident is recorded in the caving literature in which an individual descending a rope set his own pants on fire with his carbide lamp! He quickly solved his problem by swinging under an adjacent waterfall.) First-aid measures for burns in which the blisters are unbroken include the application of cold water to the site. A clean wet cloth laid over the burn and periodically remoistened by the addition of water or application of a second, soaked cloth above the first may be helpful. If the burn is open (broken blisters or deep burns), canteen or boiled water should be used rather than cave water or chemically purified water.

A second type of burn that may be incurred is a chemical burn due to leakage from wet cell batteries. First-aid measures consist of immediate and continued flooding of the burn with copious amounts of water for at least five minutes and the addition of a neutralizing agent appropriate to the specific electrolyte solution spilled (see Chapter 8). The American Red Cross states, "The essential first aid is to wash away the chemical completely, as quickly as possible, with large quantities of water, using a shower or hose if available . . . Immediate washing is more important than neutralizing the chemical and should be continued for at least five minutes. Remove the victim's clothing from the areas involved." If an eye or eyes are contaminated the Red Cross recommends continued irrigation of the eye with water for at least five minutes in case of acid contamination, or fifteen minutes in case of alkali contamination.

In the case of any serious burn, the victim should, of course, leave the cave immediately and seek medical assistance.

DISEASES RELATED TO WATER AND CAVE DIRT

For far too long where caves are concerned, man has lived by the adage "out of sight, out of mind" and has used caves as dumps and sewers, both intentionally and inadvertently. Everything from dead animals to human sewage has been dumped, diverted, or allowed to sink into caves. Intentional abuses are not as common as they once were, and as a population we are becoming smarter about what may eventually happen underground to sewage that is dumped aboveground or channeled into waterways. As our population increases, however, so does our waste, and increasingly there are threats to the underground world, caves included. Also, caves are being visited by constantly growing numbers of individuals who may add to varying degrees to the pollution of the cave waters and general cave environment. Therefore cavers should realize that potential cave health hazards may include bacteria, parasites, viruses, and other disease-carrying organisms.

Most water in caves today should be considered suspect and a potential transmitter of diarrhea, hepatitis, typhoid, and other diseases. In some caves one will have a great deal of contact with cave dust, dirt, mud, guano, and similar materials; it is important that cuts and abrasions received in the cave be thoroughly cleaned, cared for, and watched for signs of infection. If the latter occurs, see your doctor. Certainly any puncture wound should be treated immediately by a doctor, who will determine whether a tetanus injection or tetanus toxoid booster injection should be given. Cavers are advised to keep recommended immunizations current, particularly tetanus and typhoid.

Histoplasmosis

Histoplasmosis is a disease caused by a dimorphic pathogenic fungus, *Histoplasma capsulatum*, which occurs rather commonly in certain areas of the world. The fungus grows in moist soil where it eventually produces large quantities of spores, and these are transported by wind to other locations. If the spores are inhaled by a warm-blooded animal they produce yeast cells in the lungs, which proliferate through budding, causing the disease. In a more extreme form of the disease, the cells may be carried in the bloodstream to other body locations where, undergoing continued growth, they may cause the death of the victim.

The fungus occurs worldwide in tropical countries, but is also found in some temperate latitudes where conditions are suitable. The latter include annual temperatures that reach or exceed 70°F for a part of the year, and moist, undisturbed soils, particularly those enriched by the phosphate and nitrogen in bird and bat guano. Bats can be infected by inhaling the spores; in some cases the disease will cause ulcerations in the bowel, through which the fungus is released in the bats' feces. Thus some bat-inhabited caves with their undisturbed soil enriched by guano will become reservoirs of *H. capsulatum*.

Relatively few people are infected by *H. capsulatum* in caves. Cases are more often associated with soil contaminated by birds. However, because there have been several spectacular occurences in which nearly every member of a caving party has contracted the disease following a particular cave visit, it is a rather common belief that bats and caves are the sole cause of histoplasmosis, and a name commonly used for the disease is cave fever.

Caving literature includes numerous accounts of caves that were once known as sick caves because individuals entering them sometimes became ill with a respiratory illness some days after their visit. Wild tales were related about these locations—there were curses upon the caves, or there was hidden treasure protected by some force that caused treasure seekers to cease and desist in their search. The scientific explanation, *H. capsulatum*, may be less colorful but is certainly more enlightening.

Many individuals who live in areas where the fungus is common have been infected and have had very mild or undetected cases, as revealed by positive skin tests. Although the symptoms are often unapparent or very mild, there is a wide variability in the severity of the disease, and deaths do occur, most often in infants and older adults.

Cases range from asymptomatic or mild to those with symptoms similar to those of influenza, lasting one to four days. More severe infections are often mistaken for atypical pneumonia, with cough, mild chest pain, and fever present, lasting approximately five to fifteen days. Cases lasting up to six months may be classified as acute. Progressive cases, in which the fungus affects many body parts, include the acute progressive, which is usually fatal within six weeks or less, and the chronic progressive, which may continue for years.

There is a histoplasmosis strip across the center of the United States, including major portions of the Ohio and Mississippi valleys, and a long extension reaches along the Mexican border. Thus *H. capsulatum* is present in a portion of the prime cave country of the United States; further south, in Mexico and Central and South America, it is even more widely spread.

However, for the caver the odds are in his favor that he will never contract the disease, or that if he does he will have a mild or undetected case. To visit a cave with a known history of harboring *H. capsulatum* is not recommended, but neither should fear of the disease prevent the caver from pursuing his exploration elsewhere.

Some cases of the disease have been related to breathing heavy cave dust, particularly dust generated by digging in guano and soil in caves. If you are visiting a very dusty cave or will otherwise be exposed to cave dust, it would be wise to wear a face mask, as the breathing of large amounts of dust—histoplasmosis-infected or not—is done at some hazard.

Cave-Dust Pneumonitis

Cave-dust pneumonitis is a second good reason for avoiding the inhalation of cave-dust. This term is used to describe inflammation of lung tissue due to breathing in large amounts of cave dust. It is characterized by chest pain when breathing, shortness of breath, and a dry cough. Onset of symptoms is fairly rapid, often less than a day following exposure, and it disappears within a few days. Causative factors have not been pinpointed, but very possibly are related to material in the dust to which the victim is allergic.

RABIES

Rabies, or hydrophobia, has long been one of man's most feared diseases. It is fatal if not treated, and until recently the treatment was not always totally successful. Rabies is ordinarily transmitted by the bite of infected animals including bats.

Two major advances in rabies prevention have recently been made. One includes a superior rabies vaccine for the human victim receiving a bite from a known or suspected rabid animal. Whereas the previous treatment required a series of over twenty shots of duck embryo vaccine, the new rabies vaccine requires only five. Additionally, the improved vaccine is produced through use of human cell cultures (rather than duck embryo cultures) and thus avoids many of the allergic reactions suffered by some individuals who received the older vaccine. The new vaccine is given intramuscularly on days 0, 3, 7, 14, and 28.

With the initial injection of vaccine, rabies immune globulin prepared from human venous plasma is also administered. This provides the victim with immediate immunization by means of preformed rabies antibodies while the victim's body develops its own immunity over the next two weeks in response to injections of rabies vaccine.

Many individuals who run a high risk of coming into contact with the rabies virus routinely undergo vaccination against rabies by taking the rabies vaccine series. This includes veterinarians and certain other animal handlers, physicians, laboratory personnel working with the virus, and similar individuals. Many cavers are now being immunized as a precaution. The manufacturers of the new vaccine recommend that persons working with live rabies virus have their rabies antibody titers checked every six months and have boosters given as needed. Persons with a continuing risk of exposure should receive booster doses every two years or have their blood serum tested for rabies antibodies every two years and then be given a booster dose if the titer is inadequate.

Rabies is most commonly transmitted by inoculation with infectious saliva when an infected animal bites another animal or human. However, it can be transmitted through open wounds, scratches, abrasions, or mucous membranes contaminated with saliva, brain, or similar infected matter from a rabid animal. Additionally there have been two cases of airborne rabies contracted in the laboratory, and probably airborne rabies has been contracted in bat-infested Frio Cave, Texas.

Following the deaths from rabies of two individuals after visiting Frio Cave, scientific studies were undertaken regarding airborne infectivity of rabies virus. Certain mammals, including foxes, coyotes, opossums, and hamsters, were held in Frio Cave for varying periods in such a manner that they could not be bitten by cave-inhabiting animals; yet some developed rabies even when exposed only to the cave air. This virus transmission to the experimental animals occurred only when bat populations were present in the cave. Other experiments in a second bat-inhabited cave had similar results. In later experiments, rabies virus was isolated from the atmosphere in Frio Cave by means of a mechanical air sampler. Studies have shown that rabies virus can multiply and persist within the brain, brown fat, and salivary gland tissue of bats that outwardly give no obvious indication of having the disease and that do not die due to its presence.

It is obvious that cavers should take sensible precautions where rabies is concerned. Avoid handling bats and avoid other mammals, such as foxes and skunks, that one may meet in cave entrances or on the hike to the cave, especially if they appear unafraid of humans or are otherwise acting in an unnatural manner.

If you regularly visit caves with bat populations, you should consult with your doctor and consider the possibility of taking the new immunization series and boosters as necessary. Always confer immediately with medical authorities if you are bitten or scratched by any bat or other suspect animal.

INSECTS, SPIDERS, AND SCORPIONS

Insects, spiders, and scorpions may be encountered in caves, and bites or stings from certain of these are a potential danger to the caver. In the United States these creatures are most often found in and around cave entrances. In more tropical caves, such as in Mexico and further south, the number of species present is much greater; their habitation reaches greater distances within the cave; and the potency of their venom for the human victim may be greater. In this discussion we are considering U.S. caves only.

Insects

With the exception of those bees, wasps, and occasionally mosquitoes hovering, resting, or nesting near cave entrances, insects pose few serious problems for cavers in the United States. There is one type of insect, however, in the southwestern states than can cause human disease farther south in its range, although the disease has not yet been reported within the United States. The insect is known as the kissing bug, cone-nosed bug, or assassin bug (*Triatoma spp.*). It is ½ to 1 inch in length and has an elongated cone-shaped head. The mouthparts are of the piercing and sucking type. Kissing bugs may produce a painful, itching, venomous bite, and are carriers of the causative agent of a serious illness, Chagas' Disease, in southern Mexico and Central and South America.

Kissing bugs feed on the blood of their hosts, which may include man. Normally they live in rodent nests, particularly those of pack rats. In early and midsummer they often leave these locations and can then become a nuisance or problem to man.

The severity of the bite varies according to the susceptibility of the victim. Normally a hard welt ½ to 3 inches in diameter develops. More sensitive individuals may develop extensive swelling of the affected area, and some experience systemic symptoms such as nausea, rapid heart action, and increased rate of respiration.

In its southern range *Triatoma* is host to a small flagellate microorganism that can, in its extended stage, cause Chagas' Disease in humans. Symptoms of the disease are often delayed for long periods. The parasite may eventually invade the human blood system and migrate into tissues, commonly those of the heart, spleen, and lymph nodes. No cases of Chagas' Disease have been recorded in the United States, but a trypanosome very similar to the one that causes the disease has been found in kissing bugs and small animals in the southwestern states. The kissing bug often defecates on the skin as it bites, and the trypanosome is carried in the feces. If it has been defecated onto the skin or is released there as the human smacks and smashes the biter, and the victim then scratches the bite, the trypanosome enters the wound.

As kissing bugs are well known from pack rat nests and such nests are not uncommon near cave entrances, cavers may occasionally encounter kissing bugs. If bitten by one, wash the bite and surrounding area well to remove the feces.

Spiders

Black widow spiders are the best known of America's venomous spiders. They occur almost worldwide in tropical and temperate regions, including every state in the contiguous United States. The familiar female of the species is fairly large, a deep shiny black in color, with a globular abdomen displaying a red hourglass marking on the underside. The black widow spins a messy-looking, non-geometric web to trap its prey.

This spider is extremely venomous. However, it is also retiring and unaggressive and ordinarily will bite a human only when the victim brushes against the spider or a similar contact is made. Initially the human victim may feel local pain when bitten, but may not see the spider and thus may not be aware of what caused the pain. The spider's venom is neurotoxic; that is, it is toxic to the nerves or nervous tissue. Symptoms of envenomation include sweating, conges-tion of the face and eyes, salivation, nausea, vomiting, feeling of apprehension, severe muscular cramps, boardlike rigidity of the abdomen, abnormally high blood and spinal fluid pressures, and pain settling in the abdomen and legs. Progression of the symptoms is rapid, but effects begin to regress after several hours. Poisoning may be fatal to small children or to people with hypertension or coronary problems. Antivenin is available.

Cavers would be most likely to receive a black widow bite in or near the entrance, so medical assistance can and should be sought immediately.

The second type of potentially dangerous spider the caver might encounter near cave entrances is the brown recluse. These spiders of the genus *Loxosceles* are distributed fairly widely in the United States; several species are represented, particularly in the southern and western states. These small to medium-sized spiders, approximately $5/16$ inch in body length, are dark brown to fawn color, with a darker, violin-shaped mark on the upper side of the cephalothorax. This mark gives rise to one of their common names, "violin spider."

The venom is hemolytic; that is, it destroys red blood cells. When bitten a person may feel little or no discomfort or may have a local stinging pain. Within a few hours, a hemorrhagic blister appears at the site and gradually increases in size. Over a period of days, the affected area centered about the bite becomes gangrenous, tissue sloughs off, and a draining ulcer forms. The ulcerous condition may continue to spread outward, destroying adjacent tissue due to the fact that the toxin remains in the tissue around the bite for a long period. Physicians may find it necessary to excise the bite area to remove the infecting source, after which the ulcer begins to heal. If left unchecked, the ulcer may continue to grow to a size several inches in diameter. In some cases the victim may experience chills, fever, aching, a generalized skin rash, and nausea. Death is rarely associated with the bite of the brown recluse. No antivenin is available.

Ordinarily the primary problem associated with the bite of this spider is that of the ulcer. Its bite does not present an emergency situation, since several hours may elapse before the first symptoms appear. Such a bite should, however, be handled by a physician.

Scorpions

Scorpions are found in many of the tropical, subtropical, and desert areas of the world, and approximately 800 species have been described worldwide. In the United States, scorpions are more widespread than one might presume. They are distributed over three-fourths of the nation. Approximately forty species occur in the continental United States; in the state of Arizona alone there are approximately twenty species. Scorpions range across the southern states from Florida to California; they occur as far north as Washington and Montana and have been collected in southern Canada. In general they are not found in the New England and Great Lake states. Florida and California have the most species.

All scorpions are venomous to varying degrees; some are of great danger to man. The sting of many nonlethal species is often equated with that of a yellow jacket or hornet. In the United States only a single species is considered potentially lethal to humans; this is *Centruroides sculpturatus*.

Because its venom is potentially lethal and it may

occasionally be found in and around cave entrances, cavers caving within its geographical range should be able to identify *C. sculpturatus*. Unfortunately this is not the largest or the most imposing of the scorpions in its range, nor is it brightly marked. It is quite small by comparison to some other scorpions, such as the giant, hairy scorpion, a nonlethal species of the southwest. Dr. Herbert Stahnke, an authority on scorpions, suggests the following points for identification:

1. *C. sculpturatus* is yellowish or greenish-yellow to straw color over the entire body.

2. In size, *C. sculpturatus range from* ½ inch in length at the time they leave the mother to an average adult length of 2 inches, although certain individuals may be almost 3 inches when fully developed.

3. These scorpions are slender. The adult female's body at its greatest width is not wider that ⅜ inch; the male's is only ¼ inch or less.

4. The adult female's tail may be slightly more than $\frac{1}{16}$ inch in diameter; the male's is even more slender.

5. The pincers are very slender, about six times as long as the broadest part.

6. *C. sculpturatus* possesses a subaculear tooth. This very small tooth, or tubercle, at the base of the stinger may be discernible to the naked eye if it is silhouetted against the light, or may be seen with a hand lens. There are, however, also other species belonging to this genus that display the subaculear tooth and are nonlethal.

One behavioral trait also helps to differentiate *C. sculpturatus* from many other scorpions. *C. sculpturatus* is often found clinging to the underside of a covering, rather than resting on the ground or substratum like many other scorpions.

Symptoms that follow a scorpion sting also aid in differentiating the lethal from the nonlethal. Reaction to the nonlethal sting is largely localized. One can expect pain, swelling, and discoloration of the tissues in the immediate area; in some cases, pain extends up the affected extremity. The sting of the potentially lethal species may cause immediate severe pain at the site; this pain soon recedes, and swelling and discoloration do not occur. Instead, the reaction is systemic, the venom being a convulsant neurotoxin (affecting the nervous system and leading in some cases to convulsions). The sting site tingles, prickles, and becomes hypersensitive. The presence of this sensation at the sting site is one means of identifying the sting of *C. sculpturatus*. If the patient immediately draws away after a gentle tap on the sting site, the sting is very likely to have been that of *C. sculpturatus*.

Symptoms that develop following a *C. sculpturatus* sting include the following: numbness travels up the affected extremity; tightness develops in the throat; the tongue has a thick feeling; the victim may drool and exhibit a fever and breathing difficulties. Great restlessness may develop, which in severe cases may cause convulsions. Even after recovery, the original site of the sting often remains hypersensitive for from several days to a week.

If stung the victim should be kept as quiet as possible and transported to a medical facility. If possible, the scorpion should be captured in order that positive identification of the species involved can be made. If ice is available before reaching medical help, use an ice pack or ice separated from the victim's skin by cloth layers. Periodically remove it; for example, five to ten minutes on, followed by five minutes off, and so on. *Do not use ice directly on the skin. Do not immerse the body in ice, ice slush, or ice water.* An antivenin is available.

Although we are not discussing tropical caves, a particular word of caution is in order with regard to scorpions that may be encountered in Mexico and farther south. Some species of scorpions in those areas are far more dangerous than *C. sculpturatus*. An antivenin is available in Mexico for treatment of victims of stings of scorpion species found in that country.

SNAKES

Snakes may be encountered in the entrance and near-entrance portions of caves. In winter these areas may provide hibernation sites, in summer a cool retreat. Cavers should take proper precautions.

As far as poisonous snakes in the United States are concerned, it is the rattlesnakes that cavers are most likely to encounter. Generally rattlesnakes will attempt to flee from humans, but the snake that is suddenly startled or is in an enclosed or trapped situation may instead attempt to protect itself by striking.

Cavers in their caving garb with boots and long, durable pants are partially protected from snakebite by their clothing. However, in a cave entry snakes may be located on ledges and in niches in the walls as well as on the floor. Be cautious in this regard. Look where you put your hands and refrain from peering at ledges at close range in a way that may put you eyeball to eyeball with a resting reptile.

In case a rattlesnake bite does occur, severity of the bite is dependent on many factors including size of snake, amount of venom injected (bites are occasionally received without injection of any venom), species of snake, location of bite, depth of bite, and age, size, and physical condition of the victim. Bites are rarely received directly into a blood vessel, in which case generalized systemic symptoms—changes in heartbeat and respiration, shock, unconsciousness, and the like—may occur almost immediately. However, in the majority of cases the venom is injected under the skin and usually not to any great depth into muscle, thus providing a good chance for removal of a certain quantity of the venom through shallow incisions in the skin. Also, approximately 98 percent of the bites are estimated to occur on the extremities, where use of constricting bands, incision, and suction is often possible.

Symptoms of rattlesnake bite include pain at the site; rapid onset of swelling and discoloration, which extend toward the heart; weakness and giddiness; respiratory difficulty; nausea and vomiting; low blood pressure; subnormal temperature; numbness and tingling of face, lips, and other body parts; double vision; and blindness. Death due to respiratory or circulatory failure may occur within one to two days.

First aid for rattlesnake bite includes the following:

1. Do not panic.
2. Keep patient quiet.
3. Immobilize bitten part, if possible. If not, keep movement of bitten limb to a minimum; muscular-action increases the spread of the venom. Keep bitten body part below level of heart, if possible.
4. Some authorities believe that if the victim can be rapidly moved to a hospital or doctor for professional treatment, this should be done and no first aid should be administered. However, many bites are sustained some distance from medical help, in which case the following first-aid measures should be considered.
5. Apply constriction. This does not mean a tourniquet. A constricting band should be placed two to three inches above the bite—between the heart and bite—to restrict the flow of venous blood and lymph, but not to restrict arterial blood flow. A distal pulse, signifying arterial circulation, should be present in the extremity at all times and should be monitored. The constricting band should be loose enough to allow insertion of a finger or pencil-sized object between the band and the body part. If swelling progresses up a limb, advance the constricting band above the swelling. Improper use of a band can be dangerous; applied too tightly, it restricts arterial flow to the area beyond it and causes severe tissue damage.
6. If it is determined that the victim was definitely bitten by a rattlesnake and that envenomation has occurred, immediately carry out incision and suction.
7. If some doubt exists as to whether the victim was bitten by a venomous snake or whether envenomation has occurred, watch the bite for the first three to five minutes. If during this time pain occurs and swelling appears at the site, assume that envenomation by a poisonous snake has occurred and consider incision and suction. Pain and swelling at the site are signs of a rattlesnake bite. The bite of a nonpoisonous snake or a poisonous snake that has not injected venom will not produce swelling.

8. Cut and suction the bite:

a. Use a cutting instrument that has been sterilized, if possible—wipe the instrument with antiseptic or hold it over a flame. If available use iodine, alcohol, or a similar disinfectant to clean the skin area to be cut.

b. Make a small, longitudinal incision over each fang mark. The incision should be parallel with the long axis of the bitten limb. *Do not cut across the limb.*

c. Incisions should be approximately ¼ to ⅓ inch in length, and not more than ⅛ to ¼ inch in depth.

d. No additional incisions should be made.

e. Making incisions involves the danger of cutting nerves and blood vessels, particularly on the hands, wrists, neck, ankles, head, and groin. If in doubt, do not make a bad situation worse by causing further damage through first-aid incisions.

f. Apply suction with a suction device, if available.

g. If the mouth suction is used, suck and spit.

h. Continue suction for at least thirty to sixty minutes.

9. Transport the victim by litter, if possible.

10. If the bite is on a hand or arm, remove rings and so forth before swelling makes their removal difficult.

11. If possible to do so without causing further problems, capture the snake in order that positive identification as to exact species can be made (treatment may vary accordingly). However, do not take chances on a second bite or delay first aid or transport in an attempt to capture the snake.

12. Keep patient as quiet as possible and rush to medical aid.

There are four types of poisonous snakes in the United States: rattlesnakes, copperheads, water moccasins, and coral snakes. The first three are all pit vipers. In general, pit viper venom is neurotoxic (toxic or acting like a poison in regard to nervous tissue); hemorrhagic (tending to cause hemorrhage); thrombogenic (tending to cause thrombus, or blood clot); hemolytic (inducing the liberation of hemoglobin from red blood cells); and proteolytic (producing hydrolysis of proteins with formation of simpler soluble products, as in digestion).

The coral snake is a member of the cobra family. The eastern species is a large snake; the western species is small and seldom encountered. The coral snake's venom is potent and affects the victim's nervous system. Symptoms of coral snake bite include blurred vision, drooping eyelids, slurred speech, drowsiness, sweating, salivation, nausea, vomiting, shock, respiratory difficulty, and may include paralysis, convulsions, and coma. The American Red Cross recommends similar first-aid measures for the bites of all four types.

Since poisonous snakes in the United States rarely venture any great distance inside caves, any bites that might be incurred would probably be received near the entrance, and in this location a rapid exit from the cave could be accomplished. Many types of snakes, both poisonous and nonpoisonous, may range inside caves to varying distances in areas elsewhere, particularly in tropical country. Cavers are advised to acquaint themselves with any information available regarding reptiles common to caves they plan to visit.

18
CAVE RESCUE

RESCUE IS AN EX-
tremely complex sub-
ject, and complete
written about it. We
books have been
cannot attempt to cover the entire subject; instead, we
wish to pass along some basic rescue techniques that
are versatile and effective. Rescue is a response to a
critical, unusual, and unplanned situation. In caving it
is through knowledge and experience that a party ordinarily avoids situations in which a rescue becomes
the only course of action.

Rescue operations can be broken down into two
basic types—those that require outside assistance and
those in which the members of the caving party carry
out evacuation by themselves. The latter is more common, and even in those cases in which outside help is
required, the caving party must provide the initial rescue and first-aid operations.

Following an accident or similar emergency, the
caving party must act immediately and precisely, for a
caver who is but slightly injured one minute may become a caver who is fighting to stay alive a few minutes later due to hypothermia, shock, or other factors.

Hypothermia is the killer in many caving accidents, either as the primary or secondary cause. Hypothermia may be a contributory cause of an accident
resulting from impaired reaction time and judgment;
or, following an accident, hypothermia may set in
once the injured caver cannot operate normally to
maintain body temperature.

Immediately upon assessing the situation after an

accident occurs, the remainder of the caving party should stabilize the victim, stop any bleeding, and monitor vital signs: breathing and cardiac output. Strive to maintain his body temperature through all means available. At least one and probably additional cavers in the party should be carrying a space blanket in their pack or helmet, and this is extremely efficient in maintaining body heat. Follow other procedures noted earlier to ward off hypothermia.

Once initial action has been taken, a decision must be made whether to begin evacuation of the victim immediately or send for help and await an outside rescue operation. Many times, quickly initiating the movement of the victim toward the entrance will allow him to give some assistance, which may not be possible later. This activity may also aid the victim in warding off the chilling effects caused by remaining inactive. The victim's condition must be evaluated thoroughly, however, before the final decision to move him is made, for moving the injured individual may increase his injuries or possibly prove fatal to him if the caving team lacks sufficient knowledge, skill, or equipment to carry out the move correctly. A caving victim who has received neck, back, or any spinal injury should not be moved until a proper stretcher, backboard, or other immobilizing instrument can be obtained or constructed.

If there is a rescue team located within a reasonable distance from the cave, the call for the organized rescue team would be made for less severe injuries than if the team were distant. Oftentimes, however, even in the case of severe injury, the decision to leave the victim in the cave while awaiting an organized rescue team may prove fatal. By the time the rescue team arrives, the victim's condition may well have deteriorated to the point of no return. The final decision to move or not to move the victim out under the party's own means rests upon their shoulders. There are many factors to be considered, and the decision is often difficult to make. Members of the party must evaluate the situation and do the best they can.

SELF-RESCUE

We will consider first the case in which self-rescue is the course chosen. If the cave is in a remote location or in a foreign country that has no trained cave rescue teams, self-rescue may be the only possible rescue. Once the situation has been evaluated and the decision to use self-rescue decided upon, the rescuers must work methodically and carefully.

Horizontal Travel

The easiest method of horizontal evacuation is through the use of a rescue stretcher. One of the best is the Neil Robinson; however, any stokes-type stretcher will generally work well. If none of these is available, a simple piece of plywood can be formed into an immobilizing stretcher by cutting holes and notches in it. The victim can be strapped to the makeshift stretcher, thereby immobilizing him. Many mobile campers and trailers contain enough wood to construct a backboard stretcher in an emergency.

Another method used to construct an emergency stretcher makes use of a piece of rope approximately 150 feet long. If a single length is not available, personal slings and short sections of rope can be tied together to obtain sufficient length. Rocky Mountain Rescue Group (1973) describes two types of rope litters. One is actually crocheted around the victim. A second type of rope litter that seems to work well is described by Halliday (1974). Two small loops are tied about 18 inches apart in the middle of the rope. More loops are tied the same distance apart until the rope is knotted on either side of the center for about 7 feet. The rope is laid out to form a U and the open end is closed with a secure knot. The rope ends are then woven back and forth through the loops from side to side, securing them occasionally with knots to aid stability. The victim is laid on the stretcher and the loops are used for handles by the rescuers.

If it is not possible to construct a litter, the party must improvise to carry the victim out. Piggyback methods work to some extent. Fireman's carry (that is,

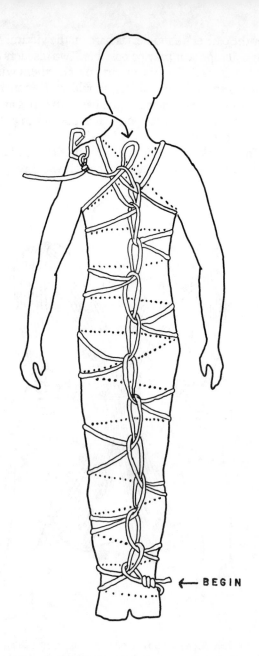

← BEGIN

Improvised rope litter. *This is used for transporting an injured caver in an emergency situation.*

over the carrier's shoulder) is hard on the victim. A split coil rope seat may be possible. Two rescuers can join hands and allow the victim to sit on them with his arms around the rescuers' shoulders. If enough cavers are present they can join hands in series and form a rough stretcher upon which the victim can be laid and carried.

In crawlways the victim can sometimes be laid on the back of a prone caver who then crawls through the

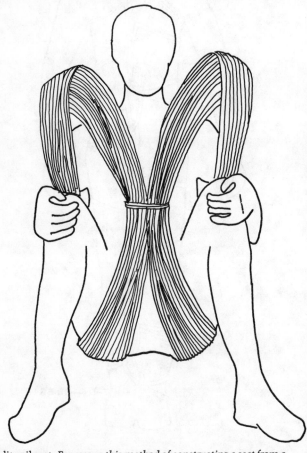

Split coil seat. For rescue this method of constructing a seat from a coil of rope may be employed. The seat can be carried backpack-style by a rescuer by placing his arms through the upper loops; the victim sits in the lower loops.

constricted area carrying the victim on top of his body. When possible the other members will need to assist the caver on the bottom through the squeeze. Obviously no rescue is an easy, enjoyable proposition.

Vertical Travel

Moving a victim up a drop is often a complicated process, and almost always requires construction of some type of mechanical advantage system. The only exception to this would be if the drops are quite short and/or manpower is readily available.

The hauling system decided upon will be influenced to a great extent by equipment available, the existence of anchors, their location, and the cave passage configuration. In all hauling systems security is of foremost concern. See that the victim (and many times the rescuers) are connected to belay or safety lines.

Hauling Systems Theory. The idea behind hauling systems is to accomplish the lifting of a victim in a safe, smoothly controlled manner. Mechanical advan-

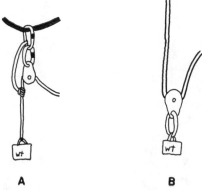

A   **B**

Hauling systems.

A. *Basic direction change for a hauling system. Note safety prusik on weighted line, rigged such that when pulling is stopped the weight is held in place.*

B. *The basic two-to-one advantage haul system is used in moving weighted objects from a lower to a higher level, and is commonly used in rescue and equipment hauling.*

tage systems for lifting are rated as giving a mechanical advantage of two-to-one, three-to-one, four-to-one, and so on. A two-to-one system would theoretically allow you to lift a 100-pound object by exerting a lifting force of 50 pounds; a three-to-one system would require a 33⅓-pound force. These figures are true for an ideal system, but vary in practice. The major reason for this deviation is friction. Every pulley creates some friction. When it is necessary to substitute a carabiner for a pulley, friction is increased dramatically. Every point of contact on the rope increases friction.

In cave rescue the hauling system must be secure, safe, and efficient. Simplicity leads to versatility, which is of primary importance in this type rescue operation. The larger the mechanical advantage, the easier it is to lift the load; but at the same time this sacrifices simplicity because of lines running back and forth, which tend to get tangled and inhibit rescue activity.

Two-to-One Hauling System. The two-to-one hauling system is quite simple and versatile. This system can be rigged so that a horizontal pull raises an

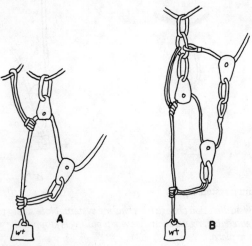

Hauling systems.

A. *Schematic setup for a three-to-one mechanical advantage system;*
B. *Schematic setup for a six-to-one mechanical advantage system.*

object vertically. The two-to-one system can also be rigged so that the rigging pulley is attached to the victim along with a safety Jumar. A rescuer at the top can then pull up on the free end of the haul rope. With the other end of the haul rope anchored at the top, the victim moves upward. As the safety Jumar will hold the victim's weight, the rescuer can rest at any time.

Three-to-One and Other Hauling Systems. When more lifting force or ease of pulling is needed, one can set up a system with a greater mechanical advantage. As mentioned above, the greater the advantage, the more cumbersome the system.

The rope must be positioned in Zs to obtain the mechanical advantage. The bottom prusik or ascender should be positioned as close to the victim as possible. This will reduce the number of times the bottom prusik or ascender needs to be reset. It should be noted that the hauling should stop before pulley 2 reaches pulley 1. If the pulleys meet, the rope will straighten, losing its Z configuration and hence its mechanical advantage.

Hauling continues until the pulleys nearly touch each other. At this point the safey prusik or ascender is engaged while the tension is transferred from the haul line to the safety ascender. Once the safety prusik or ascender is holding the load, the bottom prusik or ascender is moved back down for another bite as close to the load as possible, and hauling begins again as the safety prusik or ascender is unweighted and disengaged.

It is wise to remember that hauling systems using dynamic nylon rope become very inefficient in long hauls or systems of high mechanical advantage. The stretch must be overcome in the system itself, and this stretch makes resetting the lower prusik or ascender much more difficult. Static rope should be used whenever possible.

Another point to remember is that the greater the mechanical advantage, the more rope will be required to raise an object a given distance.

Counterweight System. In this simple hauling system, a pulley and safety ascender are anchored just

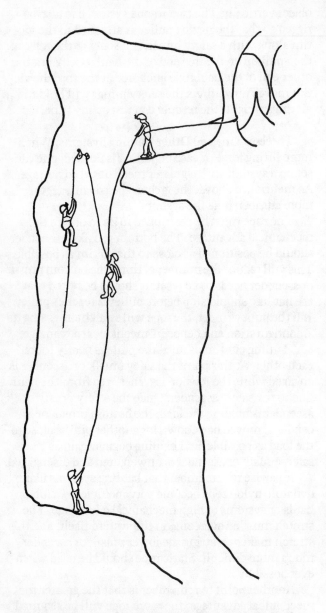

Counterweight hauling system. *This provides a method whereby a victim can be raised through the use of a counterweight. A heavier caver will climb on the opposite end of the haul rope, which runs through a pulley. The victim should have an additional belay.*

above the top of the drop up which the victim is being hauled. The haul rope is positioned through the pulley and safety ascender. The victim is tied into one end. A rescuer clips himself in on the other side of the pulley. He attaches his ascenders to the rope and ascends up the rope just below the pulley and safety ascender. As he climbs the rope, he should stay essentially in the same position while the victim begins his upward journey and the rope is pulled through the pulley by the rescuer's weight. The ascending rescuer must also be clipped into the anchor for the pulley, and should be a minimum of 20 to 30 pounds heavier than the victim so that he offsets the victim's weight sufficiently.

Prusik or Mechanical Ascender. In most cave rescue efforts mechanical ascenders or material to construct prusik knots are generally available. Mechanical ascenders are easy to work with and work well for limited loads and stresses. If, however, higher stresses or increased loads are expected, prusiks are better. When tied correctly prusiks are stronger than many mechanical ascenders. They also have the advantage that they rarely experience catastrophic failure, as mechanical ascenders sometimes do. That is, prusiks generally slip before they break, giving warning that the system is overweighted.

Lowering. Lowering the victim is obviously much easier than hauling him upward. In lowering, the setup is generally quite easy and straightforward. A descender is anchored and a rope is then rigged through it. The victim is tied in to the end and lowered as rope is fed through the descender.

If the victim is accompanied by a rescuer, be sure the descending device used possesses sufficient friction for a slow, controlled lowering. The victim should always have a belay. Many times a rescuer can rappel down next to the victim instead of accompanying the victim down while tied into the same rope. As anchors and space available for the setup are often limited, ingenuity is generally required when a system is being set up.

Victim on the Rope. It is possible in a caving accident that the victim could be on the rope while unconscious or unable to move up or down. If the caving party is above the victim and the situation can be assessed, it is usually best to set up a haul system and haul up the rope to which the victim is attached, starting the victim up and out rather than lowering him down farther into the cave.

If, on the other hand, the caving party is below the victim, a rescuer must ascend the standing rope to the victim and bring him down on his descender. The rescuer ascends and places an extra ascender and pulley above the victim and threads a 6-foot rope through the pulley. One end is clipped into the victim's harness, the other to the rescuer's harness. The rescuer unclips his ascenders and acts as a counterweight, lifting the victim up, and unclips the victim's ascenders. The rescuer threads the standing rope through the descender, locks it off, clips the victim into it, and eases him down until he is supported by the descender. The rescuer then clips himself into the descender, detaches the ascender and pulley, and abseils down. Remember that the rescuer will be abseiling with twice the normal weight and must assure that his descender produces enough friction for a controlled descent.

When extra rope is available, the rescuer may thread one end of this rope through the pulley to the victim. The other end will be positioned through an anchored descender at the bottom of the drop. With this setup the rescuers on the floor can then lower the victim down by feeding rope through the descender.

OUTSIDE RESCUE

If outside assistance for the rescue is decided upon, it is important that it be sought, controlled, and delivered in as rapid and efficient a manner as possible. Preferably two cavers should make their way out of the cave and seek help. At least one caver must stay with the victim; he should be the most medically qualified member of the party.

Even when outside help is clearly necessary and is

being summoned, the caving party itself can accomplish a great deal in the interim by preparing the victim for transport. Oftentimes the party can also prepare the cave to some extent for the evacuation to come, and in some cases may possibly be able to start the victim on his way to the surface.

To report a caving accident in the United States, call the local law enforcement agency, fire department, Forest Service, Park Service, or similar agency. The following information must reach competent authorities:

1. The location and number from which the call is being made.

2. The exact location of the cave, including precise directions as to how to reach it.

3. The victim's name, address, condition, and injuries.

4. The names and addresses of all other cavers in the party and their present locations.

5. A brief idea of distances, time needed, and difficulty of evacuation.

Attempt to avoid publicity, as cave accidents and rescues attract large crowds and make sensational news. Crowds not only impede rescue operations, which could prove fatal for the victim, but also set the stage for potential accidents.

It is extremely important that organization of the rescue be structured immediately upon a decision to request a full-scale rescue. One member of the caving party should take immediate control of the situation and act a director until he feels a more competent person has arrived, at which time he can transfer his authority.

During rescue, there should be a communication team with a leader, a cave rescue coordinator stationed at the cave entrance, an assistant cave rescue coordinator who stays with the victim, a press secretary, a few competent belayers and riggers, and many stretcher bearers and haulers. All information must be released through the press secretary.

In emergencies, worldwide, the National Cave Rescue Commission (NCRC) of the NSS is capable of supplying rescue teams and expertise as well as coordination liaison with the United States Air Force. For this purpose there is a toll-free number manned twenty hours a day: 800-850-3051.

REFERENCES

BREISCH, Richard L., ed. *American Caving Accidents, 1975: A Report of the National Speleological Society.* Speleobooks Press, Albuquerque, N.M., 1977.

BREISCH, Richard L. "Fatal Caving Accidents in North America Since 1940." *NSS News* XXXV, #11, Nov. 1977.

EXLEY, Sheck. *Basic Cave Diving: A Blueprint for Survival.* NSS Cave Diving Section, Huntsville, Ala., 1980.

GURNEE, Russell and Jeanne. *Gurnee Guide to American Caves: A Comprehensive Guide to the Caves in the United States Open to the Public.* Zephyrus Press, Teaneck, N.J., 1980.

HALLIDAY, William R. *American Caves and Caving: Techniques, Pleasures, and Safeguards of Modern Cave Exploration.* Harper & Row, New York, 1974.

HALLIDAY, W. R., and C. H. Anderson. "Glacier Caves, A New Field of Speleology." *Studies in Speleology* 2 (part 2): 53–59, July 1970.

Hand Signals for Cave Diving. National Association for Cave Diving, 1980.

HENRY, Charles D. "The Pathophysiology of Heat stroke," *Critical Care Update*, July, 1980.

HILL, Carol A. *Cave Minerals.* National Speleological Society, Huntsville, Alabama, 1976.

Human Performance and Scuba Diving. Scripps Institute, La Jolla, Calif., 1970.

ISENHARD, K. "Roller Cam." *Nylon Highway* 1:22, 1974.

KREIDER, Marlin B. "Physical and Physiological Factors in Fatal Exposures to Cold," *Bulletin of the National Speleological Society*, Huntsville, Alabama, 1976.

KREIDER, Marlin B. "Physical and Physiological Factors in Fatal Exposures to Cold," *NSS Bulletin* 29 (#1): 1–11, Jan. 1967.

MAGNUSSEN, C. "How Strong Is A Stitched Splice in Nylon Webbing?" *Off Belay* 5: 6–8.

McCLURG, David. *Exploring Caves: A Guide to the Underground Wilderness.* Stackpole Books, Harrisburg, Pa., 1980.

MONTGOMERY, Neil R. *Single Rope Techniques.* The Sydney Speleological Society, Sydney, Australia, 1977.

MOORE, George W., and G. Nicholas Sullivan. *Speleology: The Study of Caves.* Zephyrus Press, Teaneck, N.J., 1978.

MOUNT, Tom. *Safe Cave Diving.* National Association for Cave Diving, 1973.

National Speleological Society. Quotations taken from membership promotional and cave conservation-oriented publications.

PETERSON, Donald W., and Donald A. Swanson. "Observed

Formation of Lava Tubes During 1970–71 at Kilauea Volcano, Hawaii." *Studies in Speleology* 2 (part 6): 209–221, Jan. 1974.

POULSON, Thomas L., and William B. White. "The Cave Environment." *Science* 165: 971–981, 5 Sept. 1969. Copyright 1969 by the Association for the Advancement of Science.

SMUTEK, R. "The REI Field Tests of Chocks." *Off Belay* 32: 18–20.

SWEETING, Marjorie. *Karst Landforms*. Columbia University Press, New York, 1973.

THOMPSON, Lonnie G., and Garry D. McKenzie. "Origin of Glacier Caves in the Quelccaya Ice Cap, Peru." *NSS Bulletin* 41: 15–19.

THRAILKILL, J. "Chemical and Hydrological Factors in the Excavation of Limestone Caves." *Bulletin Geological Society of America* 79: 19–46, 1968.

THRUN, Robert. *Prusiking*. National Speleological Society, Huntsville, Ala., 1973.

ULLIN, J.G. "More on Using Jumars." *Off Belay* 9: 3–4.

WALRAVEN, Gail, Josie Harding, Karen Milazzo LeBlanc, Ginger Murphy, and Margaret F. Nerney. *Manual of Advanced Prehospital Care*. Robert J. Brady, 1978.

WARWICK, G.T. "Geomorphology and Caves." In T. D. Ford and C. H. D. Cullingford, eds., *The Science of Speleology*. Academic Press, New York, 1976.

WOOD, C. "Caves in Rocks of Volcanic Origin." In T. D. Ford and C. H. D. Cullingford, eds., *The Science of Speleology*. Academic Press, New York, 1976.

RECOMMENDED READING

American Caving Accidents, 1967–1970: Reports of the National Speleological Society. Speleobooks Press, Albuquerque, N. Mex., 1974.

BARBOUR, Roger W., and Wayne H. Davis. *Bats of America.* University Press of Kentucky, Lexington, 1969.

BREISCH, Richard, ed. *American Caving Accidents, 1975: A Report of the National Speleological Society.* Speleobooks Press, Albuquerque, N. Mex., 1977.

BRUCKER, Roger W., and Richard A. Watson. *The Longest Cave.* Alfred A. Knopf, New York, 1976.

BURGESS, Robert F. *The Cave Divers.* Dodd, Mead & Company, New York, 1976.

CASTERET, Norbert. *Ten Years Under the Earth.* Greystone Press, 1938.

CONN, Herb and Jan. *The Jewel Cave Adventure: Fifty Miles of Discovery Under South Dakota.* Zephyrus Press, Teaneck, N. J., 1977.

CULLINGFORD, Cecil, ed. *Manual of Caving Techniques.* Routledge, London, 1969.

EXLEY, Sheck. *Basic Cave Diving: A Blueprint for Survival.* NSS Cave Diving Section, 1980.

FORD, R. D., and C. H. D. Cullingford, eds. *The Science of Speleology.* Academic Press, New York, 1976.

FREEMAN, John P., ed. *Cave Research Personnel Manual.* Cave Research Foundation, Columbus, Ohio, 1975.

GURNEE, Russell and Jeanne. *Gurnee Guide to American Caves: A Comprehensive Guide to the Caves in the United States Open to the Public.* Zephyrus Press, Teaneck, N. J., 1980.

HALLIDAY, William R. *American Caves and Caving: Techniques, Pleasures, and Safeguards of Modern Cave Exploration.* Harper & Row, New York, 1974.

HALLIDAY, William R. *Depths of the Earth: Caves and Cavers of the United States.* Harper & Row, New York, 1976.

Hand Signals for Diving. National Association for Cave Diving, High Springs, Fla., 1980.

HILL, Carol A. *Cave Minerals.* National Speleological Society, Huntsville, Ala., 1976.

JENNINGS, Joe. *Karst.* Australian National University Press, Canberra, Australia, 1971.

JUDSON, David. *Ghar Parau.* Macmillan, New York, 1973.

LAWRENCE, Joe, Jr., and Roger W. Brucker. *The Caves Beyond: The Story of the Floyd Collins' Crystal Cave Exploration.* (Reprint of the 1955 edition, with a new introduction by Roger W. Brucker.) Zephyrus Press, Teaneck, N. J., 1975.

LEEN, Nina, photographer; text by Alvin Novick. *The World of Bats.* Holt, Rinehart and Winston, New York, 1969.

McCLURG, David R. *Exploring Caves: A Guide to the Under-*

ground Wilderness. Stackpole Books, Harrisburg, Pa., 1980.

MITCHELL, Robert W., and James R. Reddell, eds. *Studies on the Cavernicole Fauna of Mexico and Adjacent Regions.* Association for Mexican Cave Studies, Bulletin 5. The Speleo Press, Austin, Tex., 1973.

MOHR, Charles E., and Thomas L. Poulson. *The Life of the Cave.* McGraw-Hill, New York, 1966.

MOHR, Charles E., and Howard N. Sloane, eds. *Celebrated American Caves.* Rutgers University Press, New Brunswick, N. J., 1955.

MONTGOMERY, Neil R. *Single Rope Techniques.* The Sydney Speleological Society, Sydney, Australia, 1977.

MOORE, George W., and G. Nicholas Sullivan. *Speleology: The Study of Caves.* Zephyrus Press, Teaneck, N. J., 1978.

MOUNT, Tom. *Safe Cave Diving.* National Association for Cave Diving, 1973.

MURRAY, Robert K., and Roger W. Brucker. *Trapped!* G. P. Putnam's Sons, New York, 1979.

POULSON, Thomas L., and William B. White. "The Cave Environment." *Science* 165: 171–181, 1969.

REDDELL, James R., ed. *Studies on the Caves and Cave Fauna of the Yucatan Peninsula.* Association for Mexican Cave Studies, Bulletin 6. The Speleo Press, Austin, Tex., 1977.

REDDELL, James R., and Robert W. Mitchell, eds. *Studies on the Cavernicole Fauna of Mexico.* Association for Mexican Cave Studies, Bulletin 4. The Speleo Press, Austin, Tex., 1971.

RUSSELL, William H., and Terry W. Raines, eds. *Caves of the Inter-American Highway: Nuevo Laredo, Tamaulipas to Tamazunchale, San Luis Potosi.* Association for Mexican Cave Studies, Bulletin 1. Austin, Tex., 1967.

SLOANE, Bruce, ed. *Cavers, Caves, and Caving.* Rutgers University Press, New Brunswick, N. J., 1977.

SWEETING, Marjorie M. *Karst Landforms.* Columbia University Press, New York, 1973.

THRUN, Robert. *Prusiking.* National Speleological Society, Huntsville, Ala., 1973.

VANDEL, A. *Biospeleology: The Biology of Cavernicolous Animals.* Pergamon Press, New York, 1965.

WALTHAM, A. C. *The World of Caves.* G. P. Putnam's Sons, New York, 1976.

WALTHAM, Tony. *Caves.* Macmillan, New York, 1974.

WATSON, Patty J., ed. *The Archaeology of the Mammoth Cave Area.* Academic Press, New York, 1974.

Canadian Caver. Published by the Department of Geography, University of Alberta, Edmonton, Alberta, Canada.

NSS NEWS. Monthly publication devoted to speleology. National Speleological Society, Huntsville, Ala. 35810.

The NSS Bulletin: Quarterly Journal of the National Spele-
ological Society. Huntsville, Ala. 35810.
Nylon Highway. Vertical Section of the National Speleological
Society, Huntsville, Ala. 35810.

INDEX

Abrasion, rope: 140–41, 156–57, 168–71, 231

Acrophobia, 81

Air supply, diving, 243–44, 250

Anchors, 154–65, bolts, 161–65; chocks, 159–60; choice of, 155, 160, 161–62; multiple, 157, 158, 159, 166; natural, 155–59; pitons, 160–61

Animals, cave, 7, 57, 60, 72–80

Ascending, 202–36; knots, 203–5; mechanical devices, 128–29, 201, 205–15; mechanical systems, 215–29; special techniques, 229–32; systems for rescue, 295–300

Backpacks, 83, 115; in waterfalls, 236

Belay, 123, 125–30, 200–201, 215–16; defined, 125; devices for, 128, 129; with ladders, 134, setting up, 125, 145–46; signals for, 130; uncontrolled falls during, 138

Biota, cave, 7, 57, 61, 72–80; characteristics of, 76–77; classifications of animals, 73; conservation of, 79–80; darkness a determining factor for, 75; effects of genetic isolation on, 77, 78; effects of Ice Age on, 77; food a determining factor for, 73–77, 79; plants, 74; zones of, 72

Bolts, 161–65; permanent place-

ment of, 163; Rawl type, 164–65; self-drilling shield type, 162–63

Carabiner, 180–83, 204–12 *passim*; failure, 182, 183; maintenance, 182–83; uses, 155, 159, 196; wrap, 187–88, 190

Cave development, 5–6; in cold regions, 21; in dolomite, 29; in glaciers, 58–59; in lava, 52–54; in limestone, 10–28, 61; in marble, 29; in salt and gypsum, 29; in sandstone, 62; under the sea, 60; in talus, 62; in tropical regions, 25

Caves: breakdown of, 20–21; conditions in, 6–7; definition, 4–5; flooding in, 57, 251–52; types of, 5–6, 22

Caves, names of: Carlsbad Caverns, 25, 43; Flint Mammoth Cave System, 13; Frio Cave, 279; Gouffre Jean Bernard, 13; Jewel Cave, 48; Lehman Caves, 43; Paradise Ice Caves, 58; Pumpkin Cave, 154

Caving, 8; history, 1–2; permissions, 86; preparing for, 81–87; rules of, 82–90

Climate, effect of: on caves, 21, 24–25, 59; on karst formation, 28

Clothes, caving, 57, 91–96;